MARCHING TO COLD HARBOR

VICTORY AND FAILURE, 1864

By

R. Wayne Maney

 WHITE MANE PUBLISHING COMPANY, INC.

This White Mane Publishing Company, Inc., publication was printed by:

Beidel Printing House, Inc.
63 West Burd Street
Shippensburg, Pennsylvania 17257
United States of America

The acid-free paper used in this book meets the guidelines for permanence and durability of the Committee on Production Guidelines for Book Longevity of the Council on Library Resources.

For a complete list of available publications please write:

White Mane Publishing Company, Inc.
Post Office Box 152
Shippensburg, Pennsylvania 17257
United States of America

Library of Congress Cataloging-in-Publication Data

Maney, R. Wayne, 1952-
    Marching to Cold Harbor : victory and failure, 1864 / by R. Wayne Maney.
        p.   cm.
    Includes bibliographical references and index.
    ISBN 0-942597-65-6 : $29.95
    1. Cold Harbor (Va.), Battle of, 1864.   I. Title.
E476.52.M36 1995
973.7'37--dc20   94-27111
                                                              CIP

PRINTED IN THE UNITED STATES OF AMERICA

Dedicated to Kris and Katie

Contents

Maps, Photographs, and Illustrations

Introduction

Soon after his appointment as General-in-Chief of all Union forces in early 1864, Lieutenant General Ulysses S. Grant began the movements of the Army of the Potomac from the Rapidan River in central Virginia to meet General Robert E. Lee's army. His goal was to defeat the Confederates militarily and end the war once and for all. Many historians consider that phase of the Civil War to be the most violent of the entire struggle, the beginning of the transition of the war into one of total cruelty and absolute commitment on the parts of both armies. There was little trace of romanticism anywhere in what Northern generals called "The Campaign from the Rapidan to the James"; there was no hint of ideals nor mention of the war's philosophy by the Southern defenders. The story of that series of battles and maneuvers was the unfolding of incomparable suffering and destruction. From the fiery Wilderness woods to the approaches to the last citadel at Petersburg, those bright weeks of 1864 held scenes of recklessness and determination that were almost beyond description. It was a death match of giants who clawed and tore each other as they wrestled through the Virginia lowlands toward Richmond.

In several recent studies of the great Virginia campaign of the spring of 1864 – known traditionally as the Wilderness Campaign – there has been no concentrated treatment of the Battle of Cold Harbor, the last major confrontation before the fighting sank into the trenches before Petersburg. This book presents a new view of those overlooked engagements along the Chickahominy in June of 1864 in Lee's last victory. The great assault by the Army of the Potomac upon the Confederate entrenchments on June 3 was the largest and deadliest of the entire war, outdoing even Pickett's ill-fated charge on the third day at Gettysburg.

There are many witnesses of the events and historians since who have considered the actions at Cold Harbor hardly a battle at all. In the aftermath of the Wilderness fighting and Spotsylvania Court House, and projecting toward the ten-month siege of Petersburg, the savage struggle at Cold Harbor has provoked slight interest. There is no air of gallantry or glamour to be found here, although that place along the sluggish Chickahominy still holds a feeling of death and disquiet. In my visits to that small battlefield park just outside of Richmond, I have become fascinated and even haunted by my knowledge of the forgotten men who fought there. My personal searching has convinced me of their dramatic impact on the entire war. This book is in great part a personal memorial to them.

For Southerners, there are two battles of Cold Harbor. The first is often used to designate part of the Seven Days' Battles of 1862 that Northern writers refer to as Gaines' Mill. I have blended the primary accounts of that second encounter into a general battlefield study that covers the thirty-six days from Grant's first movement from winter quarters to the withdrawal of both armies from the Cold Harbor fronts.

Much of the language is as I have found it; I have retained the old spelling for "Spottsylvania" throughout the description of that part of the campaigning in the relevant quotations.

Cold Harbor Battlefield is a tiny part of the Richmond National Battlefield Park. The National Park Service holds only 149 acres of the scenes that encompassed an area in 1864 of more than fourteen square miles. The one surviving portion of Cold Harbor Battlefield is dissected by Virginia Route 156 (Old Cold Harbor Road) barely to the east of the thriving residential area of Mechanicsville. The preserved section contains some of the best examples of entrenched works that can be found of the war in Virginia. I encourage readers to visit them before the growth of Richmond overtakes the area. Please support historic preservation.

R. Wayne Maney

Chapter One

Part One
Our Turn Has Come

"He doesn't ask me to do impossibilities for him, and he's the first general I've had that didn't."

　　　　　　　　　　　　　　- Abraham Lincoln[1]

"It shall be my earnest endeavor that you and the country will not be disappointed."

　　　　　　　　　　　　　　- Ulysses S. Grant[2]

In the first week of May 1864, the Army of the Potomac left its reasonably comfortable hibernation in the canvas and log city of Brandy Station and, led by cavalry, moved toward the traditional Rapidan crossings at Germanna and Ely's Ford. That would be the seventh time in less than two years, if Major General George Meade's attempt at Mine Run of the previous November is included, that a Federal army would enter the hazardous country of central Virginia. Almost 116,000 men with more than 50,000 horses and 6,000 supply wagons headed away from winter quarters, leaving the litter of sedentary army life and rich memorials of rebuilding and preparations for what many hoped was the last campaign of the war.[3]

The Army of the Potomac had rested at Brandy Station for almost five months. The men had time to write, play baseball, and even engage in boyish snowball fights while they anticipated the arrival of Lieutenant General Ulysses S. Grant, conqueror of Vicksburg and hero of victories in eastern Tennessee.

Those months had been put to good use. Units, some of which had formed the original nucleus of the Army of the Potomac in the summer of 1861, had been rebuilt or reformed or consolidated out of existence. Major General George G. Meade, in command since July 1863, had long wished for consolidated larger units that required fewer politically connected generals in command. It might have seemed that Meade's lack of subtlety, with his frequent and legendary explosions of temper, had not helped his cause, but with the arrival of Grant deep changes were made. They reorganized that huge army from five corps to three. The I Corps and III Corps had never recovered from the Battle of Gettysburg and their brigades were distributed among the other three corps. Many of the proud veterans wearing the deactivated corps' badges were outraged.

Changes were also made in the leadership of the remaining corps and there were some loud complaints. Of particular embarrassment was the near loss of their beloved Major General John Sedgwick from the VI Corps. Being politically suspect as both a Democrat and admirer of McClellan, he was slated for command in the Shenandoah, but was kept by Lincoln at the last moment with the men who adored his simplicity and concern.

Major General Winfield Scott Hancock remained in command of II Corps. A wounded hero of Gettysburg, he had the largest appetite for the attack of all the Union corps commanders.

Major General Gouverneur Warren received command of V Corps. Thirty-four and regarded as a pedant of great personal bravery, he had saved the day at Little Round Top at Gettysburg. He had also incurred the wrath of the unforgiving Meade for failing to possess enough of the "spirit of the offensive" at Mine Run that previous fall.[4] He was, as the great army stretched and began to move, an undetermined quantity.

The IX Corps was led by the one officer who most embodied the disasters of the past, Major General Ambrose Burnside. He still retained such political support in the Cabinet that his command was allowed to remain independent of Meade. Now at full strength, IX Corps was coming down from Annapolis by train.

There were also dramatic changes in the army's personnel that marked a clean break from traditions. For much of the first half of the war, there had been a familiarity between men and officers. Many had been neighbors before joining the army and had retained a provincial flavor. The identification of units and brigades by local colors had been maintained. The atmosphere of a volunteer force raised by free states with democratic discipline still existed at least up to mid-1863. Those had been the units decimated at Antietam and Gettysburg and Chickamauga.

But by the spring of 1864, the Army of the Potomac was no longer a volunteer army even in pretense. Both draftees and bounty men were filling its ranks. Conscripts, by far the minority, were men too honest or too poor to evade the draft by paying a commutation fee or by hiring a substitute to go in their places. They tended to have better discipline records and hold more reliably under fire. More recruits came in as volunteers rewarded by their states, or counties, with cash bonuses or bounties for their patriotism. A system of brokerage developed, particularly after 1863's draft riots, that helped produce the necessary numbers of soldiers. Reports of subsequent abuses resulted: men kidnapped or "shanghaied" into service; asylums and hospitals picked clean to fill quotas,[5] prisons emptied and street gangs admitted in full-force; and poor immigrants tricked into signing an X for their name. Many of those "volunteers" made good soldiers; many did not, and the worst cases of all, the "bounty-jumpers", proved to be useless in the eyes of the veterans. They were "professional recruits" who collected a bonus in one district and immediately deserted to rejoin and recollect in another. "Bonusmen" were guarded as closely as enemy captives, and none generally were allowed picket duty for risk of easy escape. The remaining old veterans were often sharply indignant about those "depraved and desperate human beings as never disgraced an army."[6]

That record of complaint, perhaps exaggerated at times, is strong and unanimous toward the high-bounty system. Artilleryman Private Frank Wilkeson wrote that the cause for demoralization in the last year of the war was "the worthless character of the recruits who were supplied to the army...the weak, the diseased, the feeble-minded...the faint-hearted and stupid...They were moral lepers...the clean-minded would not associate with them."[7] A cavalry officer told about his unit's reception of some 300 recruits. "The most thorough-paced villains...of New York and Boston...cutthroats and thieves" who, having deserted time after time did so from winter quarters in 1864. Fewer than fifty of them remained after three weeks.[8]

The North had sustained such staggering losses by the autumn of 1863 that even those men were needed. The three-year enlistments of thousands of veterans were expiring that spring, and not enough of them would reenlist to even replace the Union's wounded and sick. For example, the entire 13th Massachusetts refused reenlistment save for a handful who joined other regiments.[9] "I have no desire to monopolize all the patriotism," said one man from the 25th Massachusetts. Grant even reduced the Washington Garrison, transferring in heavy artillery regiments from their safe emplacements in the defenses of The District of Columbia. Those infantry trained as artillery were in oversized regiments of 1,800 and more.[10] For two years they had enjoyed light duty and regular rations and real beds. Now they shouldered their muskets and joined the army along the Rapidan. Some cavalry commands based in Maryland met a similar fate as their horses and sabres were taken away and they marched to Virginia with arms in surprised hands. A popular story described how a Connecticut heavy artilleryman, when meeting dismounted Maryland cavalry, asked, "Where are your horses?" and a Marylander replied, "Gone to fetch your heavy guns." The hazing the veterans in camp gave the "Heavies" would be slight compared to the greetings that those untested regiments received from the Southern army in the weeks ahead.

More dramatic was the Army of the Potomac's cavalry transformation. Now men like Philip Sheridan – small and grim – and hell-bent skirmishers like George Custer and Ulric Dahlgren directed their mounted troops as solid fighting units. Given charge of Grant's cavalry on April 4 in a meeting with President Lincoln, Sheridan did not cut the figure of a great warrior. Horace Porter, of Grant's staff, wrote that Sheridan was barely five feet six inches and was so worn down from the hard work of the field that he weighed less than 115 pounds. Lincoln, always having a joke ready, asked the young general, "Who ever saw a dead cavalryman?" Later, Sheridan made it unjokingly clear that he foresaw much death. "I am going to take the cavalry away from the bobtailed brigadiers. They must do without their escorts. I intend to make the cavalry an arm of the service."[11]

Strict regulations were now applied to the formerly unhurried horsemen. Officers checked on even the most routine jobs, an air of "spit and salute" appeared along with businesslike weapons such as the seven-shot Spencer carbine. Sheridan's force numbered almost 12,000 increasingly ready troopers in four divisions.

The artillery went through endless maneuvers during those months in camp. Target practice was constant and gun crews went through drill after drill of assembly, charge, disassembly, and withdrawal. Likewise, the infantry improved its marksmanship.

Drill, discipline, and harsher punishments became centralized. With the passing of a genuine volunteer army, so passed the concept of each unit keeping its own house clean. There was a quaintness about the individualism of the old days, when artillery units meted out their own punishments for "slacking" and infantry units made offenders carry heavy logs or wear placards.[12] Severe punishments for being absent without leave or drunkenness (one of the most common derelictions for both men and officers) became standardized. Just as the colorful individualism of Zouave finery or the wearing of bucktails on hats[13] was toned down in the army's growing conformity, the necessity of dealing with wholesale disciplinary management made courts martial and military punishment more regular and impersonal. Firing squads were used with much greater frequency.

There was a new spirit by May of 1864 along with reorganization and new commanders. Men finished their baseball games, packed, and made ready to leave Brandy Station and Culpeper. There were still expressions of doubt and foreboding. One officer said, "What will Lee's magnificent fighters do to an army of conscripts and bounty men? They will not even pause for a deep breath."[14]

The Army's leadership had hoped that inducements of furloughs and cash awards might cause whole regiments to reenlist, but that had not happened. April and May would bring new fighting, and many veterans were simply worn out by previous campaign seasons. There was a feeling of new unity, but somehow not of thorough confidence as the lead units readied to pass into the green countryside of central Virginia, into that familiar territory where so many had earlier been left behind. Private Robert Carter of the 22nd Massachusetts wrote his parents: "The summer days are almost here, when we shall be plodding over the roads once more in search of victory or death. Many a poor fellow will find the latter. I dread the approaching campaign. I can see horrors insurmountable through the summer months."[15]

Part Two
New Man, New Plan

"General Grant's habitual expression is that of a man who has made up his mind to drive his head through a stonewall..."
> - Colonel Theodore Lyman[16]
> Meade's Headquarter's Staff

"This man will fight us every day and every hour till the end of the war."
> - Lieutenant General
> James Longstreet[17]
> First Corps

"Only time will tell if this new general's first name is really Ulysses or Useless."
> - Charles A. Page[18]
> Correspondent
> New York Tribune

"I was much pleased with Grant. You may rest assured he is not an ordinary man."
> - Major General George G. Meade[19]

"The feeling about Grant is peculiar - a little jealousy, a little dislike, a little envy, a little want of confidence - only brilliant success will dissipate the elements. If he succeeds, the war is over. For I do assure you that in the hands of a General who gave them success, there is no force on earth that would resist this Army."
> - Captain Charles Adams, Jr.[20]
> Assistant Secretary of War

"Great confidence is felt in the plans that General Grant will adopt, and the means that he will have to use in crushing the last vestige of this Heaven accursed rebellion."
> - Private Wilbur Fisk[21]
> 2nd Vermont Regiment

"Grant impresses me well, but it is doubtful whether he can do much more with the army than his predecessors have done..."
> - Major General John Sedgwick[22]
> VI Corps, USA

It was difficult for anyone who met Ulysses S. Grant in March of 1864 to know who he actually was. He said little about his background and his physical stature (five feet eight inches and 135 pounds) gave little to measure. Observers during his first Washington visit described him as ordinary and unkempt with a slightly seedy look, resolute and stern-visaged, a man not to be trifled with, little and scared looking. He was not overly concerned with fashion and was almost never without a lighted cigar. His closest friend and confidante was his wife, Julia, who hated public life in any manner. He was well-liked by fellow officers and had a reputation befitting a common soldier – often one too common, some believed.[23]

Grant was the hero of Vicksburg and Chattanooga. He had defeated major Southern armies in the field and had taken objectives that no one else seemed to be able to conquer. Lincoln's own estimation of him is summed up in the often-used accolade, "He fights." Lincoln pressed forward the formal resurrection of the title of lieutenant general for him, with a doubling of salary, and handed to Grant control of a well-fed and superbly equipped military machine numbering more than 662,000. He was expected to take it and win the war.

Grant's promotion came as the war was about to enter its fourth year. After so many casualties and so much struggle, the war was at its most crucial stage. In both the political and military senses, the war could still be lost.

But the North's three years of punishing labors had accomplished much. Nowhere were the rebel forces on the attack in any strategic manner. The North had repelled attempts in Pennsylvania, Kentucky, and Maryland to shift the focus of the war out of the South. The naval blockade of Southern coasts and port cities was a successful and possibly the most conducive to victory of all aspects of Lincoln's war strategy. The Confederacy was short of foodstuffs, equipment, and medicines. She had few resources for an extended war effort.

Texas and whatever material resources it might bring towards Confederate survival was practically detached by that time. Most port cities were in Federal hands and Confederate naval power was almost nonexistent. Federal gunboats had control of the Mississippi and its primary branches. Including Rear Admiral David Farragut's fleet outside of Mobile Bay, there were no less than seven powerful Federal forces poised against the South.[24] But Lincoln's government needed more time to bring those punishing forces together.

Militarily, 1864 opened upon a mixture of unsettling scenes. In Richmond, where economic conditions were so bad that beggars could scarcely be found anymore, the upper class struggled to find greens, or anything else, for the dinner table. But celebrations arose to hail the destruction of Colonel Ulric Dahlgren's Union cavalry raiders, as well as the reported escape of Brigadier General John Hunt Morgan from a Federal prison in Ohio.[25] General Pierre Beauregard's forces held firm along the South Carolina coast and were about to begin successful operations at New Bern in North Carolina. Lieutenant General James Longstreet was poised to strike at Knoxville, while Lieutenant General Kirby Smith's outnumbered army held at Shreveport. Union hopes of destroying Louisiana cotton and isolating Texas came to grief as the Red River expedition collapsed. Major General William Tecumseh Sherman's drive into Georgia was stalled, and General Joe Johnston grew stronger each week. Confederate cavalry roamed freely in Kentucky and Mississippi; raiders attacked "Free-Soiler" towns in Missouri and Kansas;[26] and Colonel John Mosby's men ranged in Fauquier and Loudon Counties north of the Rappahannock.[27] Large resources, commanded by Major General Benjamin "Spoons" Butler, were stuck on the James River below Petersburg. Brigadier General Truman Seymour's strong force was driven from north Florida early that year in the only major battle of the war fought on Florida soil. Southern horsemen and infantry, though small in number, had retained a confident presence in the vital Shenandoah Valley since the fall. Major General George Pickett had been given the task of deploying his meager regulars and militia in the defense systems of the Confederate capital. The first Northern prisoners of war were being pushed into the open-field prison camp in southern Georgia soon to be known as Andersonville, while newspaper accounts of the "Massacre at Fort Pillow" near Memphis, where Major General Nathan B. Forrest's men were alleged to have murdered more than two hundred black soldiers after capture, revulsed and outraged many.[28] French Imperial troops had brazenly entered Mexico and rumors of France's alliance with the Confederacy were reborn. Meanwhile, Prime Minister Lord Palmerston of Great Britain was loudly supporting Southern efforts to acquire weapons and munitions, although European recognition of Southern independence was a dying hope. Most worrisome of all to Union leadership, Robert E. Lee's Army of Northern Virginia was still in the field, hungry and weakened but intact.

President Lincoln in February called for 500,000 more troops for the coming campaigns with results less successful than his earlier call in October for 400,000. Many Northerners who had been the most energetic supporters of the war were now expressing the bitterness of their disillusionment.

Divisions and conflicts were rampant within both Lincoln's Republican Party and the opposition Democrats. The President was solidly in charge of the "Moderate" Republican bloc – those who wished to pursue the war to its limited objectives of Union, Emancipation, and mild Reconstruction. The so-called "Radical" branch of the governing party demanded, well before any victory could be realistically projected, a delayed Reconstruction program which would place severe penalties and terms upon the defeated rebel states. There was a potent force of war Democrats such as Andrew Johnson of Tennessee and John Dix of New York who represented the ideal of restoration of the Union under no fixed conditions.

Alarming to all of those interests was the rising and formidable coalition referred to as the "Peace Democrats" – those disparate and emotional voices that called for an immediate end to the war behind a shield of reasons. By the early spring of 1864, they were growing in strength and visibility, clearly the beneficiary of the lengthening casualty lists that for many Northern families represented the only tangible result of the efforts of their generals.[29]

Outlawry within areas under Federal control, financial corruption spreading throughout the war economy, and the seemingly endless shuffling and second-guessing in the Congress and War Department gave little hope to people who had already given more measure than they felt was warranted. A story was told of a speculator who once exclaimed in a crowded railcar, "I hope the war may last six months longer, as I have made a hundred thousand dollars in the last six." A woman moves suddenly to slap him, crying, "Sir, I had two sons – one was killed at Fredericksburg, the other at Murfreesboro!"; the other passengers shoved the man from the door.[30] Charles Francis Adams said in 1863, "Jefferson Davis is perhaps in some respects superior to our own President."[31] And James G. Bennett of the *New York Herald* argued that Lincoln and his cronies had gravely lengthened the war.[32]

The President was accused of trying to become a dictator because of his cavalier approach to habeas corpus protections and use of courts martial in civilian realms. Within the Republican Party leadership planning the upcoming election campaign, there were sharp differences of support and opinion for him. As embarrassing to the ruling clique was the fact that the most vivid anti-war sentiments were being flamed in the Midwest heartland of the Republican Party. In Ohio, Indiana, and Illinois was rising the harsh point that the prize was no longer worth the cost. The extremists in the Democratic structure, known as "Copperheads," presented a threat to all those interested in the war's prosecution.

Their objective was to bring an end to the war as quickly as possible without settling the questions of union or emancipation or political compromise. The Copperheads represented a growing weariness of profitless bloodshed; they stood at the front of those who saw continuation of the war for whatever purpose to be vacant of moral base. Some were simply outright Southern sympathizers, while some had religious or moral justifications. The movement's members might be anti-draft or anti-black or simply caught up in the memories of dashing George McClellan, who would be their candidate posed against Lincoln in the fall. Some sought their own taste of conspiracy and upheaval based on any possible number of emotions.

Horace Greeley declared in early summer, "The life of the republic is still in imminent peril, and its bitterest enemies are of its own household."[33] He could have been referring to anyone, even himself.

✳ ✳ ✳ ✳ ✳

Shortly after Grant's promotion to lieutenant general, Secretary of War Edwin Stanton told him that as of that spring, there would be no more exchanging of Confederate prisoners for Union prisoners as standard war policy. Stanton explained that, despite the expected unpopularity of that policy, his great concern was that the Southern authorities refused to recognize escaped slaves in Federal uniforms as soldiers. Captured black soldiers were put back into servitude and their white officers were subject to prosecution under fugitive slave acts. Furthermore, after the parole of the prisoners of war at Vicksburg, the South had returned them to active service, contrary to their terms. And the South's continuance of that practice was helping to solve its manpower shortage. Grant agreed with the Secretary:

> We ought not to make a single exchange or release on any pretext whatever until the war closes. We have got to fight until the Military Power of the South is exhausted, and if we release or exchange prisoners captured it simply becomes a war of extermination.[34]

At almost the same time, Grant told Butler, who was responsible for exchanges in the eastern theatre:

> It is hard on our men held in southern prisons not to exchange them, but it is humanity to those left in the ranks to fight our battles. Every man we hold, when released on parole or otherwise, becomes an active soldier against us at once, either directly or indirectly. If we commence a system of exchange which liberates all prisoners

taken, we will have to fight on until the whole South is extermi-
nated. If we hold these caught they amount to no more than
deadmen.[35]

Grant was to remain so firmly in support of Stanton's stand that it
came to be seen as his own policy, rather than that of the Department
of War. It added to Grant's reputation for being inhuman, and as the
last campaign began, Northern journalists were writing lurid reports
of conditions in Southern camps that horrified families in the North,
inflaming anti-government sentiments.

Many years after the war, Sherman summed up Grant's outlook
for the spring of 1864. "He was to go for Lee and I was to go for Joe
Johnston. That was his plan."[36] Grant himself later observed that, as
he took charge, the trouble with the Northern war effort thus far had
been its lack of coordination. Grant had early on developed a philosophy to finish the military task. "I was convinced that no peace could
be had that would be stable and conducive to the happiness of the
people, both North and South, until the military power of the rebellion was entirely broken."[37] That was simple and not far removed
from what Brigadier General Irwin McDowell felt in July 1861 before
the First Battle of Manassas.
    Grant's plan for breaking the power of the Confederate rebellion
was to launch all parts of his army simultaneously in coordinated action in May of 1864. Banks would drive upon Mobile and Major General Franz Sigel would advance through the Shenandoah. Sherman
would move against Johnston's western forces to penetrate the interior of the deep South to wreck its war resources. Grant himself would
oversee a triple-pronged attack upon Lee's Army of Northern Virginia
through Meade from the Rapidan, Butler from the tidal James, and
Brigadier General George Crook from a distance directly west of Richmond. It was total war against not only field armies but also against
Southern communications, food sources, territory, and her people.

    Exactly what role as planner of that final grand assault President
Abraham Lincoln served has never been clarified. When he referred to
events many years later, Grant gave very little credit to Lincoln as a
tactician; he in fact delivered the sense that the President gave him
uninterrupted responsibility for general war strategy. There was an
evident condescension that underlines a great deal of the relationship
between the two. Horace Porter, one of Grant's aides, wrote: "The President," Grant said, "told me that he did not pretend to know anything

about the handling of troops, and that it was with the greatest reluctance that he had ever interfered with the movements of army commanders." Grant added that the President was concerned primarily with prudent speed because the nation's morale and resources were limited, and that "he believed that I knew the value of minutes, and that he was not going to interfere with my plans."[38] Grant himself wrote that on one occasion Lincoln brought out a map of Virginia and said that he wanted him to hear about a plan of his. Pointing to where two rivers emptied into the Potomac, the President suggested that Grant's army might advance between the safety of the rivers. Grant listened respectfully and told Lincoln that the idea was impracticable. "It was not brought up again in our conversations."[39]

Lincoln was pleased to share his burdens. When asked by a member of his secretariat about Grant, Lincoln said:

> Stoddard, he's the first General I have had! I'll tell you what I mean. You know how it's been with all the rest. As soon as I put a man in command of the army he'd come to me with a plan of campaign and as much as say, 'Now I don't believe I can do it, but if you say so I'll try it on,' and so put the responsibility of success or failure on me. They all wanted me to be the general. It wasn't so with Grant. He hasn't told me what his plans are and I don't want to know. I'm glad to find a man who can go ahead without me.[40]

Though he had seen five other armies go toward Richmond with poor results, Lincoln was confident that Grant would deliver. An officer in the 2nd Corps expressed a more common attitude:

> There is no enthusiasm in the army for General Grant; on the other hand there is no prejudice against him. We are prepared to throw our hats up for him when he shows himself the great soldier here in Virginia against Lee and the best troops of the Rebels.[41]

Grant's view of the job in Virginia was simple: to pin down Lee's army quickly and make it fight the kind of war that Lee could not win. Grant did not elaborate about how that might be done more than to order Meade: "Lee's army is your objective point. Wherever Lee goes, there you will go also."[42]

✻ ✻ ✻ ✻ ✻

During the Seven Years' War in the mid-18th century, William Pitt the Elder was reported to say that armies should not try to conquer a map. He was speaking about small-scale professional bodies of men on the British model that could not physically occupy countrysides with any effectiveness. Many Southern hopes in 1864 were founded on their sheer geographic presence, greater in size than the North with few vital urban centers, much the same region that had exhausted Lord Cornwallis and led to British defeat in 1781.[43] Jefferson Davis said that the enemy "must be beaten out of his vain confidence in our subjugation." Any settlement of the war short of unconditional surrender would give his Confederacy the victory.

While Abraham Lincoln knew that, the true determiner of the South's fate was not solely Lincoln. Behind him were the Northern soldiers and behind them the Northern population, and if either of those lost the will to continue, the war would be ended.[44] What remained, as Davis saw it and as William Pitt might, was the huge center of the Confederacy stretched from Richmond to Mobile to Savannah, the massive agricultural, geographic, and industrial – as scanty as it was – core of an uncertain nation. How long would it take to physically conquer and occupy that region of considerable resources and facilities? How many more names would family members in New England or Iowa or Maryland trace out with a fingertip on the casualty lists that would be tacked up as soon as the telegraphed reports were filed?

Grant was set upon destroying the enemy on the field of battle. In order to do that, the plan of war that Grant and Sherman shared had to be more than the wishful-thinking maneuvering that had ruined McClellan, Hooker, and Pope. Grant had to move over hundreds of miles of perplexing physical challenges in the hope that the Southern forces would stand and meet them. "I know nothing about maneuver," Grant was once heard to admit to Meade not long after arriving in Virginia.[45] Lee and Davis could both hope that would prove true as Grant's forces headed out at the now familiar topography of central and eastern Virginia, the first of several "maps" that the weary Union soldiers were given to overcome.

At the end of April 1864, Lincoln wrote to Grant:

> Not expecting to see you again before the Spring campaign opens, I wish to express in this my entire satisfaction with what you have done up to this time, so far as I understand it. The particulars of your plans I neither know nor seek to know. You are vigilant and self-reliant; and, pleased with this, I wish not to obtrude any constraints or restraints upon you. While I am very anxious that any great disaster, or the capture of our men in great numbers, shall

be avoided, I know these points are less likely to escape your attention than they would be mine. If there is anything wanting which is in my power to give, please do not fail to let me know. And now with a brave army and a just cause, may God sustain you.[46]

Lincoln's words were unlike any other message to any other general or associate in the war. Grant's reply of May 1 was:

> Your kind letter received...I have never had cause for complaint – have never expressed or implied a complaint against the Administration or the Secretary of War, for throwing any embarrassment in the way of my vigorously prosecuting what appeared to be my duty. And since the promotion which placed me in command of all the armies, and in view of the great responsibility and the importance of success, I have been astonished at the readiness with which everything asked for has been yielded, without even an explanation being asked. Should my success be less than I desire and expect, the least I can say is, the fault is not with you.[47]

Therefore, with a plan as substantial as his cigar's smoke, Grant and his army moved out. On May 3, Elisha Hunt Rhodes of Getty's division, VI Corps, wrote:

> Our turn has come...We shall probably cross the Rapidan River again and make another push for Richmond...While I do not feel that I am more safe than others, yet I have a firm reliance upon my Heavenly Father and am willing to leave it all to him.[48]

Chapter Two

Part One
All Is Bright and Blowing

"We wanted to see Grant introduced to General Lee & the Army of Northern Virginia, to let him have a smell of our powder. For we knew we simply could never be driven off a battle field, that whatever force Grant brought, his luck would have to accommodate itself to that fact."
- Brigadier General
Edward P. Alexander[1]
Chief of Artillery
First Corps

"General Lee was conversing with two of his officers, one of whom was known to be not only a hard fighter and a hard swearer, but a cordial hater of the Yankees...The latter officer, looking at the Yankees with a dark scowl on his face, exclaimed most emphatically, 'I wish they were all dead!' General Lee, with the grace and manner peculiar to himself, replied, 'How can you say so, General? Now, I wish they were all at home, attending to their own business, and leaving us to do the same.'"
- Edward Pollard[2]
Editor
Richmond Examiner

"General Lee appears to have reasoned thus: 'What will I gain by retreating? I cannot expect any material gain in strength. This is as good a time and as good a place to settle this issue as I can expect to find.' General Lee, I have always thought, was the most belligerent man in his army."
- Major General Henry Heth[3]
Third Corps

Across the Rapidan, Lee and his army had spent the winter concerned more with food than with Grant. In January, Lee complained, "Unless there is a change, I fear the army cannot be kept effective and probably cannot be kept together."[4] The Army of Northern Virginia had been asked to withstand punishments and discomfort from the onset, but by the early months of 1864, it was on the verge of starvation. Lee told Davis on April 12, "There is nothing to be had in this section for man and animals."[5]

Lee's winter quarters that year was near Gordonsville, Virginia. Pleasant pasture country, the outlying grassfields located less than thirty miles directly south of Brandy Station on the Orange and Alexandria rail line, gave the Southerners some meager sanctuary to heal. In what during peacetime was a fertile and productive agricultural region, there was little to sustain Lee's thin ranks. A staff officer in the Second Corps, McHenry Howard, described the land as,

> greening in the forest and neglected field, not in springing grain...A rich country in neglect; fences gone; barns vanished into the fires of soldiers; live-stock killed, eaten, or taken off. As at Fredericksburg, what had been wide-spreading woods were stripped of trees; war was on the land.[6]

Lee appealed with as much dignity as he possessed for the bare essentials, knowing that there was little for the government in Richmond to send. It particularly depressed him to see the deterioration of the horses. "Fully half of them were incapable of getting up to a gallop," one cavalry officer said. The spring grass offered some improvement for the animals, but the men, already resembling scarecrows, continued to weaken. President Davis had managed to deliver 90,000 pounds of meat earlier in the winter, but it had little effect on the hunger as artilleryman William Dame wrote, "We were always hungry." In the letter of April 12, Lee went so far as to offer Davis a private ultimatum:

> My anxiety on the subject of provisions for the army is so great that I cannot refrain from expressing it to Your Excellency. I cannot see how we can operate with our present supplies. Any derangement in their arrival or disaster to the railroad would render it impossible for me to keep the army together, and might force a retreat into North Carolina.[7]

Lee's Army of Northern Virginia also reorganized that winter. A tired and angry James Longstreet and the remains of the First Corps came back from a mauling in east Tennessee. Now in early April, Longstreet's corps of not more than 11,000 effectives cleaned themselves up for review by Lee. Longstreet's experiences in semi-independent command had been a failure of military strategy and coherent leadership. He had so much trouble with subordinates, particularly Brigadier Generals Daniel H. Hill and Evander Law, that he felt undermined by conflicting higher authority;[8] he had become bitter and discouraged toward Davis's administration to the point of being preoccupied. He was less the "Old War Horse" and more the aggrieved field commander who trusted no one except Lee himself. Of his veteran division commanders, Major General Lafayette McLaws, whom Longstreet blamed for helping lose the fight in Tennessee, was appealing to be restored to his post after a noisy court martial. John B. Hood, who had lost a leg at Chickamauga, was promoted to Lieutenant General in hopes of his retirement, but would soon return to command Confederate forces opposing Sherman.[9] His old divisional command was given to Major General Charles Field, who had never led a division in action and had held no field position since Second Manassas. Major General George Pickett, who had never gotten on well with Longstreet, had been sent to eastern North Carolina to continue operations around New Bern, and had afterward been put in charge of a skeleton force near Bermuda Hundred. Those wholesale command changes would have much effect later on in Virginia.[10]

Lieutenant General Richard Ewell of the Second Corps was in failing health by that time, both in body and mind. Unable to recover from wounds, a recurring malady had left him confused and exhausted. Dispiritedness from receiving the greatest share of the blame for Gettysburg had made him a risk at corps level. Few trusted that he could deliver. His divisions were led by the tempestuous Major General Jubal Early, the popular Major General Robert Rodes, and the steady Major General Edward Johnson. Third Corps was led by Lieutenant General Ambrose P. Hill who had known little beyond frustration and humiliation since Gettysburg.[11]

A. P. Hill was seen as inconsistent and unsure. However, he had three of the finest division leaders in the army in Major Generals Richard Anderson, Henry Heth, and Cadmus Wilcox. All totaled, the Army of Northern Virginia mustered approximately 62,000 effective soldiers and 227 guns by May 1, 1864. The grim numerical odds were reflected in the grimmer spirit of command that had pervaded Lee's army since July the previous year. The aftereffects of Gettysburg were still being felt. Ewell was enfeebled, Hill unsure in his own mind about his real capabilities, and the valiant First Corps shaken down by Longstreet's anger and depression. Early, as arrogant as ever, provoked more than a few fights within Lee's cadre. By the spring of 1864, the Army of Northern Virginia was riddled by doubt, empty-bellied and commanded by bellicose officers who could hardly stand the details of organization before the fight to come.[12]

Of the 77,000 men that Lee had brought back into Virginia six months before, more than 11,000 had disappeared, many because of illness and the results of bad food and inadequate medical care. The urge to finally give up had caused others to drift away and seek some personal form of peace. Yet there was a strength of will and optimism that came from somewhere. Brigadier General Dodson Ramseur wrote on April 15, "I feel so hopeful about the coming campaign. I have never felt so encouraged before." One notable quality of those remaining was that they would never admit that there was nothing available, whether ammunition or flour or hay. They blamed someone for holding it up and damned commissaries or quartermasters with conviction. It was that resourcefulness of focus that allowed the remaining shoeless, emaciated veterans to stand firm. A Louisiana infantryman, Charles Batchelor, wrote to his sister, "The army of Northern Virginia is anxious to meet the Yankees' greatest general under the immortal Robert E. Lee."[13]

✳ ✳ ✳ ✳ ✳

As Grant said in late April, "General Lee filled a very high place in the estimation of the people and press of the Northern states. His praises were sounded throughout the entire North after any action he was engaged in."[14] Union officers anticipated another rough trip through Virginia, fearful of testing Lee again in his home territory. Some referred to their "annual Bull Run flogging."

If there was uncertainty among the Northern military and civilian leadership, there was never any lack of confidence felt by them toward Lee. His reputation was never higher than in the spring of 1864, whether among his own troops or in the Army of the Potomac. Lee's reputation was worth another corps, as estimates of his genius, real or not, took on superhuman qualities in the minds of many. The sense of inferiority which was always a factor in Grant's self-image, especially when his thoughts went to Lee, would shortly have dramatic results in the unraveling of plans and strategy.

Lee was dramatically showing the effects of arduous campaigning. His physical condition – legendary in strength and endurance since the war with Mexico – was weakened by recurring fatigue and arthritis. Lee might have suffered some form of stroke or seizure in the spring or summer of 1863, and was frequently in need of rest.[15] A South Carolina officer noted that Lee appeared faded and drawn compared to his countenance of a year before. Another from Georgia mentioned that though Lee was a bit grayer and displayed a few more wrinkles, he looked remarkably the same as he did two years ago.[16] However changed or not, Lee's appearance was enough to encourage the hungry and dispirited, and his men wrestled for the chance touch of his saddle, bridle, or his boot as he went among them.

Lee was now committed to the defensive, much against his nature. His belligerent spirit was restless. "If I was able to move, the enemy might be driven back from the Rappahannock and obliged to look to the safety of his own capital instead of the assault upon ours."[17] He observed the stripped land of Orange County and the poor condition of his army. "We shall have to glean troops from every quarter to oppose the combination of the enemy." His scouts brought in reports every day of Union build-ups and cavalry movements. He expected Grant and Meade to lead their assault as soon as the wet weather abated. "Colonel," he said to a member of his staff, "we have got to whip them! We must whip them!"[18]

On April 3, Lee requisitioned the strongest and best-tended horses from Richmond. He checked his intelligence reports concerning the options the Army of the Potomac might choose from. He even monitored rainfall and water levels in the Rapidan and Rappahannock in case he needed to cross either river.[19] "We are not in condition," he told President Davis, "and never have been, in my opinion, to invade the enemy's country with any prospect of permanent benefit. But we can alarm and embarrass him to some extent, and thus prevent his undertaking anything of magnitude against us."[20]

Lee had often remarked that one help for his situation in Virginia would be aggressive action in the West, possibly in Texas or Tennessee, by the Confederate forces remaining there. But there was little hope of that by spring of 1864. Lee knew of the condition of General Joe Johnston's forces. His letters to Davis are filled with expressions of resolution and tightly worded confidence in his veterans. Every day of rain and warmer weather brought grass for his animals and one less day of tiring campaigning for his men.

Lee repeatedly appealed to Davis for the return of Major General Robert Hoke's division from its triumphs in eastern North Carolina, along with reminders about food and fodder. There was little that Davis could do that he had not already done. He had attempted to convince the British government to deliver warships; he had rearranged the meager resources that his states provided and had, contrary to what biographers have submitted, left his commanders alone for the greatest part to meet challenges as they came.[21] Davis had attempted to deal evenly with reluctant and prickly military leaders such as Joe Johnston and Longstreet. After Lincoln's most recent call for 500,000 additional men to arms, more than the entire Confederacy could muster, Davis's only available action was to widen the draft age for Southern men to between 15 and 57. Afterwards Davis wrote that the necessary action was robbing both the cradle and the grave.[22] Members of his own Cabinet, leaders of the Confederate legislature, and leading journalists leveled acrimony and insult at him right and left. On the last day of April his five-year-old son, Joe, fell thirty feet from a window of the presidential mansion and died of his injuries that same day.[23]

Richmond itself could give only poor response through that third winter of the war. Food and necessities of every kind remained scarce and inflation had crippled the Southern economy. Beans went for sixty dollars a bushel, coffee for ten dollars a pound, and good cloth for ten dollars a yard. Confederate currency devalued each business day. Some citizens combined their scant resources and held "starvation parties." Fresh meat had vanished and eggs sold for more than two dollars a dozen. All the news was of Grant's inevitable concentration on their city and over it all lingered the specter of starvation.[24]

Lee's scouts brought him word by the end of March that the wives of Federal officers had begun to leave Brandy Station and on April 7, the army sent away sutlers and private merchandisers. "Everything indicates a concentrated attack on this front, which renders me the more anxious to get back the troops belonging to this army, and causes me to suggest if possible, that others be moved from points at the south, where they can be spared, to Richmond," read Lee's message to Davis.[25] From Clark's Mountain his signalmen were able to watch the Union army in movement, just as they had once watched Hooker and more recently, Meade, try to come through.

On April 18, Lee ordered all unnecessary baggage moved to the rear. On May 2 on the summit of the mountain, Lee and his staff and lieutenants could look north toward Culpeper and imagine the Union army driving directly south at them, following the Orange and Alexandria railroad tracks. Barely visible ten miles beyond was the Rappahannock that in ten more miles reached the old battlegrounds of Fredericksburg. They could see Meade's tents pitched by the Rapidan and looking eastward could study the green, eighty-square-mile expanse called the Wilderness on the river's northern rim.

That was the last time that Lee would climb that mountain, where he had first gone with Lieutenant General Thomas "Stonewall" Jackson in August of 1862. Jackson had been killed in battle here in the Wilderness a year before, and since then the army had dramatically changed. But Lee knew that whoever commanded them, the men were still capable. "Never was the army in better trim than now," said Colonel Walter Taylor of Lee's staff, "There is no overweening confidence, but a calm, firm, and positive determination to be victorious, with God's help."[26]

Lee studied the terrain through his field glasses and pointed at Germanna and Ely's Fords on the Rapidan. "Grant will cross by one of those fords," he said. Still, for safety, Lee sent instructions to Longstreet to move one of his divisions to the northwest of Gordonsville in case that avenue was taken.

Lee expected three simultaneous attacks from three different directions. The main assault would come across the Rapidan against his front. Butler's forces would threaten Richmond from Bermuda Hundred on the James River and a diversionary movement launched in the Shenandoah would complete the scheme. All those actions seemed to be clear to him because Lee had developed an affinity for the region, having fought at so many adversaries along the two rivers in the less than two years at the head of his army.

On April 28, Lee told his cousin, Margaret Stuart:

> You must sometimes cast your thoughts on the Army of Northern Virginia, and never forget it in your prayers. It is preparing for a great struggle, but I pray and trust that the great God, mighty to deliver, will spread over it His almighty arms, and drive its enemies before it.[27]

The next day the signal station reported heavy dustclouds and columns of men on the march. Billows of thick smoke, as if fires were being lighted to destroy equipment and personal belongings that could not be carried, blew over the river. Lee ordered Ewell's Second Corps to be ready to move at the next daylight.[28]

Part Two
Toward the Poison Fields

"I cultivate hope and patience, and trust to the blunders of our enemies and the gallantry of our troops for ultimate success."
                                        - President Jefferson Davis[29]

"If I mistake not, Grant will shortly come to grief if he attempts to repeat the tactics in Virginia which proved so successful in Mississippi."
                                        - Officer on Lee's Staff to
                                          Colonel Charles Venable[30]

"We have just received marching orders...all is bustle and confusion...I feel sure of a victory..."
                                        - Colonel James Wadsworth[31]
                                          Meade's Headquarters

"Bob Lee will drive you-all back just as he has done before!"
                                        - Northern Infantrymen to
                                          Cavalry at Germanna Ford[32]

President Davis felt that the next six months were vital. The prospect of adding to the North's war weariness, to contest every movement fiercely and show the people of the North that no matter what gains they might seek, the price would be far too costly, gave him a certain determination. Davis pondered how much the North could stand to watch as more armies disappeared in the name of the Union. How much was their sacred "Union" worth? In six months the voters of the Northern states would decide.

Davis was convinced that his nation could not be defeated as long as his armies suffered no military disaster within the redoubt of Richmond and the central South. He must prolong the action and even on the defensive, control the development of the coming campaigns.

There were even those who felt that Grant's aggressive spirit would actually serve the interests of those wanting a political solution to the war. The heavier the losses, the more fearful the carnage in Virginia or in Georgia, the more would be the effect on the Northern peace movement. A commander who moved cautiously and counted his casualties would not be so shattering on Northern nerves. With those visions of an angry electorate that would declare peace over the heads of politicians and armies, Davis waited.[33]

On April 29, the last formal review of the Army of Northern Virginia was held to officially recognize the return of the First Corps. Near Gordonsville, Lee and his headquarters staff made a formal visit and inspection. The remnants of that once fearsome body did their best to make themselves presentable. Captain Augustus Dickert of South Carolina wrote in his journal:

> Guns were burnished and rubbed up, cartridge boxes and belts polished, and the brass buttons and buckles made to look bright as new. Our clothes were patched and brushed up, so far as was in our power, boots and shoes greased, the tattered and torn old hats were given here and there a "lick and a promise," and on the whole I must say we presented not a bad-looking body of soldiers.[34]

The reviewing party went down the ranks of the two divisions, battalions of artillery on the flanks. At the head of McLaw's division was their new commander, Brigadier General Joseph Kershaw. Highly religious, a lawyer from South Carolina, Kershaw had already had a distinguished record in every engagement he had shared, and added poise and coolness in combat to his command. With him was the commander of the famous Texas Brigade, Brigadier General John Gregg, the only newcomer to Virginia. It was said that while there were no native Virginians in the entire corps, the men rejoiced as if at homecoming and cheered loudly at General Lee's presence, tattered hats thrown high into the air.

Chapter Three

Part One
Roads Through the Wilderness

"The Wilderness was our favorite fighting ground."
> - Brigadier General
> Edward P. Alexander[1]
> Chief of Artillery
> First Corps

"The Confederates are shooting to kill, this time..."
> - Private Frank Wilkeson[2]
> New York Artillery

"All circumstances seemed to combine to make the scene one of unutterable horror. It was as though Christian men had turned to fiends, and hell itself has usurped the earth."
> - Colonel Horace Porter[3]
> Grant's Headquarter's Staff

"A butchery pure and simple it was, unrelieved by any of the arts of war..."
> - North Carolina Infantryman[4]

The "Wilderness" is the name given a large region of central Virginia west of Fredericksburg. In 1864, it was a district of dense multi-layered growth, with thickets of oak, hickory, and scrub pines ranging from fifteen to thirty feet in height. The sandy soil, worthless for extensive agriculture, was veined with creeks, brooks, and countless dry gulches and ravines, making it hazardous to walk at a calm pace. The heavy spring rains of 1864 had turned its creeks into little rivers and left low areas like marshes. The overgrowth shielded out the sun even at its midday brightest. With the exception of a few hard-wrought farms, it was desolate. Hardwood stands and thick brush shut off vision within a few feet in any direction. There were, around the few homesteads, some cleared areas dotted here and about within the eighty or so square miles of deep forest. That dark region was often referred to by natives as "the poison fields."

Two primary crossroads dissected the sprawling wasteland: headed west from Fredericksburg was the Orange Turnpike and to its south a few miles, the Orange Plank Road; from the north ran the Germanna Plank Road which crossed the Turnpike and ran to the second perhaps two miles farther; a wagon road called the Brock Road traveled up from Spotsylvania Courthouse. Wilderness Tavern was a group of houses at the upper crossroads, amidst swampy lowlands cut through by runs of pitch-black water. There, in a place of no apparent consequence, twice before Union advances had been decisively stymied. Almost exactly a year before, those woods and gullies had been the site of perhaps Lee's greatest victory near the way station of Chancellorsville.

In the spring of 1863, Hooker had advanced toward Richmond with an immense army to draw out Lee's forces. Instead, Hooker was soundly defeated, losing 18,000 men and retreating northward in humiliation. Grant was taking his soldiers, as heavy-laden with ammunition and short rations as the wagons coming in the rear, into the same dark passage.

When Lee told Ewell to move east, he had guessed that Grant would not assault his left where decisive results might be quickly achieved. Grant was instead moving his army east and south, without a real battle plan and, as he explained later, depending on Providence and his cavalry to keep his supply lines from Brandy Station and later from the Potomac secure. Grant planned to link with Butler's forces moving up from the James River. Meade had strongly opposed that plan but was overruled.[5]

It was Wednesday, May 4. At Germanna Ford, the V and VI Corps moved steadily across the Rapidan on freshly placed pontoon bridges. Six miles east of them, II Corps went across at Ely's Ford. Coming behind from Rappahannock Station was IX Corps. Meade's Chief of Staff, Major General Andrew Humphreys, defined Grant's tactical plan: "By starting the whole army in motion at midnight, it might move so far beyond the Rapidan the first day that it would be able to pass out of the Wilderness and turn, or partially turn, the right flank of Lee before a general engagement took place."[6] Into the Wilderness, where artillery maneuvering would be impossible and useless and where no open area existed, went the Army of the Potomac. At midday, Grant and his staff joined the army, coming over the upper ford. He was pleased at the uneventful movement of his army into enemy territory:

> The Cavalry seized the two crossings before daylight and by 6:00 a.m. had the pontoons ready for the crossing of the Infantry and Artillery. This was undoubtedly a surprise to Lee. The fact that the movement was unopposed proves this.[7]

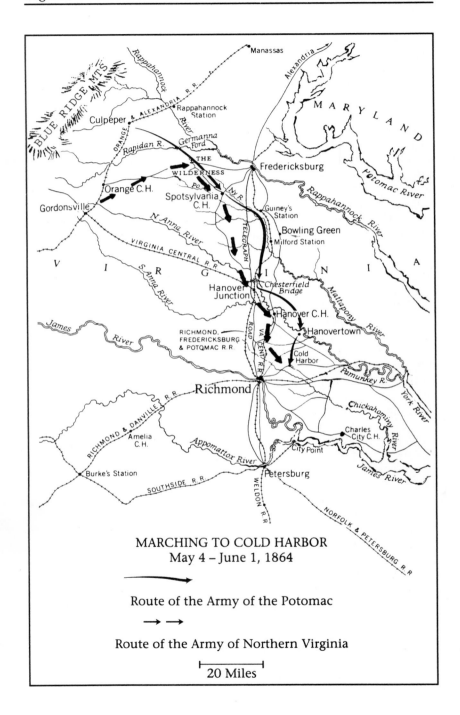

MARCHING TO COLD HARBOR
May 4 – June 1, 1864

Route of the Army of the Potomac

Route of the Army of Northern Virginia

20 Miles

A reporter asked Grant how long it would be until he reached Richmond, to which the General answered, "I will agree to be there in four days, that is, if Gen. Lee becomes a party to the agreement. If he objects, the trip will undoubtedly be prolonged."[8] In that relatively affable mood, after reporting to Washington, Grant went to sleep at Wilderness Tavern.

He had received enthusiastic telegrams announcing that the other parties in that great concert of military action – Sigel, Butler, and Sherman – were ready to begin operations. His soldiers camped on Hooker's old battlefield itself, and more than a few could see the remains of hastily buried skeletons poking from washed-out graves, or bones scattered about in the brush. "We wandered to and fro," one soldier wrote, "Looking at the gleaming skulls and whitish bones, and examining the exposed clothing of the dead to see if they had been Union or Confederate soldiers."[9]

Early the next day, Lee gave Second Corps commander Richard Ewell simple directions: to head down the Turnpike and engage the enemy when he reached them. Lee was placing the two corps he had on-hand in a blocking position against Grant's army to see what might happen.

Part Two
May 5

On the Orange Plank Road, Lee rode with Ambrose "Little Powell" Hill. Hill was sick and in some discomfort, and Lee would have to assume field command of his divisions in the hours to come. He sent word to Ewell to slow down, as progress on the rough road was tedious, and Longstreet's corps was still a day away to the west.

Ewell's lead division under Edward Johnson made first contact with Brigadier General Charles Griffin, whose division had been placed by Warren to guard the Turnpike. Those Federals had thrown up quick breastworks near Parker's Store. Another division was to move through the trackless underbrush and help Griffin meet the Southern threat. At about noon, led by the colorful 140th New York Zouaves and parts of five Regular Army regiments, Griffin's battle line came roaring out of the trees at the Southerners near Sander's Field. They were driven back by a curtain of fire from three Confederate brigades. More Zouave regiments from Pennsylvania and New York then attacked. Their lead elements were annihilated by close range fire from both flanks on the field's border.

Still, the New Yorkers plunged across and into the foliage, meeting the enemy with bayonets in the smoke and dogwood blooms. Almost at that time, the high grass and field bramble, dry as tinder, caught fire. In that weird atmosphere of daytime darkness, in smoke and flames, the 140th and 146th New York regiments lost 567 of 1,600 men in two hours. Brigadier General Romeyn Ayres's Zouave brigade suffered 936 casualties in less than thirty minutes.[10]

Across the Turnpike, one of Griffin's brigades, with the famous Iron Brigade of Brigadier General James Wadsworth's division, crossed the clearing and smashed through a Virginia brigade. Just as they were set to exploit that large gap, they became lost and confused in the marshes and thick brush. Brigadier General John Gordon's Georgians and Brigadier General Junius Daniel's North Carolinians came up to attack the confused and stationary units. The Iron Brigade and others retreated while other units were pinned in the wiry undergrowth, bullets coming from several directions.

Farther south on the Orange Plank Road, the main battle was developing. At mid-morning a footrace had begun for the crossroads where Brock Road met the main passage. If A. P. Hill's divisions could reach that intersection first, Lee would be able to cut off Hancock's II Corps to the south. He hoped to slice Grant's army in two and defeat it in detail. While Meade ordered 6,000 men under Brigadier General George Getty to drive south, Lee ordered a division led by Henry Heth to rush ahead faster than Getty and Hancock, whose strung-out forces were far below the Orange Plank. Behind Heth came Cadmus Wilcox's division, and the two began to push the Federal line backward. Getty's forces were having a tough time getting down the narrow, hacked-out, clogged wagon trail. At a clear spot called the Widow Tapp Farm, Lee and Hill counseled with their staffs. Lee wanted a full assault on the crossroads, but first ordered Wilcox to move his division to Heth's left to close up with Robert Rodes' division in the depth of the deepwoods. That left Heth, with about 7,000 at ready, against 17,000 under Hancock on the road.

At about four o'clock, Meade ordered Getty to advance two support divisions. Heth's men had constructed light breastworks on a thickly wooded hillside. As the Union troops came over a low ridge, volleys from Heth's brigades stopped them. Brigadier General Lewis Grant later said, "As soon as the first volleys were over, our men hugged the ground as closely as possible and kept up a rapid fire and the enemy did the same. The moment our men rose to advance, musketry cut them down with such slaughter that it was impracticable to do more than maintain our position."[11] Further attacks by Brigadier General Gersham Mott's division met the same end. As Wilcox moved up to support Heth, his front lines were hit by Hancock's fresh divisions coming in from the south. The Confederates made several counter-charges of their own, once reaching the support artillery of II Corps before being driven back.

By five o'clock, the exhausted men of both sides prayed for darkness. Wright's division of VI Corps had attacked around three o'clock and for two hours there had been attacks and counterattacks in the bushes and smoke. None had any real result other than to add to the day's misery. As black evening came down, sounds of chopping and shoveling went on all along the battle zone as men tried to build earthworks and cover for the next day. Fires erupted everywhere, flaring up in the leaves and bramble. The cries of the wounded went on through the night. No one could rise to help without drawing fire upon themselves.

The testimony of the participants of that first day's combat reveal the meaning of "The Wilderness" far better than the words of the historians. Captain Samuel Buck of the 13th Virginia Infantry was with his brigade north of the Wilderness Turnpike. He remembered the green curtain of foliage that reduced visibility to less than fifty feet as line after line of blue-uniformed figures crashed through. From behind barricades of dirt and dead trees, the Southerners waited until their enemies were within "pistol-distance" before opening fire:

> Nothing could stand that fire and in a few moments the blue line swayed and fell back only to be replaced by another and another until fire had tried our mettle. Each one melted as did the first; death was in every shot and we held fast to our works...

Captain Buck muttered a prayer for night to come and recorded the noises about him as the violence gave way to the chilling after-effect:

> Shall that terrible night ever be erased from my memory, the terrible groans of the wounded, the awful sound of the owl and the awful shrill shrieks of the whippoorwill – the most hideous of all noises I ever heard on a battle field after the firing had ceased? The terrible loneliness is of itself sufficient and these birds seemed to mock our grief and laugh at the groans of the dying.[12]

Private Warren Goss, an infantryman with Hancock's II Corps, wrote:

> The scenes of savage fighting with the ambushed enemy...defies description. No one could see the fight fifty feet from him. The roll and crackle of the musketry was something terrible, even to the veterans of many battles. The lines were very near each other, and from the dense underbrush and the tops of trees came puffs of smoke, the "ping" of the bullets, and the yell of the enemy. It was a blind and bloody hunt to the death, in bewildering thickets, rather than a battle.

Goss recalled how the dense undergrowth broke up the individual units in spite of their efforts to stay together. Briars and thickets cut their faces and hands as the men tripped forward, and soon after their advance the fires began to sweep into the Union lines:

The uproar of battle continued through the twilight hours. It was eight o'clock before the deadly crackle of musketry died gradually away, and the sad shadows of night, like a pall, fell over the dead in these sanguined thickets. The groans and cries for water or for help from the wounded gave place to the sounds of conflict...Thus ended the first day's fighting of the Army of the Potomac under Grant.[13]

Part Three
May 6

"I am happy. I have felt despair for the cause for some months, but now I am relieved, and feel assured that we will put the enemy back across the Rapidan before night...We will smash them now."
- Brigadier General
Micah Jenkins[14]
Field's Division

Both generals planned for attacks to begin early that morning. Meade was aware that Longstreet and Anderson had not yet caught up to Lee, and gave orders that A. P. Hill's divisions on the Orange Plank Road be destroyed. Sedgwick and Warren were to renew their assaults on the Turnpike. Burnside's four divisions were now on the field. Brigadier General Thomas Stevenson took one to assist Hancock and two more were sent to back up Wadsworth on the northern movement.

At the Tapp Farm, Lee waited for the First Corps and Anderson's division, together some 20,000 of the finest men in his army. Longstreet had moved out along the Catharpin Road south of Orange Plank at about one in the morning, heading toward Hill's positions. The violence broke around four hours later when Ewell's divisions opened up and were soon answered by Hancock's skirmishers. Coming in three lines of battle, 20,000 Union soldiers assaulted Wilcox's Confederates along on a mile-long front. Then, as Wadsworth's men again hit Heth's flank, the Southern units began to fall back, some to develop a better position, but others, like the 11th North Carolina, withdrew because their flanks had collapsed in the brutal assault. As the rebel line faltered, Hancock jubilantly declared to Meade's staff, "Tell Gen. Meade that we are driving them most beautifully!"[15] As more divisions hit the line, by seven o'clock the Southerners were pushed back more than a mile with remnants trying to re-group at the upper end of the Tapp Farm. Lee himself directed the line, ordering Colonel William Poague's twelve guns to open fire. The battery's canister staggered the II Corps' lead units but they pushed on. Lee ordered his wagons readied for withdrawal.

Then, the terrain and cover of the Wilderness once again took control of the maneuvering. Wadsworth's unlucky brigades became disoriented once again and threw themselves as well as Major General David Birney's units into a misdirected tangle. Burnside's two divisions, caught in the dark and trackless center of the Wilderness forest, never found the fight. They struggled for hours to cut through. During that time, Longstreet's forward units were coming in parallel columns, Field's division on the left and Kershaw's on the right. They shouldered through the splintered remains of Hill's corps to meet the faltering Union front.

Seeing men charging forward Lee rode up to Brigadier General John Gregg to ask what brigade was moving by him. "The Texas Brigade," Gregg responded. "Hurrah for Texas!" Lee bellowed, "Go and drive those people out!" Then he watched as Gregg took them forward. "Texans always move them." Lee impetuously began to ride toward the front with the Texans and they almost panicked to see him in close firing range. They shouted for him to get to the rear but he seemed to not hear them. Longstreet later recalled that he rode up to Lee and told him, "Your line will soon be recovered if you will permit me to handle the troops," and convinced Lee to move to safety.[16] The Texans advanced, and within the next ten minutes lost nearly 400 of their 800 men while driving the Federal line backward.

Next, Longstreet sent in four brigades including two from Kershaw's division that began to punish Hancock's bewildered right front. Brigadier General John Gibbon's division, which had the job of protecting Hancock's left along the Brock Road, became fragmented and failed to join in the counter-attack. By the middle of morning, Longstreet had driven the Federals back to their dawn starting place. Then, learning of a gap in Hancock's lines created by Gibbon's miscues, Longstreet sent his own Chief-of-Staff, Lieutenant Colonel Moxley Sorrel and four brigades to turn Birney's exposed flank. They followed an unfinished railroad bed that gave excellent cover. That was the same railbed that had shielded Jackson's smashing flanking movement against Hooker exactly a year before.[17] Charging through the screening bramble, the Confederates rolled up several Union brigades.

On the right, Wadsworth tried to keep his offensive moving and ordered Massachusetts troops directly down the Plank Road. Within minutes, Wadsworth was mortally wounded and his lead brigades dissolved. At that point, the Southern momentum also began to sputter and Hancock's men withdrew to the safety of their breastworks. It was now almost twelve-thirty in the afternoon.

Longstreet and his staff were riding along the Orange Plank Road, planning the continuation of their attack, when confused soldiers of Brigadier General William Mahone's Virginia brigade opened fire on them. Three officers were killed, among them Brigadier General Micah Jenkins of South Carolina; Longstreet took a ball that plowed through his neck and into the right shoulder. It would take almost six months for Lee's "Old War Horse" to recover, and Lee assumed command of the First Corps himself.[18]

The fighting seemed to pause around three o'clock. Grant, sitting upon a tree stump whittling and chewing his cigar, was told of Hancock's reversal and quietly ordered reinforcements thrown into the battle. He scheduled a large-scale attack against Hill and Longstreet for six that evening, but Lee struck first. Led by Anderson's Georgians and South Carolinians, the Southerners drove against Hancock's tightly packed divisions holding behind their defensive line. The woods all around and even the breastworks themselves caught fire as the Union line broke and ran. But Colonel Samuel "Sprigg" Carroll's brigade of Gettysburg veterans held. By about five that afternoon, the Southern offensive slacked off in the heavy smoke and confusion, but the chances for Grant's scheduled attack were destroyed.

Lee, at his most belligerent, asked Ewell if anything might be done to the Federals astride the Turnpike. Brigadier General John Gordon insisted that he could find the enemy's right flank and turn it in. Lee, seeing another manifestation of Chancellorsville and Jackson, agreed and scheduled Gordon's attack for about six o'clock. As it so occurred, Gordon's and Brigadier General Robert Johnston's brigades hit Sedgwick's least-prepared units. Sedgwick, well-loved and preoccupied, had in his fashion taken no preparations for defense, and the result was predictable. Shortly, Grant and Meade received word that the entire VI Corps was collapsing. Staff officers approached, warning that Lee would hurl his whole force to drive them back into the river. Horace Porter recorded:

> The General rose to his feet, took the cigar out of his mouth, turned to the officer, and replied with a degree of animation which he seldom manifested: "Oh, I am heartily tired of hearing what Lee is going to do. Some of you always seem to think he is suddenly going to turn a double somersault and land on our rear and both our flanks at the same time. Go back to your command, and try to think what we are going to do ourselves, instead of what Lee is going to do."

Grant sent in reinforcements from Warren's corps like tossing chips onto a fire. Growing darkness ended Gordon's attacks. He had destroyed two brigades, taking hundreds of prisoners, but it was all too little and too late in the day. Lee went back to his headquarters at the Tapp Farm as fires burned through the dry ravines. Grant gave his last cigar to Meade and turned in for sleep. Porter later wrote that Grant went through more than twenty long cigars that day and that he never again saw the general use tobacco so heavily.[19]

Private Benjamin Franklin Jones of the Surry Light Artillery wrote of that day in the Southern lines:

> May 6 – Our battery was engaged nearly all day, and had some very warm and dangerous work on hand just on the right of General Longstreet's line...The fierce, sharp roar of deadly musketry filled our ears from morning til night, and a thick white cloud of battle smoke hung pall-like over the fields and woods all day along the battle lines. The smoke was so thick and dense sometimes during the day that it was impossible to discern anything fifty yards away, and at midday the smoke was so thick overhead that I could just make out to see the sun, and it looked like a vast ball of red fire hanging in a smoke-veiled sky. The country all along the lines, which is mostly timber lands, was set on fire early in the day by the explosion of shell and heavy musketry; a thousand fires blazed and crackled on the bloody arena, which added new horrors and terrors to the ghastly scene spread out over the battle plain...[20]

In a letter written on the battlefield, Private Wilbur Fisk of the 2nd Vermont volunteers gave his account of those two days:

> We saw nothing of the enemy, and heard nothing of them until just before we reached the latter point, when our column unexpectedly came upon a column of rebel troops coming this way. After a little skirmishing, the rebels fell back. Here was a high point of land where the roads cross at right angles, and it is in the midst of an endless wilderness – "a wilderness of woe," as the boys call it. The rebels gave us a warm reception. They poured bullets into us so fast that we had to lie down to load and fire. The front line gave way and we were obliged to take their places. We were under their fire over three hours before we were relieved. We were close in on them, and their fire was terribly effective. Our regiment lost 264 men killed and wounded.

Fisk told of his being sent forward on the second day of combat into the same sector, where he found the stacked bodies of his comrades just as they had been left. The 2nd Vermont took prisoner a number of North Carolina soldiers, but after delivering them, was hit by the Confederate assault on the II Corps. The Vermonters were thrown into confusion, and Fisk found himself seeking a safe place in the rear like any other straggler that he so often derided in his letters to his family:

> I was tired almost to death and hungry as a wolf. I had been fighting for Uncle Sam's Constitution to the best of my ability, and now I thought it of about as much importance to me individually, to pay a little attention to my own...My objective was to find a safe place in the rear...My patriotism was well nigh used up, and so was I...
>
> (May 7)...the next day there was no fighting of any consequence...We had been assigned to the Second Corps, under General Hancock, during this fighting, and that afternoon we went back to our own corps...How much we have accomplished I cannot tell. You never need ask a private soldier for general information. He is the last man to get that. He sees but little of what is going on and takes a part in stillness...[21]

Horace Porter wrote this in his recollections:

> There are some features of the battle which have never been matched in the annals of warfare. For two days nearly 200,000 veteran troops had struggled in a death-grapple, confronted at each step with almost every obstacle by which nature could bar their path, and groping their way through a tangled forest the impenetrable gloom of which could be likened only to the shadow of death...It was a battle fought with the ear and not with the eye. All circumstances seemed to combine to make the scene one of unutterable horror. At times the wind howled through the treetops, mingled its moans with the groans of the dying, and heavy branches were cut off by the fire of the artillery, and fell crashing upon the heads of the men, adding a new terror to battle. Forest fires raged, and ammunition trains exploded; the dead were roasted in the conflagration; the wounded, roused by its hot breath, dragged themselves along, and with their torn and mangled limbs, in the mad energy of despair, to escape the ravages of the flames; and every bush seemed hung with shreds of blood-stained clothing. It was as though Christian men had turned to fiends, and hell itself had usurped the earth.[22]

Theodore Lyman of Meade's staff heard Grant say, "Tonight Lee will be retreating south."[23] It is hard to believe that a man not given to dreamy projection, who had been a calm witness to the previous two days' carnage, could have said that. Lee had no such plan, and the Northerners who were convinced that they had been through another Chancellorsville wondered what might be their own next direction of travel.

The confrontation in the Wilderness, like a clawing and tearing wrestling match between desperate giants, had cost Grant 17,666 men killed, wounded, and missing. Reliable figures for Lee's losses are given, by some counts, at a minimum of 7,500. Grant said to a newspaper correspondent before he retired that night, "If you see the President, tell him, from me, that whatever happens, there will be no turning back."[24]

After the war, some person asked Romeyn Ayres if his famous old division of regulars was still in service at the time. He answered that most of the regulars had been killed in the fighting:

> I had regulars – what were known as the regular division – before I went into battle at Gettysburg. I left half of them there, and buried the rest in the Wilderness. There are no regulars left.[25]

Chapter Four

Part One
Racing to Spotsylvania

"This month might be called 'Bloody May'..."
- *Richmond Examiner*
May 14, 1864

"If this scene had been presented to me before the war, anxious as I was for the preservation of the Union, I should have said: 'The cost is too great; erring sisters, go in peace'."
- Senator Henry Wilson
of Massachusetts[1]

"Yanks and Rebels, covered with their blood, lay clinched in the arms of death. Ghastly faces upturned, eyes staring out of their sunken sockets, countenances betokening the desperation of the conflict, told a story never told before on this continent."
- Sergeant Francis M. Thrasher[2]
108th New York

"The brush between the lines was cut and torn into shreds, and the fallen bodies of men and horses lay there with the flesh shot and torn from their bodies."
- Lieutenant Colonel
John Schoonover[3]
11th New Jersey

On the day after the Wilderness fighting ended, Brigadier General James Wilson of the cavalry visited Grant's headquarters. He was told by Chief-of-Staff John Rawlins that the Southern attack of the previous evening had tested Grant's self-control more than anything ever seen before. Grant had slept fitfully as men with singed and blistered faces fought both fires and renewed Southern attacks far past sunset. Grant's closest aides, all from the Western theatre, said that their fears of the poor fighting qualities in the Army of the Potomac were true, and that only Grant's personal efforts had prevented his army from retreating at dawn.[4]

At six-thirty that morning Grant told Meade: "Make all preparations during the day for a night march to take position at Spottsylvania
Court House with one corps..."[5]

Artilleryman Frank Wilkeson remembered an incident in the confused exiting from the morass of the Wilderness. Southern skirmishers
were posted in the turn of a road and a battery was brought up to
scatter them. Shortly after the gunners sent the first rounds off, Grant
and Meade appeared together and posted themselves under a tree to
watch the exchange as it turned into a noisy fight. Meade seemed to
fret nervously, pulling on his beard and moving about on his horse
when the fighting went badly. Grant, Wilkeson observed, only watched
quietly, his cigar firmly in his teeth as the smoke furled about his head
and shoulders, expressionless like a bored man forced to watch something that utterly disinterested him. After the shooting stopped and
the open field in the front was littered with bleeding corpses from
both sides, both generals mounted and rode away. Grant still had not
flinched a muscle.

"The enlisted men looked curiously at Grant," Wilkeson remembered, "And after he had disappeared they talked of him, and of the
dead and wounded men who lay in the field; and all of them said just
what they thought, as was the wont of American soldiers."[6]

Charles Dana, Jr., who was Lincoln's and Halleck's observer with
Grant's forces, witnessed a conversation about the battle's casualties.
Meade there offered his superior the comforting observation:

Well, General, we can't do these little tricks without losses.[7]

The picture of the impassive and remorseless dealer of death has
been firmly planted, yet among the Union commanders it was Grant
that winced at the incredible losses, who seemed so personally affected
at times that he could hardly leave his tent. He found it barely possible
to defend himself against charges of his inhumanity.

There had been so many resemblances to the defeats that the Army
of the Potomac had endured that, for some time, it was impossible to
predict Grant's next move. The battles in the Wilderness had been
fought out of control, and on the next morning, filled with fog, the
soldiers expected a withdrawal. One of them said, "...most of us thought
it was another Chancellorsville, and that the next day we should re-
cross the river."[8] Grant himself felt:

While it is in one sense a drawn battle, as neither side has gained or lost ground substantially since the fighting began, yet we remain in possession of the field, and the forces opposed to us have withdrawn to a distance from our front and taken up a defensive position. We cannot call the engagement a positive victory, but the enemy have only twice actually reached our lines in their many attacks, and have not gained a single advantage. This will enable me to carry out my intention of moving to the left, and compelling the enemy to fight in a more open country and outside of their breastworks.[9]

As Grant told Halleck that same morning:

At present we can claim no victory over the enemy, neither have they gained a single advantage. The enemy pushed out of his fortifications to prevent their position being turned, and have been sooner or later driven back in every instance. Up to this hour, the enemy have not shown themselves in force within a mile of their lines.[10]

As the Confederates had from the beginning held substantially to the defensive, there was little glory in saying that Lee had not gained the battlefield. Conquering the Wilderness had not been his objective. Still in 1863, Joe Hooker had accepted his set-back as a strategic defeat and had taken his army back the way it came. Grant saw his losses as incidental and was planning to move even closer to Richmond.

The New York Tribune of Horace Greeley published philippics against what was already called "Grant's Tactics of Butchery." Daily, under a standing headline – "The Great Contest" – readers were given raw battle reports, some with great exaggeration and many that ran counter to Lincoln's government's wishes.

In an editorial that ran on May 13, Greeley offered:

Our own conviction is that the opening of the Presidential canvass should have been postponed until after the fourth of July, and that it is advisable for the Union Party to nominate for President some other among its able and true men than Mr. Lincoln. We think the events now transpiring in Virginia and Georgia add force to all that has hitherto been urged in favor of postponement of the Presidential canvass.[11]

Meanwhile, Meade put his army in motion. He sent his supply train first toward Chancellorsville, then south. Then after dark, Warren was to take his corps down the Brock Road toward Spotsylvania, while Hancock's divisions held the charred works where Lee's last assaults had delivered such destruction. Sedgwick and the VI Corps were to veer east, then proceed south along with Burnside's relatively unharmed divisions. Burial parties attempted to recover the corpses and the wounded, who were loaded onto the ambulance wagons stringing eastward to Fredericksburg. Southerners came out for similar work, hurriedly interring the dead of both armies as they were found. After the relief of realizing that they were not being attacked again that day, many were overwhelmed at the chance to rifle haversacks for food and collect the war material left on the field. Always on lean rations, many of Lee's units had not eaten in three days.

Lee attempted to figure out what was going to come next. His younger officers seemed ebullient about the efforts of the last days, almost cocky in their attitude towards Grant's poor strategy. They almost relied upon a Federal retreat. Lee agreed with some of them that Grant might be drawing his left back toward Mine Run in some form of regrouping or even withdrawal. But soon, sporadic gunfire to the east and cavalry reports from Lee's nephew, Major General Fitzhugh Lee, showed Lee that the Federals had started a flanking movement south. Lee even ordered a rough track cut toward the Catharpin Road to ease his army's maneuver toward Spotsylvania Court House. He directed then Major General Richard Anderson, who had taken over Longstreet's corps, to begin a night march to the crossroads town. Those veterans from Georgia, South Carolina, and Mississippi had eleven miles across rough country to race. That, after having quick-marched from Gordonsville in time to counter Hancock's corps on the Orange Plank Road on May 6 in the most savage fighting in the Wilderness. They moved fast, many still without shoes even after stripping the Union dead, all of them lean and light. They moved along the rough-cut military road, tripping on stumps and debris and choking on the smoke from hundreds of fires, not yet knowing that a Federal column was rushing parallel to them but a few miles away.

Grant had not selected quiet Spotsylvania as his objective anymore than he had chosen the Orange Plank Road. He had insisted from the first that Lee's army, not Richmond, was his true target. He reasoned that Spotsylvania rested on the routes of several railroad lines and on his access to supplies from Hanover Junction. It was the crossroads on the best approach to Richmond, and if Grant arrived first, Lee would be forced out into the open.

Warren's corps in the lead, the Federals had almost a three-hour head start. Brock road was a terrible pathway to take, however. Thick smoke from smoldering wood and the odor of burned bodies hung in the air; fires burned sporadically all along the upper length. Hancock's exhausted II Corps clogged the narrow road. Men, ambulances and horses crowded the way raising choking dust. Warren's corps had to shoulder through the congestion of II Corps, who by now realized that they were going south and not into retreat.

Grant reached Todd's Tavern, a country clearing, ahead of his infantry. The army's progress was painfully slow, in part due to their advance cavalry. Sheridan with two of his divisions had pushed aside a small contingent of Stuart's cavalry earlier that day and bivouacked on the roadway. When Meade discovered that was causing Warren's corps to be stalled, he flew into a trademark rage. Sheridan's objective was the bridge at Blockhouse Road, but he lost the race to Anderson's fast-moving brigades. Meade and Sheridan had a fiery confrontation over who was in the other's business.[12] Wherever Warren's spent soldiers came to a halt, they slept, and it took hours to get them moving again.

At about six that morning, the fight started when cavalry led by Wilson and Brigadier General Wesley Merritt ran into that of Major General Fitzhugh Lee and Brigadier General Thomas Rosser. The latter force had been holding inside the town of Spotsylvania Court House itself. Anderson then received an appeal from Stuart for help and sent a brigade to both Lee and Rosser while the remainder of his exhausted units secured the Block House Bridge. Meanwhile, Warren hurriedly sent Brigadier General John Robinson's infantry division down the road where one brigade ran head-on into Kershaw's division that had just reached the hasty breastworks Rosser's cavalry had tossed together. Both sides began moving into Alsop's Farm, two miles from Spotsylvania.

Meade was surprised and angered at losing the race to the crossroads. He moved Sedgwick to the left of Warren and attacked immediately. With VI Corps moving with its characteristic slowness, Meade saw that they could not be in place before five that afternoon, by which time Ewell's 17,000 men would be coming in on Anderson's right. The Southern line jelled against the weak Federal assault late that afternoon. The Northerners had been marching and fighting for four days and their fatigue, along with their commanders' lack of knowledge about their situation, combined to cause the assaults to dissipate. The way to Spotsylvania was blocked and the Army of the Potomac was still as far from Richmond as from Washington. They were moving toward territory with names like Gaines' Mill, Mechanicsville, and Seven Pines that echoed with past bloodshed.[13]

The Southerners were becoming masters of defensive alignment and fortification. Their engineers had designed a prototype of flexible entrenchments that would enable the South to continue the war in the face of preponderant Northern strength. Their lines of rifle pits and trenches began to form instantly as soon as units took position. Within an hour after halting, logs, stones, fence rails, and other materials were piled into ramparts and covered with the dirt from a trench, giving protective cover for a kneeling man. "It is a rule," Colonel Theodore Lyman later wrote, "that, when the rebels halt, the first day gives them a good rifle pit; the second, a regular infantry parapet with cannon in position; and the third, a parapet with an abatis in front and entrenched batteries behind. Sometimes they put these three days' work into the first twenty-four hours."[14]

The battles of Spotsylvania Court House lasted more than a week and surviving combatants from both sides felt they had endured some of the most terrible fighting of the war. Descriptions of the conditions and ferocity of that week in a country village north of Richmond are like nothing else spoken or written from that conflict. There is a spirit bereft of hope, of depressing and darkened resolution, and of confusion and the acceptance of the chaos that doomed so many men. Newspaper reports began to reach their readers describing the almost unbelievable occurrences in the Wilderness.

As *The Army and Navy Journal* on May 14 reported:

> The great battle of the Wilderness was no essential part of Grant's plan. He did not avoid it, but he did not seek it...The advance was substantially analogous to that of General Hooker. The battle-ground was the same. The tactics were the same. But the results were diverse. And on familiar ground, while our army had yet failed to get into a maneuvering position, the enemy fought three days and then hastily withdrew.

On May 9, headlines in *The New York Tribune* and *The Philadelphia Inquirer* proclaimed Lee's retreat after a smashing victory.

On the already hot morning of that same day the Confederates continued to burrow in, while Meade ordered Hancock's corps to move to Warren's right. Sedgwick's units entrenched upon Warren's left while Burnside swung his divisions around to come at Spotsylvania from the northeast. Sheridan moved his cavalry to the south to draw out Stuart's cavalry brigades and to attach Lee's supply line from Richmond.

Lee again restructured his command, placing Early in charge of the ailing A. P. Hill's corps. The Confederate line was around a high ground salient on which Ewell had entrenched his corps. Streaming from the left was Anderson's corps, facing directly northwest with Mahone and Heth holding the far flank. On the right, Early's divisions were spread thinly down to Massaponax Church to confront Burnside, when and if he came. The layout resembled an inverted "V", with Lee himself posted behind Ewell's front along with John Gordon's brigades. Snipers and skirmishers prevented Grant's engineers from being able to clearly scout out Lee's positions. One of those snipers killed VI Corps Commander John Sedgwick as he supervised artillery placements in the forward lines. The genial, personal officer was joking with the artillerymen dodging the pinging bullets, when he was struck beneath the left eye and died almost immediately.[15] Informed of the incident, Grant seemed to disbelieve the loss of one of the army's most senior commanders. Twice he asked, "Is he really dead?"[16]

Grant spent part of the afternoon looking for a soft attack point in the Southern lines. He sent Hancock's three divisions toward the Block House Bridge. Although impeded by nearby woods and darkness, they were able to circle the extreme left and by the morning of May 10 were in a position, if reinforced in strength, for turning Mahone's brigade along the Po River. Grant, by whatever reasoning, ignored that option and concentrated hopes upon a direct assault recommended by Warren on Anderson's middle early in the afternoon. After three hours and the loss of more than 3,000 men, that was given up. Another assault, directed by Sedgwick's successor, Brigadier General Horatio Wright, was to deliver a hammerblow to the uppermost section of the Confederate salient.

Called by soldiers on the forward line "the Mule Shoe," the salient was a half-mile arc of deep trenches, solidly emplaced cannon, bristling with obstacles such as an abatis, chopped trees, and breastworks; behind was a second trenchline and deep traverses defending both flanks. Wright's charge would be led by 121st New York commander Colonel Emory Upton who had seen possibilities during an earlier attack upon the Confederate line. A force of some 5,000 troops plunged from within two hundred yards of the attack point, massed together in four lines, three regiments shoulder-to-shoulder. They held fire until right against the rebel works. Within a few minutes of the attack start, a little after six, Upton's men had breached the salient's outer defenses and had crushed the Georgians there.

Just as he was on the brink of a great tactical success, Upton's support from a IX Corps division did not arrive. He had to escape from the trenchlines he had worked so strenuously to capture. Brigadier General Gershom Mott was punished for the failure to reinforce Upton but the Federal assault had cost almost 1,000 men. The 49th Pennsylvania alone withdrew without 246 of its 474 soldiers and officers.

The effect on the Southerners, besides their also high casualties, was one of fear and learning. The success of the attack made Lee prepare harder in case of something similar, and extra ammunition stores were distributed for the next day.

Grant was impressed with Upton's idea, saying to Meade, "A brigade today – we'll try a corps tomorrow." He decided to take an extra day to plan that even greater assault. That evening, Grant seemed to be optimistic. The next morning, he sent a message to Halleck at the War Department:

> We now have ended the sixth day of heavy fighting...the result up to this time is much in our favor...I propose to fight it out along this line if it takes all summer.[17]

Part Two
Looking for the Last Ditch

Meade directed Hancock to shift to a zone north of the enemy salient, moving behind the tightly aligned brigades of V and VI Corps. They would smash the apex of the "Mule Shoe" in concentration at dawn on May 12. Their hammering on Lee's powerful defenses would be supported and exploited by Warren and Wright moving into Anderson on the right of the line. Burnside's men would go straight into the base of the salient from the far left, at Wilcox's brigades.

Lee met with his corps commanders and staffs. He was not certain of anything, but expressed his belief that Grant was searching for another approach to Richmond. His way was soundly blocked, and the large scale movements that had been observed all day on the quiet 11th told him that Grant was about to follow his ambulances back to Fredericksburg. He surprised even the young staff officers who continued to belittle Grant's handling of his army with the announcement that, if that movement toward Fredericksburg was the case, the Southern army should move to the attack. A. P. Hill, ill and unusually silent before now, begged Lee to keep to the defensive works that had served so well. "General Lee," he implored, "let them continue to attack our breastworks – we can stand them very well." Lee was sincere. He made his own resolution: "This army cannot stand a siege. We must end this business on the battlefield, not in a fortified place."[18] So decided, Lee ordered his guns moved back and readied to move out in pursuit, thereby dismantling some of the salient's defenses.

Rumbles of movement after midnight carried into the Confederate lines. Directly north of the salient, less than half a mile away, 15,000 men made ready to move before light. Hancock gave his final directions, and in a torrential rain and thick ground fog, the lead divisions began to slog through the deep woods. At about four-thirty that morning, Brigadier General Francis Barlow at the army's point breached the Southern picket line and easily smashed through the spiky abatis and tree barriers. Almost with no resistance, and certainly no cannon to answer, the Louisiana brigade of Colonel William Monaghan and the famous "Stonewall" brigade were overwhelmed by a charge of ranks fifty deep. Barlow's division, without any form or order, streamed into the trench lines as a packed mass. Large numbers of Confederates were taken captive in the first hour, and Major General Edward Johnson's division evaporated. The fighting was hand-to-hand and body-on-body in the tightly packed gullies filled with water. The Southerners had by now managed to get some of their guns back up to the line, but they were captured immediately.

Lee had been up at three-thirty and by the streams of fleeing men going by him he realized that battle was underway. He shamed several units into slowing and reforming just as John Gordon was working to stabilize a secondary line with his three brigades. With Lee at his side, Gordon began a counter-attack against the formless Federal infantry. That was the first of several times that Lee had to be forcibly detained from charging into the melee with the infantry.[19]

Gordon's well-directed assault staggered the Union onrush. But more Federals were jamming into the salient's frontal area. There was not control or direction, and many did not know which way to move. They were soon driven back from the first trench line of the "Shoe" but held against that counter-attack. As the two sides fired at each other at close range, the battle assumed unimaginable qualities of personalized savagery.

While the struggle within the salient turned into a chaotic brawl, even uglier fighting broke upon the western face of the trenchline, where Wright's VI Corps struck at Rode's brigade at about six. Led again by Upton, several brigades moved up the fortified slope to be raked by concentrated cannon fire. There began the worst of it – hand-to-hand and muzzle-against-muzzle violence on a scale never seen before or again. Lewis Grant of the 2nd Vermont Volunteers recalled:

> Many were shot and stabbed through crevices between the logs; men mounted the works, and with muskets rapidly handed to them, kept up, a continuous fire until they were shot down, when others would take their places and continue the deadly work.[20]

More VI Corps brigades went into the jammed earthworks, even bringing up artillery firing canister until most of the gunners themselves became casualties. For hours the struggle went on in the heavy rain, bodies piled to the sides by the living to get better advantage, and some using the rigid hands of dead comrades to cup extra ammunition. That volume of fire consumed unheard of quantities of ammunition, and trees and men alike were hit so many times that they literally fell apart.

Lee poured his own reinforcements into the center, bringing Mahone's division from the far end of the Confederate line. That time, Mississippians held Lee back when he rushed to join the fray. Burnside threw his divisions in along the eastern sector, losing great numbers of Brigadier General Robert Potter's and Brigadier General Orlando Willcox's ranks but keeping Early's brigades busy and unable to reinforce Lee's center. Warren took up the heavy assault against Anderson, gaining little at enormous costs.

As John Noonan of the 69th new York wrote:

> There was only a log revetment between the combatants through which they fired into each others' faces...men brained and bayoneted each other over the top. The rain poring down but could not chill the ardor of the combatants.[21]

The day was running out as exhausted men on both sides, having gone without food or rest, held on to wherever place they could kneel or lie in the mud. Confederate engineers slaved to finish a secondary trenchwork for withdrawal of the forward units, but it was not completed until after midnight; Union men waited for darkness, immobile and spent. Grant told Halleck that evening, that though things had begun auspiciously, the enemy seemed to find the "last ditch."[22]

On the morning of May 13, the Northerners awoke to find nothing but pits filled with corpses in a landscape torn apart. The rebels had moved back silently, leaving the forward end of the Mule Shoe, known thereafter as "the Bloody Angle," for the Union to nervously watch that entire day.

Grant told Meade that morning, "I do not desire a battle brought on with the enemy in their position of yesterday," and advising his field manager that they must move to Lee's right for their next attack. Warren's V Corps was ordered to move behind the army placements to the east of Spotsylvania Court House that night. Grant's plans were set for Warren, along with Wright's corps, to renew the assaults at dawn on the 14th. But the mud and slime of two days of incessant rain made those plans impossible to carry out.

Grant then decided that, having observed the Southern command shifting over to meet his slow flanking operation, he could weaken the lines on the left face of the original trench lines. Grant told Wright to countermand his divisions back across to his old lines. Hancock's II Corps would support an attack on the blood-covered earthworks north of Spotsylvania village. When the attack was launched, the Federals took position in the Bloody Angle inside Lee's original defensive lines.

They met the full force of Ewell's corps and 29 pieces of artillery. Seeing their opponents thickly massed inside their abandoned works, the Southerners opened up with canister. In less than two hours the Federals withdrew with over 2,000 killed and wounded.

General Meade later said to his wife: "Even Grant thought it useless to knock our heads against a brick wall," and that they would now try to maneuver and draw the Southerners out.[23]

On the next day, May 19, it was General Lee's turn to throw men into a futile offensive effort as Ewell cut through what Lee guessed would be a weakened Union right. His idea was to punch toward Fredericksburg and disrupt Grant's lines of communications and supply. The Second Corps discovered that the Union right had just been reinforced by some 7,500 troops from five heavy artillery regiments and John Gordon's division lost almost 1,000 men before Ewell retrieved his forces. That encounter brought an end to the combat near Spotsylvania.

Losses in the spring campaign were sickening. The most accurate Union count was 18,399 casualties at Spotsylvania, added to the 17,666 at the Wilderness. In addition, more than 4,000 were evacuated due to illnesses and provosts estimated that at least 14,000 were missing as deserted or mustered out. As Sheridan's cavalry was detached, the Army of the Potomac was left with 56,200 effectives and could expect few replacements.[24] Ulysses S. Grant had lost almost half of his army in nine days.

The Confederates suffered almost 17,500 losses in the same period since May 4, including possibly 5,000 as captured in battle. But Beauregard's victory at Drewry's Bluff stopped Butler's offensive, and enabled Beauregard to send Lee an entire division of 6,000 men. Sigel's rout at New Market, Virginia, allowed John Breckinridge to deliver another 2,600 to the Army of Northern Virginia. Lee's army was still a formidable weapon, but the losses in command, such as Longstreet, and those of the irreplaceable veterans who had fallen on the Orange Plank Road and at Bloody Angle, could not help but be felt in the coming weeks.

Perhaps the Second Corps had paid the dearest price for holding at Spotsylvania. Major General Edward Johnson's trustworthy old division had been weakened beyond salvage. Its four brigades had manned the center of the Mule Shoe cauldron, and had, by some reports, lost more than half of their numbers. Some regiments could muster less than a dozen effectives. The remnants of the units of Brigadier General John Jones, along with a few of William Monaghan's Louisianans and the remainder of Brigadier General George Steuart's "Stonewall Brigade," were attached to a new division placed under John Gordon. If there was a hero in Lee's army at the Bloody Angle, it was Gordon, and he made major general for his contributions. Without fanfare, some of the most familiar names in the entire army were being erased away.

※ ※ ※ ※ ※

Colonel Lewis Grant, commander of the 2nd Vermont brigade of VI Corps, wrote about the Bloody Angle:

> It was not only a desperate struggle, it was a hand to hand fight. Nothing but the piled up logs or breastworks separated the combatants...It was there that the celebrated tree was cut off by bullets, there that the brush logs were cut to pieces and whipped into basket stuff...there that the rebel ditches cross sections were filled with dead men several deep...I was at the angle next day. The sight was terrible and sickening, much worse than at Bloody Lane – Antietam. There a great many man were lying in the road across the rails of the torn down fences, out in the cornfield, but they were not piled up several deep, their flesh was not so torn mangled as at the angle.[25]

Captain Isaac Seymour of the Louisiana Tigers, who was hit directly by the first impact of Hancock's assault on May 12, remembered:

> All eyes turned to the angle's apex, and one of Monaghan's men jumped up, pointed and yelled, "Look out, boys! We will have blood for supper!" Through a break in the fog in front of Jones's brigade could be seen wave after wave of madly cheering Federal troops bearing down on the angle. In the rear of Jones's men came Johnson's missing artillerymen galloping back to their position just in time to be overwhelmed by the Yankee flood. Jones's brigade was swallowed by that tide with hardly a shot fired. Grant's screaming Yankees then fanned out to both sides of the angle and came tearing down the trench with a vengeance...the Louisianans managed only a few shots before being swallowed by the federals...Monaghan ordered his men to slide to the left...the brigade had barely gotten into position along a small hill when the federals swept upon them yelling like devils. Monaghan roared, "Fire!" and the Tigers obliterated the first blue line. But others took their place, and the Yankees continued pushing forward. When Monaghan reassembled his shattered brigades in the morning, he found the 2nd Louisiana almost annihilated.[26]

Private Wilbur Fisk of Vermont wrote:

> But the most singular and obstinate fighting that I have seen
> during the war, or ever heard or dreamed of in my life, was the fight
> of last Thursday. Hancock had charged and driven the enemy from
> their breastworks, and from their camps, but the enemy rallied and
> regained all but their first line of works, and in one place they got a
> portion of that. The rebels were on one side of the breastwork and
> we on the other. We could touch their guns with ours. They would
> load, jump up and fire into us, and we did the same to them. Al-
> most every shot that was made took effect. Some of our boys would
> jump clear up on to the breastwork and fire, then down, reload and
> fire again, until they themselves were picked off...I visited the place
> the next morning, and though I had seen horrid scenes since this
> war commenced, I never saw anything half so bad as that. Our men
> lay piled one top of another, nearly all shot through the head. There
> were many among them that I knew well, five from my own com-
> pany. On the rebel side it was worse than on ours. In some places
> they were piled four and five deep, some of whom were still alive. I
> turned away from that place, glad to escape from such a terrible,
> sickening sight. I have always hoped, that if I must die while I am a
> soldier, I should prefer to die on the battle-field, but after looking at
> such a scene, one cannot help but turn away and saying, "Any
> death but that."[27]

On May 13, Elisha Hunt Rhodes of the 2nd Rhode Island Volunteers wrote:

> Yesterday we had another fearful day of battle...It turned out
> that the Second Corps under Gen. Hancock had charged the rebel
> works and taken their entire line with several thousand
> prisoners...On the right side of our line the works formed an angle,
> and our regiment found itself enfiladed by the enemy. Soon the
> horses and gunners of a battery posted in the angle were killed or
> disabled, and the enemy charged with loud yells upon the guns to
> the woods...A brigade of New Jersey troops were brought up and
> attempted to enter the angle but were driven back. Gen. Sickles' old
> brigade were then brought up, but the men could not stand the
> terrible fire and instead of advancing in line only formed a semi-
> circle around the guns...I took a position in the rifle pit, and the
> boys would load their guns and pass them to me to fire...And the
> fight went on and continued until nearly 2 A.M. this morning
> (13th)...I never saw even at Gettysburg so many dead Rebels as lay
> in front of our lines. I laid down to sleep about 3 A.M. today but did
> not rest much, for the wounded were all about us...[28]

Benjamin Washington Jones of the Surry Light Artillery offered:

> During the battle I saw a Yankee shell explode in front of one
> of our batteries. The butt end of the shell struck one of our drivers
> in the chest and went through him; when it struck him he jumped
> about a foot from the saddle, then fell to the ground stretched out
> full length, and never struggled. It rained nearly all day...It looked
> as if Heaven were trying to wash up the blood as fast as the civi-
> lized barbarians were spilling it.

> May 14 – We were in position in front of the enemy's works all
> day...there was some sharpshooting along the lines during the day,
> and some artillery firing...I think that General Grant has arrived at
> the place where he does not know exactly what to do, nor how to
> do it. The stubborn and unyielding wall of bayonets of the strate-
> gical and ubiquitous Lee is forever interfering with, and very seri-
> ously interrupting, every step of the blue host's onward march to
> Richmond. Thunder-showers this evening.[29]

Ambulance wagons and burial details worked, handling entire brigades. Bewildered officers and enlisted men surveyed the landscape,
and evidence points to a great deal of drunken solace sought by many.
Charles Dana, Lincoln's official observer, told:

> After the battle was over and firing had nearly ceased, Rawlins
> and I went out to ride over the field...I dismounted and climbed
> up the bank over the outer line of rude breastworks. Within we
> saw a fence over which earth had evidently been banked, but which
> was now bare and half down. It was here that the fighting had
> been fiercest. We picked our way to the fence and stopped to look
> over the scene.... I remember as I stood there I was almost startled
> to hear a bird twittering in a tree. All around us the underbrush
> and trees, which were just beginning to be green, had been riddled
> and burnt. The ground was thick with dead and wounded men,
> among whom the relief corps was at work. The earth, which was
> soft from the heavy rains...had been trampled by the fighting of
> thousands of men until it was soft, like thin hasty pudding. Over
> the fence against which we leaned lay a great pool of this mud, its
> surface as smooth as that of a pond.
> As we stood there, looking silently down at it, of a sudden the
> leg of a man was lifted from the pool and the mud dripped off his
> boot...It was so unexpected, so horrible, that for a moment we
> were stunned. Then we pulled ourselves together and called to some
> soldiers nearby to rescue the owner of the leg. They pulled him out

with but little trouble, and discovered that he was not dead, only wounded. He was taken to the hospital, where he got well, I believe.[30]

Chapter Five

Crossing the Streams

"The operations of this day were much embarrassed by our ignorance of the roads and the entire incorrectness of our maps."
- Charles Dana, Jr.[1]
Assistant Secretary of War

"When we reached the North Anna I think the general feeling was that we should roll on, like a wave, up to the very gates of Richmond."
- Colonel Rufus Dawes[2]
II Corps Staff

"The Rebs are getting dispirited and out of provisions, and I think would fall back if they had any place to go. We are growing more and more hopeful."
- Major General Gouverneur Warren[3]
Union V Corps

"We must strike them a blow - we must never let them pass us again - we must strike them a blow."
- General Robert E. Lee
to Colonel Charles Venable[4]

"May 24 – By reference to my map I found we are only seventeen miles from Richmond. So, we are rapidly nearing the Rebel stronghold and might reasonably expect to be thundering at its doors in a few days, or weeks at the most."
- Private John W. Haley[5]
17th Maine Regiment

Immediately after Meade and Sheridan's argument before the fighting began at Spotsylvania, Grant decided that Sheridan should be allowed to go after Stuart on his own initiative. Sheridan had boasted, "If the headquarters would stay out of our hair, I and the Calvary Corps will leave and go whip Stuart."[6] While Meade wanted to press charges of insubordination, Grant told the cavalry to move out.

Strung out for thirteen miles, with almost 10,000 horsemen and 32 artillery pieces, Sheridan's column skirted northwest around Spotsylvania toward Richmond on May 9. Like Grant, Sheridan had no specific objective but moved into new territory south of the Po and North Anna rivers to do as much damage as possible. The cavalry wanted more than anything to draw out Stuart and his vaunted troopers for a final, fateful confrontation.

Like their opponents, the Southern cavalry had been involved only on the fringes of the fighting since May 4. The most notable action by either mounted force had been at the Block House Bridge, where Fitz Lee's men fought almost as infantry and engineers to hold off Wilson's cavalry. That had proved to be a pivotal action. For the most part, however, the performances of both cavalries had been relegated to shielding infantry and conducting reconnaissance. That part of the overland campaign would have been the same had the Federal cavalry not ridden at all.[7]

Stuart's force, not more than 8,000 divided into six brigades, had spent the winter in quarters close to Fredericksburg, spread out to the maximum in order to give their hungry horses as much forage space as possible. Now that Sheridan was on the move, Stuart was left trying to guess the Federal cavalry's destination. He divided his force, sending Fitzhugh Lee south and keeping the remainder close to Lee.

On May 10, Sheridan stormed into the railroad junction at Beaver Dam Station, a quiet supply depot on the Virginia Central Railway where large quantities of provisions for the army waited. The depot guards torched it just at the sight of Sheridan's approach. Brigadier General George Custer and his Michigan troopers went on to burn more than a quarter of the Central's rolling stock. The fast-moving troopers headed on, cutting telegraph lines and uprooting rail tracks. Unable to catch up, Stuart warned the Richmond commander, General Braxton Bragg, that Sheridan might attack the capitol itself. He then sent Fitz Lee on a blocking route before Richmond and Brigadier General James Gordon to attack Sheridan's rear. Hoping to box the Union force between them and with infantry from Bragg's defenses to assist, Stuart set a collision course.

On May 11 at an abandoned coach stop named Yellow Tavern, perhaps ten miles from the Confederate capitol, the collision occurred. Heavy fighting, including engagements by light artillery, ensued as Custer and Brigadier General Wesley Merritt headed the attack with reckless violence. The outnumbered Southerners suffered hundreds of losses including Gordon, and Major General Stuart himself was shot in the melee. Sheridan's cavalry swept the enemy out of the way and toyed with the notion of ripping into Richmond. "It is possible that I might have captured the city of Richmond by assault," Sheridan later reported to Meade. He wisely decided against that and moved eastward, eventually going through the Confederate lines along the Chickahominy River. He reached General Butler's lines with several hundred Southern captives, as well as 378 Federal prisoners from the Wilderness that the Michigan cavalry had been able to liberate. He rested and announced his plans to return north to Grant on the 17th. Jeb Stuart died of his wounds on May 12, news of which reached Lee just as the Spotsylvania fighting eased.

The Army of the Potomac sidled east and a few miles south after leaving Spotsylvania Court House. A brief council of war with commanders and staffs was held at Massaponax Church after soldiers carried the pews into the muddy yard. Grant and Meade chatted amiably with their staffs in the open air, and the meeting had the atmosphere of riders preparing for a fox hunt. Plans were made to push east and south.

Hancock's II Corps, ever in the lead, moved through the green country to Guinea Station, a junction of the Richmond, Fredericksburg, and Potomac Railroad. Horace Porter wrote that on May 22:

> Headquarters moved south, following the line which had been taken by Hancock's troops...the weather was pleasant, the air was invigorating, the sun was shining brightly...the men had been withdrawn from the scenes of their terrific struggles at Spottsylvania...the deep gloom of the Wilderness had been left far behind...the roads were broad, the land was well-cultivated, and crops were abundant. The men seemed to breathe a new atmosphere and were inspired with new hope.[8]

Troops of the VI Corps told about walking through the still, isolated villages of Milford Station and Bowling Green, where they did some desultory robbing while civilians peeked from the windows.[9]

The II Corps marched down the old Telegraph Road which was the main channel between Fredericksburg and Richmond. Four to five miles to the west, Warren and Wright moved their corps on the approaches to the North Anna crossings at Jericho and Quarles Mills, while the IX Corps came down a center path towards Ox Ford. Their traveling was almost pleasant, and it gave time for Grant's soldiers to wonder aloud why their superior numbers and armaments had not had the desired effect thus far. "We fight as good as they do," a Michigan man suggested. "They must understand the country better, or else there is a screw loose in the machinery of our army."[10]

Lee had ordered Ewell's Corps away from Spotsylvania Court House first. Not long behind came Anderson's divisions, while Hill, claiming himself fit for duty, took the Third Corps on a wide westward swing south toward Beaver Dam. The Southerners had no place within that level and tranquil country to make a defensive stand, so Lee dropped his corps below the North Anna. If Hancock's forward body was bait for a Southern attack in the open, there seemed little chance that their commander would bite. Lee's forces deployed in a somewhat flattened, inverted "vee" with the Chesterfield Bridge at the right anchor and with A. P. Hill's Third Corps, which came in on May 23, a few miles west holding the far banks at Jericho Mill. One prime consideration was the protection of the vital railroad depot at Hanover Station, where promised reinforcements were already arriving from south and west. Among them was part of Breckinridge's small command, fresh from thrashing Sigel at New Market in the Valley, as well as portions of Pickett's division from the Richmond defenses.

A token Southern force left on the north bank at Jericho Mill was quickly overrun by forward units of Warren's V Corps. Meanwhile, on the evening of the 23rd, two brigades charged across the charred Chesterfield Bridge that Southern skirmishers had tried to set afire twice. That was not done bloodlessly, but both bridgeheads were established in less than two hours. Burnside's men in the center found it hard going against Anderson's entrenched works on the higher bank at Ox Ford. Brigadier General James Ledlie's 35th and 57th Massachusetts regiments made a ridiculous, unauthorized thrust at the firmly planted Southern line. Ledlie was by no means the only officer to acquire his courage from the bottle, but he was certainly one of the most notorious drunks in the army.

He sent his infantry directly into Brigadier General Edward Perry's Floridians, who shouted and hooted, "Come on, Yanks, come on to Richmond!" The brunt of the slaughter fell upon Ledlie's Massachusetts soldiers when heavy musket and canister opened up on them. The Confederate volleys appeared to be aimed deliberately at knee-level as hundreds of Federals were shot down and left to the calm work of Rebel sharpshooters.[11] That deadly combat continued until around seven that evening, the savaged regiments were chased back into their own lines by William Mahone's shock-troops and were saved only by the fall of night. Thereafter, the IX Corps lost any enthusiasm to renew the offensive for some time to come.

A few miles to the west late that same afternoon, an irresistible opportunity presented itself to A. P. Hill. Part of Warren's V Corps had become isolated on the southern bank of the North Anna after seizing the shallow ford, where Union engineers were building a bridge. Lee's own summary had noted earlier that the right wing of the Federal forces was not strongly positioned. Hill undertook no further reconnaissance. Being given, as always, a free rein to test any such opportunity, Hill sent Cadmus Wilcox's division into the attack.

Unfortunately for Wilcox and the almost 700 North and South Carolinians lost in that foray, his four brigades had been sent up against nearly 15,000 Federals in three divisions. His attack was smashed to pieces and the survivors fell back in confusion toward Hill's safer positions near Noel's Station. Later, when Lee spoke with Hill, the already ill commander unleashed an uncharacteristic and famous rebuke:

> Why did you not do as Jackson would have done - thrown your whole force upon those people and driven them back?[12]

At that point, there began a loss of confidence by Lee in the man formerly recognized as the most trusted and aggressive field commander in his army, and his faith in "Little Powell" Hill was never fully regained.[13]

By the night of May 24, Lee had established a defensive position that even Grant would recognize as invulnerable to assault. The Federal center was along the north side of the river looking up at massed artillery and infantry along a front of perhaps three-quarters of a mile. The two wings, now planted on the far banks left and right, were fixed so as to prevent any attacker on either side from giving assistance to the other without re-crossing the river.

Private John Haley of the 17th Maine Volunteer Infantry put his view of the scene this way:

> Our first brigade crossed over at Taylor's Bridge and gained a footing on the enemy's flank, causing them to vacate their front line. We thought this was key to their entire line, but in this we were seriously mistaken. They had not less than three lines of works, in a peculiar formation like a letter V with the point on the river. Although the 2nd Corps was on one side and the 5th Corps on the other, the point couldn't let go its hold on the river, and we couldn't seem to make any headway.[14]

The commander of one of the Alabama brigades entrenched near the point of the inverted 'vee,' Brigadier General Evander Law, said many years later:

Grant found himself in what may be called a military dilemma. He had cut his army in two by running it upon the point of a wedge. He could not break the point, which rested upon the river, and the attempt to force it out of place by striking it on its sides must of necessity be made without much concert of action between the two wings of his army, neither of which could reinforce the other without crossing the river twice; while his opponent could readily transfer his troops, as needed, from one wing to the other across the narrow space between them.[15]

The infantry who had attacked the Bloody Angle had no doubts about the impossibility of success against that line. One Michigan infantryman, Daniel Crotty, commenting back said, "Surely, we cannot see much generalship in our campaign so far, and the soldiers are getting tired of such butchery in such a way. Half the time the men are fighting on their own responsibility, and if there is anything gained so far it is by brute force and not by generalship."[16]

Frank Wilkeson wrote:

At North Anna I discovered that our infantry were tired of charging earthworks...Here I first heard savage protests against a continuation of the generalship which consisted in launching good troops against entrenched works that the generals had not inspected. Battle-tried privates came into our battery and sneeringly inquired if the corps and army commanders had been to see the line. Of course we replied "No." "Well," said one sergeant of the Pennsylvania Reserves, "I have fought in this army for three years, and in no other campaign have I seen so many generals shirk as I have in this one...If Grant or Meade, or Hancock, or Warren, or Wright, or Burnside would inspect these works at close range, they would see the folly of staying here where we are losing two or three hundred men every day to sharpshooters. We ought to get out of here and try it further down." He expressed what we all thought. At North Anna the rank and file of the Potomac army, the men who did the fighting, and who had been under fire for three weeks, began to get discouraged.

We lay for three days in the trenches at North Anna. Three days of woe and hardship. Three days which had cost us hundreds of men and line officers. How we longed to get away from the North Anna, where we had not the slightest chance of success, and how we feared that Grant would keep sending us to the slaughter![17]

Grant spent a day sending his commanders on probing missions and assessing his next movements. Units were ordered across at both ends of the Union line. They found layers of breastworks and trenches, with extensive piles of felled timber and sharpened saplings and the dreaded abatis. One short engagement occurred at Doswell Plantation, where part of Romeyn Ayres' brigade got itself thrown into a swamp and was severely mauled by a reinforced Confederate skirmish line. Given their reports, Grant decided that it was time to swing out again and try to push around Lee toward Richmond.

Artillery of both sides erupted haphazardly during the days and nights along the river. Little useful damage was done, but the noise lessened the dread of surprise. Alfred Scott, a Florida infantryman, told of nearly being killed by an exploding cannon, a large piece of which rose up high and thumped a few feet in front of him.

> One gunner then called out, "Bring us another gun here - this one has busted all to hell." Hearty curses arose about the Richmond homemade ordnance. Our forces much prefer that provided by the enemy.[18]

Several miles east of the Federal left position, the North and South Annas form the Pamunkey River which Grant was advised could be forded at Hanovertown. But he seemed almost afraid that Lee's army might move against him as they slid out of their own earthworks and recrossed the river. Putting his corps into motion on the night of May 26, he reported:

> To make a direct attack from either wing would cause a slaughter of our men that even success could not justify. To turn the enemy by his right, between the two Annas, is impossible on account of the swamp on which his right rests. To turn him by his left leaves Little River, New Found River, and the South Anna River, all of them streams presenting considerable obstacles to the movement of an army, to be crossed. I have determined, therefore, to turn the enemy's right by crossing at or near Hanover Town. This crosses all these streams at once, and leaves us where we can still draw supplies.

Grant had moved his supply base from Belle Plain on the lower Potomac after the shift from Spotsylvania. It moved again to Port Royal at the end of the Rappahannock, and now was to be set at White House, almost twenty miles east of Hanovertown on the Pamunkey. The White House had been the advance point and supply depot for McClellan in the Peninsula campaign of 1862. The debris from that enterprise had to now be cleared away. The white frame farmhouse there that had been the site of George Washington's wedding to Martha Custis had long been burned to the ground.[19]

Grant's report finished with these hopeful and somewhat uncharacteristic words:

> Lee's army is really whipped. The prisoners we now take show it, and the action of his army shows it unmistakably. A battle with them outside of entrenchments cannot be had. Our men feel that they have gained the morale over the enemy and attack with confidence. I may be mistaken, but I feel that our success over Lee's army is already assured.[20]

✳ ✳ ✳ ✳ ✳

"If I can get one more pull at him," Lee said to a local doctor who came to look at him at about that same time, "I will defeat him."[21] That would have been an ideal place and time for the Confederate army to unleash a smashing blow at the Union left, and a plan for a massive trap for Hancock's corps was discussed on the night of May 23. Charles Venable wrote that Lee was anxious to "strike a telling blow." As far as Lee could reckon, however, he had no one capable of making the pull or shutting the trap. A. P. Hill was sick, Ewell was physically and mentally broken, and Anderson was judged too inexperienced to handle decisions at such scale. Only Lee himself could put it together properly, but the orders for an attack never came.

Lee collapsed with possible dysentery the next day.[22] He should have been hospitalized, but could not remain bed-ridden. Instead Lee went about in a carriage to visit his staff and officers who knew his unwell state. Lee was later visited by Jubal Early and his own son, Captain Robert Lee, Jr., who was a cavalry staff officer under his brother, Major General William "Rooney" Lee. Robert, Jr. later said:

> I saw my father only once or twice, to speak to him, during the campaign, but, in common with all his soldiers, I felt he was very near, and that he could be entrusted with the care of us, that he would not fail us, that it would all end well. The feeling of trust that we had in him was simply sublime...Older heads may have begun to see the "beginning of the end"; when they saw that slaughter and defeat did not deter our enemy but made him more determined in his "hammering" process; but it never occurred to me and to thousands and thousands like me, that there was any occasion for uneasiness.

> When we found that General Lee was ill – confined for a day or two in his tent...this terrible thought forced itself upon us: suppose disease should disable him, even for a short time, or worse, should take him forever from the front of his men!...[23]

And so the battered Federal army was about to take a step back, travel hard over thirty miles of admittedly desolate back country, and try at another place. There was dejection and disheartenment caused by the wear and tear on the army's getting thus far and getting ready to move yet again. John Gibbon, commanding II Corps' 2nd division, wrote after a brief rest on the road:

> We had been on the march for some time when someone coming from the rear gave the startling information that one of my brigades was missing from the column! Sending hastily back, the absent brigade was found to be rapidly pushing forward. When the halt had been made, every member of the brigade from the commander down had sunk into a deep sleep from which they did not awake until the rest of the division was far down the road...[24]

Bruce Catton, assessing Grant and his Grand Army at that point wrote:

> The army had conquered nothing and it possessed not a foot of soil except the ground on which it actually stood. All the way back to the Rapidan, Virginia, was still Confederate territory, and the men who strayed past the army lines to the rear were quite as likely to be shot or captured as if they had strayed to the front. Rebel cavalry roamed far and wide, and it was assisted by pestiferous bands of guerrillas - informal groups of semi-official mounted men, who were peace-loving farmers half of the time and bloodthirsty raiders the rest of the time. These bands covered all the raiders the rest of the time. These bands covered all the rear, and no wagon could pass between the army and the river bases north of Fredericksburg without a strong escort.[25]

In some ways, Grant was severing connections that tethered his army to Washington and Halleck and Lincoln. The Army of the Potomac was no longer tied to that symbolic river. Grant never allowed Lee a clear idea of his options. His was a decidedly foreign body moving at will into territory not touched by the war in two years, and it would decide its own fate. The evacuation from the North Anna positions had begun with destruction of railroad line wherever it was under their control, especially that of the Virginia Central. There was some spirit of revenge in that work as farmhouses and homes were also ransacked and burned.[26]

Both Southern and Northern accounts of loses suffered along the lines at the North Anna gave the approximate figures at: Union army – 570 killed and 2,100 wounded; Confederate army – 300 killed and 1,500 wounded.

The Union army advanced downstream under cover of darkness toward the Pamunkey River which flowed into the broad York River. Lee was surprised, having stated that his own estimate of Grant's next march would have been a westward loop that would cut the Confederates' link with the provisions of the Shenandoah Valley, as well as trump Lee's old counter-movement route. Perhaps Lee would have acted that way himself had he controlled the reins of Grant's army.[27]

Grant and his forces were going onto familiar soil where almost exactly two years ago McClellan had been so unfortunate and where some veterans still in the ranks had seen Richmond from an even closer vantage point. Grant was taking his army toward what some Yankees called "the confounded Chickahominy."

In his *Southern History of the War*, published in 1866, journalist Edward A. Pollard observed that Grant's entire strategy from early 1864 to the end of the siege at Petersburg was nothing more than a repetition of the failed "On to Richmond" scenarios of his failed predecessors. At the end of May 1864, Pollard wrote this acerbic and profound appraisal:

> But for the candid and intelligent, the situation of Grant was one of considerable import to him, implied much of disaster, and was actually a consequence of his repeated disappointments. He did nothing more than hold the same ground as that occupied by McClellan in his first peninsular campaign. He had set out to accomplish Mr. Lincoln's plan of an overland march on Richmond...

> The significance of all these operations was, that Grant had utterly failed in his design of defeating Lee's army far from its base, and pushing the fragments before him down to Richmond, and had been forced to cover up his failure by adopting the dreaded scheme of McClellan. The event of the 12th of May at Spottsylvania Courthouse had settled the question of whether he could beat Lee in the field and put him to a disastrous retreat. Unable to remove the obstacle on the threshold of his proposed campaign, nothing was left but to abandon it. Grant makes his way down the valley of the Rappahannock; turns aside at Hanover Junction; to find a repetition of Spottsylvania Courthouse; deflects to the headwaters of

the York; and at last, by a monstrous circuit, reaches a point where he might have landed on the 1st of May, without loss or opposition. We may appreciate the amount of gaseous nonsense and truculent blackguardism of Yankee journals, when we find them declaring that these movements were a foot-race for Richmond that Grant was across the last ditch, and that the end of the rebellion was immediately at hand.[28]

Edward Pollard detested all Northern leaders and practically everyone in the Confederate Government, especially President Davis. He considered himself a devoted Southern Socrates, sounding patriotic complaints for every ear. Few other voices are as honestly and identifiably partisan.

Meanwhile, some weeks earlier, a reporter from *The New York Tribune*, Henry E. Wing, had followed the Union army into the Wilderness. There was no word to be had in Washington except rumors of disaster. On Friday, May 6, President Lincoln stopped in at the War Department to pick up the latest telegraphed messages, something he had done since early in the war. He learned of a news correspondent who was twenty miles away, insisting to be seen by Charles Dana before turning over any message about Grant. Secretary of War Edwin Stanton ordered the man shot the next morning as a spy.

Lincoln asked the telegraph operator to find out if that reporter would talk to the President. Henry agreed, after being allowed to send a hundred word summary to the *Tribune*. Wing was brought to a meeting of Lincoln and his Cabinet that Saturday morning, at around two o'clock. But he had little information beyond what he had written. He did tell the gathering about what he had witnessed while riding with Hancock's corps when Lee's army came out on the attack.

When he told the Cabinet that he knew nothing about events of the last twenty-four hours, they stood and left dejectedly. Lincoln looked at Wing and asked, "You wanted to speak with me?" "Yes, Mr. President. I have a message for you – from General Grant. He told me to tell it to you when you were alone." "Something from Grant to me?" Lincoln asked. "Yes," Wing answered, "He told me I was to tell you, Mr. President, that there would be no turning back." Lincoln impulsively grasped the man's shoulders and kissed him on the cheek. "Come and tell me about it," he told Wing and led him to a chair.

Henry Wing then poured loose all his feelings. He attempted to describe the fighting he had seen in the Wilderness – the confusion, the mistakes, the lack of coordination between Warren and Hancock. He described the accusations and shifting of blame that went on at

Headquarters at that day's end, and how Meade had even suggested that the Army of the Potomac withdraw back to the Rapidan. It was Grant who said, "We shall attack in the morning."

Lincoln now knew the first-hand truth and more of it than anyone else. He recognized the positive aspects of Grant's tenacity, but he also understood the gravity of what would unfold. While laudatory headlines praised Grant's "progress" in Virginia, Lincoln remained troubled at the war's costs. At about the time of Grant's movement away from the North Anna, he told correspondent Noah Brooks:

> To me the most trying thing of all this war is that the people are too sanguine; they expect too much at once. I declare to you, sir, that we are today further ahead than I thought, one year and a half ago, that we should be...As God is my judge, I shall be satisfied if we are over with the fight in Virginia within a year.[29]

As New York gunner Wilkeson later noted:

> Joyfully we received the order to march on the night of the 26th. Eagerly the tired troops fell into line behind their foul intrenchments. With pleasure we re-crossed the North Anna and resumed the flank movement to the south. That night we had a good night's sleep, undisturbed by picket firing. We of the artillery awoke next morning to find the rest of the army gone, and we started after them - being, for the first and last time during the campaign, in the rear. Before us, in the distance, rose the swells of Cold Harbor, and we marched steadily and joyfully to our doom.[30]

Chapter Six

Marching to Cold Harbor

Part One
May 27 through May 31

"Often, when depressed and disposed to question whether there is, or ever was, in me the salt of real manhood, I have looked back to the first three days of June, 1864, and felt the revival of a saving self-respect and the determination not to do or suffer anything unworthy of this heroic past of which I was a part."

- Major Robert Stiles[1]
First Corps

"May 26 – ...Made ourselves as comfortable as we could through the day. Rumors that a night march may be expected, but destination unknown."

- Sergeant Austin Stearns[2]
13th Massachusetts Infantry

"Two things up to this time had been well-demonstrated. We had never succeeded in forcing Lee, by battle, from any position he had assumed, nor had he succeeded in forcing us from any."

- Brigadier General John Gibbon[3]
II Corps

"I am more than ever determined, if I find an opening, to take the offensive in the grand object, the destruction of the enemy."

- General Robert E. Lee to
Lieutenant General
Robert Anderson[4]
May 30

"May 28/64 – We started early and crossed the Pamunkey River and marched to the vicinity of Hanover town where we were set to work building entrenchments. Great is the shovel and spade. Well I would as soon dig the Rebels out as to fight them."

- Elisha Hunt Rhodes[5]
2nd Rhode Island

*"During the night it [Grant's army] had 'folded its tents like the Arab
and as quietly stolen away'..."*
                                        - Brigadier General Evander Law[6]
                                        First Corps

Then the dance of death took another swing. Lee's army was so
solidly emplaced on the high ground at the North Anna River that
even Grant considered it unassailable. He then began his fourth strategic turn since May 4. With some delicacy, the Federals moved back
across the North Anna and marched in two columns along the left
bank of the Pamunkey River, moving southeast. With the help of cavalry demonstrations on both Confederate flanks and under cover of
darkness, the withdrawal went smoothly. At dawn, the Southern pickets found only a thin screen of pickets still holding the enemy
entrenchments.

Warren's and Burnside's corps moved down to the almost-deserted
port town of Hanovertown to cross back over; Wright's and Hancock's
stepped over about four miles west. The walk down had been relatively uneventful other than the scaring off of scattered Confederate
horsemen, and the men covered 34 miles in a day and a half. The
country itself was overgrown and as brambly as parts of the Wilderness. The men had not had a change of clothing now for almost a
month, and knowing that they were in the vicinity of McClellan's
1862 humiliations did not give them much comfort.

Grant described the tidal country:

> The streams are numerous, deep and sluggish, sometimes
> spreading out into swamps grown with impenetrable growths of
> trees and underbrush. The banks were generally low and marshy,
> making the streams difficult to approach except where there were
> roads and bridges.[7]

The duty of leading the Federal army out and away had gone to
the 1st and 2nd divisions of the cavalry, led by Sheridan himself. He
was accompanied by a division of VI Corps led by Brigadier General
David Russell. Grant's headquarters staff seemed to be uncertain about
Lee's army and plans.[8] Grant gave Sheridan the task of preventing the
destruction of the North Anna bridges that were still intact and moving as quickly as possible to secure the Pamunkey crossings. That last
task was accomplished with some excitement. Young Custer led his
1st Michigan troopers across personally, swimming his horse over while
the few Confederate pickets present shot at him. Russell's infantry ran
into a North Carolina brigade that had been guarding the fords along

the Pamunkey, but those enemy forces were soon racing back toward Hanover Courthouse. Sheridan pursued and captured some seventy prisoners before his exhausted men bivouacked for the night.

The headquarters report for May 29 said:

> The movement from the North Anna to the Pamunkey occupied only about forty hours. In that time the army marched a distance of about forty miles, over good but dusty and unknown roads, effected the passage of two large rivers, and was brought within an easy day's march of Richmond. Of all our immense transportation not a wagon was lost...The weather on Friday and yesterday was very warm, and men and animals became very weary. The comparative rest of today, however, has refreshed them both...Prisoners and contrabands brought in today render it certain that Lee's whole army left the South Anna during Friday, and marched via Hanover Courthouse again to our front, and took up a position north of the Chickahominy, to the right and left of the Mechanicsville road. Officers familiar with the ground claim that he will be able to form a very strong defensive line in that locality. No signs of the enemy appeared in our front today.[9]

Lee realized the difficult task of catching the Federals, who after getting over the Pamunkey on pontoon bridges were actually eight miles closer to Richmond than he was. He still suffered from a diarrhetic illness that had swept through the Southern ranks and was unable to ride horseback. In even worse health, Richard Ewell on the 27th asked to be relieved after two dismal days inside his tent. Ewell's health had been a source of concerns for some months and knowing that the next blocking maneuver may be the most important yet, Lee accepted Ewell's request. A debilitated Ewell accepted sick leave of undetermined length and was sent to Richmond, to take charge of the city's civilian defenses. Jubal Early was now in charge of the Southern Second Corps.

The Army of Northern Virginia had been forced to undergo additional wholesale leadership changes in the last month. The Wilderness to James River campaign became known as the burial ground of Southern high command, underscoring its impact on the future conduct of the war. Two of Lee's three corps had received new leadership, with Longstreet wounded and Ewell transferred. Four out of nine infantry divisions had command changes, as well as 16 of the 35 original brigades. Hill had been weaker than ever and relieved twice in May by Early. As painful as any losses were the deaths of Stuart and Brigadier General James Gordon at Yellow Tavern.

Lee drew his three corps out from their riverbank fortress hesitantly and began to counter Grant once again. He had no idea of the direction of the Federal forces and made tentative plans to fall further back towards Richmond, stationing his army at the village of Ashland in Hanover County. With Lee himself in a borrowed carriage and Ewell sent ahead in an ambulance, his army went south, across the South Anna River, then took a protective swing toward Atlee Station on the Virginia Central line.

Early later recounted:

> Ewell's corps, now under my command...was moved across the South Anna over the bridge of the Central Railroad and by a place called "Merry Oaks," leaving Ashland on the Richmond, Fredericksburg and Potomac Railroad to the right, and bivouacked for the night at Hughes' cross-road, the intersection of the road from Ashland to Atlee Station...The next morning I moved by Atlee's Station to Hundley's Corner, at the intersection of the road from Hanover Town (the point at which Grant crossed the Pamunkey), by Pole Green Church to Richmond, with the road from Atlee's Station, by Old Church in Hanover County, to the White House on the Pamunkey. This is the point from which General Jackson commenced his famous attack on McClellan's flank and rear, in 1862, and it was very important that it should be occupied as it intercepted Grant's direct march toward Richmond...
>
> My troops were placed in position, covering the road by Pole Green Church, and also the road to Old Church, with my right resting near Beaver Dam Creek, a small stream running towards Mechanicsville and into the Chickahominy. Brigadier General Ramseur of Rodes' division was this day [28 May] assigned to the command of my division. Ewell's corps, the 2nd of the Army of Northern Virginia, now numbered less than 9,000 muskets for duty, its loss, on the 12th of May, having been very heavy.[10]

The Southern army marched down the Richmond, Fredericksburg, and Potomac rail line, and by mid-afternoon of May 27 had reached a point somewhere between the Chickahominy River and the headwaters of the Totopotomoy Creek. Lee's columns halted for the night at Atlee Station to await further developments that might unveil Grant's intentions.

On the morning of May 28, still no better informed than the day before, Lee sent out a cavalry reconnaissance-in-strength. That was the first solid effort made by Lee's troopers since the mortal wounding of Stuart at Yellow Tavern on May 11. The senior cavalry officer leading that force was Major General Wade Hampton of South Carolina, rumored to be the richest landowner in the South. He was one of the bravest and most brilliant officers in the army. His job was to maneuver around Sheridan in order to learn Grant's plans for his infantry. Lee would then be able to block the Federal army if it had not yet crossed the river.

Part Two
Haw's Shop

The reconnaissance force was made up of Major General William Lee's division, Brigadier General Williams Wickham's brigade of Fitz Lee's division, Hampton's own brigade led by Brigadier General Thomas Rosser, and 1,100 well-equipped and healthy troopers of the 4th and 5th South Carolina brigades. They had been sent to Virginia after lengthy arguments from fretful South Carolina politicians who feared the weakening of their coastal defenses. The Carolinians rode well-fed horses and their officers wore white gloves; instead of the light carbines normally in use, they carried long Enfield muskets along with much unnecessary luggage. None had seen a day's war service other than their commander, one-legged Brigadier General Calbraith Butler, and he was yet a day away. The ragged Virginia veterans gave those new recruits such hazing that they begged to be turned loose on the enemy.[11]

At about the same time on that morning, Grant sent Sheridan's cavalry on a similar intelligence mission. His infantry had crossed to the south side of the Pamunkey hours earlier and taken up positions just behind their cavalry line at Crump Creek. He was just as ignorant of Lee's movements as Lee was of his and so directed Sheridan to reconnoiter in the direction of Mechanicsville to determine if Confederates were in the area in strong numbers. Brigadier General David Gregg took his division out first, to be followed by the rest of Sheridan's troopers once their lines had been taken over by infantry.

At around ten that morning, Gregg's horsemen reached a lonely crossroads known as Haw's Shop, named after its only landmark, a blacksmith's workshop. It was the junction for three roads from Hanovertown that connected with the main arteries to Richmond. It could be of some importance if Grant wished to move in that direction. Gregg halted and placed pickets all along the Mechanicsville road. Almost immediately, they spotted the vanguard of Hampton's force half a mile west of the crossroads.

Hampton quickly rushed Rosser and Wickham forward and chased the first cavalry line, held by the 10th New York, back towards the Shop. Just as quickly, the 1st Pennsylvania brigade caught the attacking Southerners between rail fences that lined the road and smashed them, sending Rosser's and Wickham's men in recoil. Meanwhile, Hampton formed a defensive line across the road near Enon Church, a white frame chapel, with the remainder of his force. The retreating troopers rallied there and formed as dismounted infantry, with Rosser and Wickham on the left and center, respectively, and with the two South Carolina regiments on the right.

Gregg sent four regiments of the 10th New York, dismounted, to attack the Southern position. To their left formed the 1st Pennsylvania and 1st New Jersey and on the far end, the 6th Ohio. They took cover behind timbers and broken fences and provided fire support with the assistance of six three-inch rifles by the 6th New York Light Battery. Despite that firepower, the New Yorkers began to fall back. Brigadier General Henry Davies called for reinforcements that came in the form of Colonel Irvin Gregg's Pennsylvania Cavalry. Those men fell in on the right and soon the Federal attack increased sharply in what one Pennsylvanian called "fighting of a most desperate character." One said that the shooting consumed eighteen thousand rounds and overheated the cavalry carbines enough to render them useless.

The Southerners answered volley for volley, including skillful fire by the two South Carolina regiments. Their use of the long Enfields impressed not only Hampton's veterans but also the recipients of their fire; one said, "These were the most desperate fighters we had seen among the Southern cavalry." Sheridan was convinced at the time and even years afterward that he was facing mounted infantry.[12]

In an open field north of the Mechanicsville road were two double ditches, each lined by fencing and only forty paces apart. The 1st New Jersey came charging over the first and was met by a deadly volley from dismounted rebels in the second ditch line. The artillery fire was heavy for a cavalry fight. Both Union and Confederate gunners showered the killing field, even hitting an old house being used as a hospital for Union wounded.

That fire fight rattled on for more than six hours without any appreciable advantage made by either side. Hampton learned from captives that Federal infantry was indeed on the south side of the Pamunkey and entrenching within support distance of their cavalry. As he now had learned what he needed to know, Hampton ordered a quick withdrawal just as Custer and the Michigan brigades were moving onto the Mechanicsville road. Those troopers were armed with new seven-shot Spencer carbines which the Southerners found particularly hazardous.

As Wickham's Virginians were beginning to withdraw, Custer's men, aligned in column of platoons and with their band playing, hit the Confederate line hard in the last assault of that day. Wickham's troops broke into confusion and made for their horses in the rear. Rosser's men, now in a gap, were able to mount and withdraw without great mishap, leaving the inexperienced South Carolinians on their own. They did not know how to retreat and could not break off their engagement. Their flank began to fold and take heavy casualties from the Northern troopers' repeating carbines. At one point Hampton himself had to pull some of those recruits up and out of line by their collars. The survivors managed to fall back in good order as the Federal, slowed by their own heavy losses and fatigue, did not pursue.

George T. Brooke, with the 2nd Virginia Cavalry in Wickham's brigade, barely escaped out of the thick timber. His company had suffered terrible attrition in the last month, going from sixty troopers on May 7 to "seven or eight who could barely ride, by May 28." On the forward line of fire at Haw's Shop, he later wrote:

> I was on the skirmish line when I did not realize the rest had fallen back into the woods...the enemy was barely 150 yards away. I...was shot and maimed for life, but managed to work back to my horse, which was soon after shot from under me.[13]

The Battle of Haw's Shop, practically unremembered in most accounts of the Civil War, was in fact the largest cavalry engagement since Brandy Station almost exactly a year before. It was fought in such heavy timber growth that little contact was done by mounted fighters. Many survivors considered it the most severe cavalry battle of the war, with heavy casualties taken by both participants. Federal losses were given at 340 men while numbers for Hampton's force were never known, but 127 dead and wounded were left on the field. Most were from the South Carolina regiments, and Northern burial details found dead officers still wearing their white kid gloves.

As costly as it was, that battle unmasked Federal infantry close to the Totopotomoy River. That information enabled Lee to make critical troop movements that Grant would have to face six days later, at Cold Harbor.

✳ ✳ ✳ ✳

General Pierre T. G. Beauregard was considered one of the most imaginative of the Southern leaders by his friends and one of the most unreliable by practically everyone else. President Jefferson Davis was of the latter group, but his chief military advisor, Braxton Bragg, had a higher opinion of Beauregard's usefulness. In early 1864, Bragg had ordered Beauregard to assume command of the Department of North Carolina and Cape Fear, with headquarters at Weldon, North Carolina. Beauregard, when he saw its extent, promptly called it the Department of North Carolina and Southern Virginia and assumed charge of all operations from Wilmington, North Carolina, to Petersburg, Virginia. Thus, he imaginatively placed himself second only to Lee in direct charge of field operations in the defensive efforts in Virginia. Despite the grand titles, Beauregard had no more than 21,000 bodies at his command, including the clerks that Ewell was organizing as a civil militia in Richmond. Responsible for operations around the capitol, Beauregard was most concerned with Butler's Army of the James that May of 1864.

That force consisted of two full corps, the X and XVIII, more than 36,000 strong. As suggested to Grant in early April, Butler would take the two corps and smash at Richmond from the confluence of the James and Appomattox Rivers, at the Bermuda Hundred. Grant allowed Butler to remain in charge, as long as part of the offensive was towards the capture of the port town of City Point. Grant wanted that base for his planned offensives against Petersburg if the need were to arise. That thrust against Richmond was timed to move with Grant's crossing the Rapidan.

On May 9, Butler ordered the X Corps, led by Major General Quincy Gillmore, and the XVIII headed by Major General William Farrar Smith, to move toward Petersburg. Finding all the bridges to their north blocked by artillery and the streams impassable, Smith suggested putting a bridge over the Appomattox and attacking Petersburg from the east. Butler replied that he would not build any bridges for West Point men to retreat over. After three days of arguments Butler ordered the operations to shift toward Richmond, twelve miles away.

Beauregard had his own plan to attack Butler that President Davis unenthusiastically approved, while warning Beauregard to protect Richmond's defenses at Drewry's Bluff on the James. His plan called for using all available forces to cut Butler's army off from Bermuda Hundred.

The Battle of Drewry's Bluff on May 12 through 16 was a minor disaster viewed from either side involved. Smith and Gilmore both mishandled their orders and did not come close to coordinating a single move. The Confederates mauled both corps, and led by Hoke and Major General Robert Ransom, could have delivered an overwhelming defeat on Butler if they themselves had not been confused by crossed directions and possible drunkenness by senior commanders. [14]

However it developed – charges and counter-charges continued after the war ended – the stunned Union forces went into retreat. Heavy guns mounted on the steep sides of the bluffs and the gunboats *Virginia* and *Patrick Henry* casemated in the river below prevented any Federal use of the James itself. After that fiasco, Grant had no further use for Butler, and made it clear that the Army of the James, corked up in the geographic "bottle" on the James, was expendable. On May 22, when Grant learned of the extent of the disaster to Butler (losses of almost 4,000) the commander told Horace Porter, "Butler is not detaining even 10,000 men in Richmond, and not even keeping the roads south of that city broken..."

On May 25 Grant telegraphed orders to Halleck:

> Send Butler's forces to White House, to land on the north side, and march up to join this army. The James River should be held to City Point, but leave nothing more than is absolutely necessary to hold it, acting purely on the defensive.[15]

The Army of the James would now be a storehouse of manpower at Bermuda Hundred that Grant would draw from as he needed. Lee first heard the rumor of that decision from a Northern newspaper brought to his headquarters on May 18. Butler's two corps, a Washington dispatch said, would be called into Grant's service because "they were not strong enough to take Richmond, and too strong to be kept idle."[16]

Lee soon realized that he could be facing five Federal corps. His army had not received even half enough reinforcements to make up for losses that month. Yet, the most readily available supply of troops was Beauregard's force still facing toward Bermuda Hundred. It seemed that everyone knew that Butler would never come out of the "bottle" except for Beauregard, who insisted that Butler was still a potential threat.

※ ※ ※ ※ ※

Around dusk on May 29, Grant's forces arrived at the Totopotomoy, a sluggish and swamp-fringed course of water where his corps fanned out to the south and west. The vanguard of the Army of the Potomac was less than ten miles due north of Richmond at that point. Across from them were Lee's three corps patiently aligned for battle and waiting for Grant to provide the right cue.

Private Theodore Gerrish of the 20th Maine crossed the Pamunkey River on May 28, and with his unit began to erect earthworks when it met resistance. No one had to tell the Maine soldiers anymore how or when to dig, and they used bayonets, knives, tinplates, and any tool handy to get into the ground. They had little to eat except hardtack and coffee since May 4 – no vegetables and only a taste of stringy meat from the equally exhausted cattle driven along with the army. There had been almost continuous marching, digging, fighting, and watchfulness.

Gerrish described how it would be at the end of a long day's march through the stifling heat:

> About the time the stars were coming out, the welcome order to halt and break into companies would be heard up at the front of the regiment. Then the commands, "Halt..halt...halt" coming back through the companies. Subsequent orders would follow rapidly: "Front face...order arms...fix bayonets...stack arms...break into ranks." If a company was lucky, it would have fifteen men at the end of a march. Five of these would be detailed for picket duty and would have to report to the adjutant within ten minutes; they would be out on the picket line all night without hope of rest or sleep. Of the remaining ten men, half would be so exhausted that they would stretch out on the ground and go to sleep without eating. Others would search out wood and water and prepare an evening meal. The ground of Virginia is inherently hostile, because there would be a hummock where a man wanted a hollow for his hip and a hollow where he wanted a hummock for his head; often there would be an outbreak of firing in the course of the night and the whole company would have to turn out.[17]

Lee's veterans at that point were as weakened by illness and hunger as ever before. By the time they had reached the Totopotomoy to await the Union onslaught, some units had been without rations for two days.

George Cary Eggleston, a Virginia artilleryman, recalled:

> There was no fear in the Confederate ranks of any thing that General Grant might do; but there was an appalling and well-founded fear of starvation, which indeed some of us were already suffering. From the beginning of that campaign our food supply had been barely sufficient to maintain life, and on the march from Spotsylvania to Cold Harbor it would have been a gross exaggeration to describe it that way. In my battery three hard biscuits and one very meager slice of fat pork were issued to each man on

our arrival, and that was the first food that any of us had seen since our halt at the North Anna two days before. The next supply did not come till two days later, and it consisted of a single cracker per man, with no meat at all.

We ate the pork raw, partly because there was no convenient way of cooking it, but more because cooking would have involved some waste...[18]

John Hatton of the 1st Maryland Battery, CSA, remembered part of a conversation:

"Bob, have you anything to eat? I've drawn my belt up so many holes that my front is about to cave in and plaster itself to my back!" "Eat!! Ho! Damn eat! Damn everything! I'm about to starve to death and die on this march and I don't care if I do!" "Why Bob, my boy, what's the matter? Are you about to surrender? What would the good folks say...?"[19]

Hunger was shared even by the normally well-supplied Union men. Maintaining the crippling pace of the march made eating much secondary to movement. Once beyond the Totopotomoy, digging and crawling interrupted supplying the men on the front and flanks.

Sergeant Austin Stearns, 13th Massachusetts Infantry, wrote on May 30:

I who had almost always had enough to eat and to spare, was so hungry that I actually staggered when I marched...we passed over a plowed field and the bullets striking the ground kicked up clouds of dust. We advanced down into the wood, and soon became engaged. Darkness came in and the fight ended. A ration of fresh beef was served in the night; as we were not allowed any fire, how to cook it was a question. At length a small fire or smoke (for there was more smoke than fire) was made behind the trunk of a fallen tree, and after holding it there a few minutes, we ate it.[20]

John Haley of the 17th Maine Infantry said:

May 29 – We set a lively pace, trying to keep up with the cavalry. After a mile or so we turned square to the right and went through fields and woods, pastures and bogs. Another mile brought us to the enemy's works across the Totopotomoy Creek – an insignificant stream with marshy banks, difficult to get over. Of course the first thing we did was to throw up some works and throw out some pickets, then lay down for the night, as we had little else to do. We also had little to eat, and the question of food had become as serious with us as with the Rebels. We captured one Reb not long since whose entire stock of food was a haversack of meal, the dryest kind of fodder, with nothing whatever to season it.[21]

✳ ✳ ✳ ✳ ✳

On May 27, Major General William "Baldy" Smith concentrated two divisions of his own XVIII Corps and two divisions of Gillmore's X Corps in the rear of the lines at Port Walthall on the Appomattox River. By eleven-thirty the morning of the 29th, almost all – nearly 16,000 infantry, about 100 cavalry and 16 field pieces – were embarked at Bermuda Hundred. The flotilla carrying them was seen by Confederate observers as it descended the James, and Beauregard notified Richmond that seventeen boats had passed. By eleven the next morning, Smith's forces had arrived at White House landing, about sixteen miles by road from Cold Harbor.[22]

Lee assumed that Beauregard understood the manpower situation he faced on the Richmond-Petersburg line. He felt that if his army could not stop Grant, that Beauregard could not save Richmond. Lee arranged a conference and in the early evening of May 29, Beauregard came to his field headquarters at Atlee to view the situation personally. He politely insisted that his forces, which he estimated to be around only 12,000 infantry, could not be further reduced without creating more danger for Richmond. Four brigades from Pickett's old division and three more from South Carolina had reached Lee the last week of May, and Beauregard could not be convinced that more were needed from him. He gave no promise of further assistance.

There was more movement and sporadic fire until late that evening. By early the next morning, Grant once more extended his left flank intent on placing it on the Chickahominy River. That would be catastrophic for Lee's army, yet to lengthen his own lines would weaken parts of his front beyond the point of safety. Without immediate reinforcement, the only hope was to strike Grant's outreached left hard enough to make it recoil backwards.

Porter Alexander, First Corps Chief of Artillery, wrote:

> He [Gen. Lee] was more alert than ever for some chance, or some weak spot to strike. I happened to see an instance. Some half mile in front of where our line crossed the Old Church Road, stood Bethesda Church, a locality which I remember well from May '62, when Gen. Johnston sent me with the engineers on a reconnaissance to select a line of battle north of the Chickahominy. We could

see the church dimly in the woods from our line, about noon, when I happened to go there to see Gen. Lee on some matter, for this was not part of the line for our corps; he and Gen. Early were noting the appearance of about a brigade of the enemy near the church. Their coming was to be expected, for they were extending in that direction from their right. It was clear that Bethesda Church would be soon in the very midst of their intrenchments. But these fellows were not yet intrenched. Gen. Lee struck at them like lightning. He said to Gen. Early, "Send out a brigade see if those people are in force. The chances were ten to one that they were in force, considering the locality, but Pegrem's brigade was quickly sent out to attack them.[23]

Part Three
Bethesda Church

By midday on May 30, Grant had three of his four corps over the swampy Totopotomoy and Burnside's IX Corps had begun to move across. The soldiers that Lee had been observing were men from Brigadier General Samuel Crawford's division of Warren's V Corps, who had been brought up from Haw's Shop early that morning. They had moved through the tepid lowlands taking shots from Confederate pickets hiding in the twisted briers and thickets. Some of them knew the terrain, and those who read maps knew that room for those side-steps was running out. They could not again sidle twenty miles to advance five on the approach they were taking. Any road that they took would lead them right into Richmond, and every road was filled with belligerent Southerners in rifle pits and trenches.

Lee, in a dispatch to Anderson, his First Corps commander, commented:

> After fortifying this line they will probably make another move by their left flank to the Chickahominy. This is just a repetition of their former movements. It can only be arrested by striking at once at the part of their force which has crossed the Totopotomoy in Gen. Early's front. I have desired him to do this if he thought it could be done advantageously.

Lee then told Anderson to assist Early's attack:

> If an opening be found, take the offensive in the grand object, the destruction of the enemy.[24]

Early also saw something on the extreme Federal flank along the Shady Grove Church Road. He assembled a strike force headed by Rodes' division whose purpose would be to sweep eastward along the Old Church Road toward Bethesda Church. A slice north would place Early's forces behind Warren's left wing.

Those V Corps units were moving slowly at best, disturbed by sporadic fire from enemy cavalry and isolated infantry skirmishers. Crawford's division, pushing just west of Bethesda Church, contained two recently arrived regiments from the defenses of Washington; his other two regiments were from the Pennsylvania Reserves, of which several brigades were due to be discharged that same day.

Early's corps moved past the left flank of Union Brigadier General Charles Griffin whose 22nd Massachusetts was out front in reconnaissance. Rodes' brigades formed at right angles to the Old Church Road and began to hurriedly advance to the east. At about 2 p.m. they crashed over the first of Crawford's brigades and came screaming down the Mechanicsville road. Crawford's remaining forces began to retreat, the 1st Pennsylvania going into a nearby swamp. Rodes' forward movement became bogged down as he tried to consolidate the ground past the Bethesda Church. Hundreds of prisoners were taken but the forward units sprinted right on, leaving them for others to round up. It had all the makings of a major defeat for Grant.

Early had counted on his old division, now commanded by Stephen Dodson Ramseur, to quickly move up in support of Rodes' men before Warren could shift large forces over to the left. But hours passed before communications were made, and it was not until near six that evening that Ramseur's lead brigades moved up. By now, Griffin had taken personal charge of the flank and prepared his men to meet what had become an isolated and reckless advance. The expected help from Anderson's corps never arrived.

The 13th and 49th Virginia regiments came into the attack in double lines, exposed to point-blank massed infantry and artillery fire. Their lines literally melted away until the attack sputtered itself out. Early's report after the battle said, "The enemy was found in heavy force...Pegram's brigade was compelled to retire after sustaining considerable loss."[25]

Early's narrative on that episode read:

> On the afternoon of the 30th, in accordance with orders from Gen. Lee, I moved to the right across Beaver Dam, to the road from Old Church to Mechanicsville; and thence along that road towards Old Church until we met Bethesda Church. At this point the enemy was encountered, and his troops, which occupied the road, were driven by Rodes' division towards the road from Hundley's Corner, which unites with the road from Mechanicsville, east of Bethesda Church. Pegram's brigade, under the command of Colonel Edward Willis of the 12th Georgia Regiment, was sent forward with one of Rodes' brigades on its right, to feel the enemy and ascertain its strength; but meeting from behind breastworks, was compelled to retire, with the loss of some valuable men and officers, and among them were Col. Willis, mortally wounded and Col.

Terrill of the 13th Virginia Regiment, killed. This movement showed that the enemy was moving to our right flank, and at night I withdrew a short distance on the Mechanicsville road, covering it with my force.[26]

R. E. McBride of the 11th Pennsylvania Infantry wrote:

Now the enemy was advancing. Line after line comes swinging out. Shells come screaming over...Fragments sever the flagstaff close to Jim Shaffer's head, rip open Mike Coleman's cap, tear off Culp's arm near the shoulder. One burst in the house by the recess of woods and sets it on fire...But now the rebel lines are within rifle range. Volley after volley is poured into them, and their ranks melt before the terrible fire. In our front they falter; but toward the right they see a chance for victory. They will swing around our flank and crush us as they did an hour before. With exultant yells, their left comes sweeping on, wheeling to envelop our right. But now there bursts from the underbrush a blast as if from the pit – crashing, tearing, grinding, enfilading their lines, leaving in its track a swath of dead and dying. This is decisive, and the battle is won.[27]

Reports of the action at Bethesda Church and the XVIII Corps' arrival at White House reached Lee at about the same time. Perhaps that was why neither Early or Anderson received any criticism. There were many within the ranks, however, who were angered over that waste of blood and men.

The day of May 30 ran its course as messages and dispatches went out from both camps. The day's fighting had cost Lee almost 1,200 men compared to 731 for the Federal forces. It was perhaps one consolation that Lee was in much improved health by now, because the recent news that a new corps was to soon join Grant left him desperate as never before. He quickly gave orders that Fitz Lee move his cavalry beyond the Confederate right to secure the crossroads at Cold Harbor, three miles southeast of Bethesda Church.

Grant thought about Lee's options and realized that Smith and his corps would be vulnerable to attack before they reached the main body of the army. At six forty that evening he sent word to Meade:

General Smith will debark his force at the White House tonight and start up the south bank of the Pamunkey at an early hour, probably at 3 a.m. in the morning. It is not improbable that the enemy, being aware of Smith's movement, will be feeling to get on our left flank for the purpose of cutting him off, or by a dash to crush him and get back before we are aware of it. Sheridan ought to get notified to watch the enemy's movements well out towards Cold Harbor, and also on the Mechanicsville road. Wright should be got well-massed on Hancock's right, so that, if it becomes necessary, he can take the place of the latter readily whilst troops are being thrown east of the Totopotomoy if necessary. I want Sheridan to send a cavalry force of at least half a brigade, if not a whole brigade, at 5 a.m. in the morning, to communicate with Smith and to return with him...[28]

❋ ❋ ❋ ❋ ❋

After a final appeal to Beauregard with no effect, Lee sent a message to Davis that is as blunt as his manners would allow:

Atlee's, May 30, 1864
7:30 p.m.

His Excellency Jefferson Davis,
Richmond:

General Beauregard says the Department must determine what troops to send him. He gives it all necessary information. The result of this delay will be disaster. Butler's troops (Smith's corps) will be with Grant tomorrow. Hoke's division, at least, should be with me by light tomorrow.

R. E. Lee[29]

Davis acted as soon as he received the message. He called in Bragg and the two agreed that Hoke's 7,000 men should be sent northward by train at once. Bragg arranged the transportation and sent a terse telegraph to Beauregard, which began:

By the direction of the President, you will send Hoke's division, which you reported ready, immediately to this point by railroad.[30]

After eleven that night, Beauregard replied that he had already begun sending Hoke's division to Lee and that he and Brigadier General Bushrod Johnson's brigade would be on the move shortly.

As unlikely as any place at any time in the Civil War, a race was beginning toward a place-name on the map called Cold Harbor. It was little more than the site of another ramshackle tavern, a sleepy crossroads perched on the main road that ran from Grant's supply base at White House on the Pamunkey River, then south across the

Chickahominy River on the direct way to Richmond. Cold Harbor was a place of startling emptiness that was soon glutted by tens of thousands of violent men.

Part Four
May 31

Fitz Lee had two cavalry brigades holding Cold Harbor, guarding that intersection which led to the Pamunkey, York, and Chickahominy. Lee knew Grant would move to try to step around the Confederates. The engagement at Haw's Shop and fighting along the swamps and maze of creek shallows along the Totopotomoy had cost the Federals more than two thousand casualties. There was only one likely place to try a solid push – Cold Harbor.

Fitz Lee's two brigades had thrown together a line of breastworks from fence rails and small trees. There they hoped to hold until the arrival of Hoke rushing up from south Richmond. Even though Beauregard had delayed giving up the division, Fitz Lee learned about midday that Brigadier General Thomas Clingman's one brigade was within two miles of Gaines' Mill. He urgently told Clingman to reinforce the cavalry.[31]

Sheridan with a strong cavalry force came in early that afternoon to find the Confederates, both cavalry and infantry, dug in. He was accompanied by Grant's aide, Colonel Horace Porter. They were in the van of reinforced cavalry division commanded by Brigadier General Alfred Torbert.

Torbert's three brigades, under Merritt, Custer, and Colonel Thomas Devin attacked from several of the roads leading into Cold Harbor. Even with their Spencer repeating rifles, they found going was hard against the well-protected Southerners. Sheridan was hoping for the arrival of "Baldy" Smith's men who at that time were at Old Church.

As it turned out, Smith's original orders directed him to come up the south bank of the Pamunkey from White House Landing to New Castle, and from there to the Totopotomoy line. But while Grant's plans had changed in the last two days, he had failed to keep Smith informed of the new plan. So, Smith and his 16,000 men were becoming lost in the Peninsula and were soon six miles away from the increasing struggle for Cold Harbor.

The battle for the crossroads went on all day on May 31. Charges by Custer and Merritt failed. Sheridan sent Torbert's men in as dismounted infantry to give their fast-firing weapons more effect. Sheridan then sent for help from Brigadier General David Gregg's two brigades up at Bethesda Church, after sending patrols out to search in vain for Smith's corps. Meanwhile Sheridan pressed in and prepared to make a mass charge on Fitz Lee when Hoke's lead brigade came up the road beside Powhite Creek. The exhausted Southerners decided to fall back with that new force to make a stand at the junction of the five roads that gave that place such value. Unfortunately, Hoke's tired men, seeing the grey troopers heading their way, joined in what they saw as a general retreat through and out of Cold Harbor itself.

Sheridan's men swept in to take possession. From some of the fifty prisoners taken in those last moments, Sheridan learned that three more infantry brigades were coming in. Even with Gregg's help, Sheridan said, "I do not feel able to hold this place." He told Porter that without support, the only course open to him was to fall back.[32]

Meade and Grant disagreed. Sheridan had begun withdrawing his troopers from the breastwork line just taken when orders came from Meade telling him to hold until reinforcements arrived from VI Corps. Torbert then brought his horsemen about and settled them into line. Grant sent word that Wright's corps would be sent from the opposite end of the line, around the rear of the army in a grueling night march. It would not be in place beside Sheridan until nine o'clock the next morning. Twice before that time, Hoke's men attacked, only to be thrown back with heavy losses.

Far from being discouraged by those events of May 31, Lee saw the clear confirmation of his earlier guesses about Grant's plans. The shuttle to the southeast was in progress, with Cold Harbor the point of concentration. At that time, there was only cavalry in the area. The Federal infantry was strung out along several roads, separated and ripe for attack. Lee was free to draw from his left. He ordered Anderson's First Corps, which with Pickett's division was at full-strength, to move toward Cold Harbor. Anderson pulled his force back from the Totopotomoy line, leaving Hill to fill in the line, and began a night march to join Hoke for the attack on Sheridan.

The tired commander of the Army of Northern Virginia moved his headquarters up to Shady Grove Church, two miles closer to the scenes of terrific struggle to come in the next days.

Chapter Seven

Cold Harbor

Part One
June 1

"*Hanover Town is about twenty miles from Richmond. There are two Roads leading there; the most direct and shortest one crossing the Chickahominy at Meadow Bridge, near the Virginia Central Railroad, the second going by New and Old Cold Harbor. A few miles out from Hanover Town is a third road by way of Mechanicsville to Richmond. New Cold Harbor was important to us while there we both covered the roads to White House (where our supplies came from), and the roads south-east over which we would have to pass to get to the James River below the Richmond defenses.*"

- Lieutenant General
Ulysses S. Grant[1]

"*Now Grant was tempting fate by moving his beaten troops to this ill-fated field, there to try conclusions with McClellan's old antagonist.*"

- Captain August Dickert[2]
Kershaw's Brigade

"*In fact, his [Lee's] line was shrewdly designed to take advantage of every natural obstacle, every ravine, hillock, stream and bog, so that a searing cross-fire could be laid down from several directions against any assaulting force.*"

- Virginius Dabney[3]

"*Another flanking movement would have to be made to push the enemy into its Richmond defenses, and then will begin the tedious process of a quasi-siege. That siege would last as long as that of Sevastopol in the Crimea, unless we can get hold of their railroads and cut off their supplies, when they must come out and fight.*"

- Major General
George G. Meade[4]

"They are intricate, zig-zagged lines within lines, lines protecting flanks of lines, lines built to enfilade an opposing line, lines within which lies a battery...a maze and labyrinth of works within works and works without works, each laid out with some definite design either of defense or offense."

- Charles Page[5]
New York Tribune

The weather was extremely hot for so early in June, and the thin loamy soil in the tidewater region of the Peninsula took flight in any breeze or disturbance until the air was cloudy with dust. The tramping of tens of thousands of heavy feet and hooves and churn of wagonwheels created a fogbank of dust that, when mixed with gunsmoke, shut out much of the sunlight. The marching men, already hard-caked in sweat and dirt, seemed to take on another coating as the miles passed.

There were "old" Northern veterans who had been on that way with McClellan two years before, and some remembered being close enough to hear Richmond's church bells. Every step of their trek beyond the Pamunkey was marked by bones of horses and men, or by remnants of field-pieces or wagons left in the isolated country from the unsuccessful 1862 campaign. Now the air reeked of carcasses of many horses killed in the cavalry skirmishes that had preceeded the Federal infantry's advance on May 30 and 31.

The flat lowlands typical of southeastern Virginia were cut through and poorly drained by countless creeks and swampy runs. There were farm plots and expanses of cleared land spotted with clusters of pine trees, but heavy foliage covered most of the region. There in the extreme eastern section of Hanover County and westernmost New Kent County were no population centers or rail heads. But the meeting there was not accidental like great collisions in that war had often been. Rather, it was premeditated because both Grant and Lee saw opportunity and necessity there for both armies.

The name "Cold Harbor" was a puzzler to Union commentators, and several explanations were offered. Porter says that Cold Harbor was first supposed by Grant's staff to be a simple corruption of the phrase "Cool Arbor" suggested by the thickness of shade trees in the vicinity. Lyman of Meade's staff was never able to settle on "Cool Arbor" or "Cold Harbor" or even "Coal Harbor" and used the terms randomly.[6] Because there was no coal or anything close to a harbor nearby, many accepted the explanation that Cold Harbor meant "shelter without hot meals" in the old English tradition. The tavern that carried the label had two fireplaces, giving some mystery to that solution.[7] To add more confusion, the web of intersections contained both New Cold Harbor, which was near the infamous Gaines' Mill of 1862 activities, and Old Cold Harbor. That second group of ramshackle houses was two miles farther east, and the main lines of battle would pass between the two designations.

There, Grant believed, was the place where he would end his side-stepping. At that point yet beyond the flanks of either adversary, Grant would turn the Southern army, push it into the Chickahominy and puncture the defenses of Richmond. Cold Harbor offered not so much a clear opportunity as a chance for a conclusion to the last month of constant marching, fighting, and dying in the Wilderness and at Spotsylvania. The checkmate at the North Anna had forced that latest marching and shifting, but Grant had an awesome advantage in forces over the Southerners that could settle the issue at the proper place. Both sides felt a sense of desperation, because there was no more room for shifts by Grant and no more recovery space for Lee.

In the sweltering heat, the notion of any "Cold Harbor" was too much for many exhausted Union soldiers to believe. They had little opportunity to find relief, because Grant ordered Wright's VI Corps to march directly for Cold Harbor. The distances that the soldiers had already covered since the North Anna had taken the spring out of their steps long before, and those "side-ways" movements were more than facing left and marching. The repositioning to the left was carried out in reverse order by corps. Because the far right wing of Grant's army was held by the VI Corps, orders called for Wright to fade back, swing along the rear of the line, and come up on the other end. Expecting an attack on Sheridan at any moment and receiving messages from him urging them on, Wright's men performed the gigantic leapfrog. Many recalled that night march as perhaps the hardest of the war. Those exhausted men would not reach the battle line until mid-morning of June 1, asleep on their feet.

✳ ✳ ✳ ✳ ✳

Smith received Grant's May 28 order when he reached White House Landing with his XVIII Corps two days later. Grant told Smith to take his divisions immediately to New Castle, on the south side of the Pamunkey and almost six miles west, toward Hanovertown. Finding no supply wagons at White House, Smith left a garrison at the landing and proceeded, after telling Grant:

> Fearing that there might be some urgent reason for the appearance at New Castle of such a force as I could gather...I decided not

to wait for an answer to my letter but to move at once. Leaving Gen. Ames with 2500 men at White House, I marched with about 10,000 infantry and artillery, but without wagons to carry supplies or ammunition.[8]

While Smith was on his march westward, Grant sent messages explaining to him that New Castle was indeed his objective. Grant gave him Sheridan's position and strength at the opposite end of the Totopotomoy line:

> The movements of the enemy...would indicate the possibility of a design on his part to get between you and the Army of the Potomac...This, with the care you can give your left flank with the cavalry you have and the brigade sent to you...will make your advance secure. The position of the Army of the Potomac this evening is as follows: The left flank of the Fifth Corps is on the Shady Grove Road, extending to the Mechanicsville road and about three miles south of the Totopotomoy. The Ninth Corps is to the right of the Fifth; then comes the Second and Sixth, forming a line being on the road from Hanover Court House to Cold Harbor and about six miles south of the Court House.[9]

Grant sent his message at seven-thirty the evening of May 30. Late that night Smith sent an aide to Grant to report and to ask for further orders. Smith then received another order at daylight on June 1, telling him to proceed to New Castle and place himself between the V and VI Corps. Smith moved quickly and reached the vicinity of the New Castle ferry. Dismayed, he saw no trace of the two corps, and withdrew his weary troops back into the hills there, sending a messenger to Grant to see if the confusion might be dispelled. In the midst of throwing a bridge across the Pamunkey, the itinerant XVIII Corps commander was notified that a mistake had been made and that he was to face-about and head southeast to form on the right of the VI Corps. Smith admitted that many of his men were unused to long marching and were suffering terribly in the June heat. Those soldiers had been for the most part garrisoning Butler's immutable positions on the James River or were recent arrivals of "heavy artillery" regiments from Washington guard duty. The useless tramping about the Pamunkey River ranges was exhausting them long before they met the Southern army.[10]

But William P. Derby of the 27th Massachusetts Regiment pointed out a more serious problem:

About eleven o'clock P.M., we bivouacked at New Castle, but, on the morning of June 1st, received orders from Gen'l Grant to report to New Cold Harbor. This was the original intention, but...The error was a costly one, not so much from the inconvenience and fatigue of the additional march, as, had we arrived the night previous, we could have seized important positions in advance of the rebels, and avoided the fearful loss afterward sustained in attempting to recapture them. A forced march of twenty miles was made, under a scorching sun, over a road ground to powder by the tramp of Sheridan's cavalry the day previous, and through a country fetid with putrefying carcasses of animals, the stench from which was sickening and intolerable.[11]

The tardy arrival of Smith – his units did not come on line with Wright's corps until late in the afternoon of June 1 – was never satisfactorily explained. Perhaps Grant's original intention was to deploy a substantial part of his army more to the west along the Totopotomoy. He had said in the presence of several chroniclers, "Nothing would please me more than to have the enemy make a movement around our left flank. I would in that case move the whole army to the right and throw it between Lee and Richmond."[12] Smith's corps would have offered some buffer while Sheridan's cavalry was offered as bait to Confederate assaults to the south. In his memoirs, Grant placed blame for the confusion on an unnamed individual staff person. Porter and Lyman made Rawlins, Grant's confidante and Chief-of-Staff, the source of the problem. Whoever was to blame, the next few days would reveal the price of that delay.

LEGEND

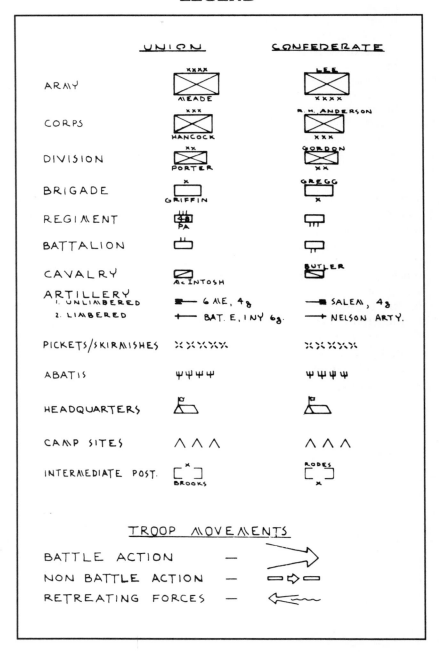

	UNION	CONFEDERATE
ARMY	MEADE	LEE
CORPS	HANCOCK	R. H. ANDERSON
DIVISION	PORTER	GORDON
BRIGADE	GRIFFIN	GREGG
REGIMENT	PA	
BATTALION		
CAVALRY	McINTOSH	BUTLER
ARTILLERY 1. UNLIMBERED	6 ME, 4g	SALEM, 4g
2. LIMBERED	BAT. E, INY 6g.	NELSON ARTY.
PICKETS/SKIRMISHES	X X X X X	X X X X X
ABATIS	ΨΨΨΨ	ΨΨΨΨ
HEADQUARTERS		
CAMP SITES	∧ ∧ ∧	∧ ∧ ∧
INTERMEDIATE POST.	BROOKS	RODES

TROOP MOVEMENTS

BATTLE ACTION   —

NON BATTLE ACTION   —

RETREATING FORCES   —

TROOP MOVEMENTS, MAY 31, 1864

Part Two
The Confederate Battle

While two more corps slowly took their places south of the Totopotomoy, the Southern forces were also receiving reinforcements, the most important of which was Hoke's division that had taken Lee such strenuous efforts to wrangle from Beauregard. A South Carolina regiment of almost eleven hundred, two Florida brigades of questionable quality, and a battalion of Georgia artillery were also filtering in. Just as important was former Vice President John Breckinridge's division that had been with Lee since late May but was yet to find a place in line. Lee had just over 60,000 men in his army by June 2.

If Grant was determined to fight it out there, so was Lee, and he was planning a stunning operation. Fitz Lee, about seven-thirty the evening of May 31, notified Lee that Federal cavalry had attacked both his own cavalry and Clingman's brigade of infantry and had driven them out of the crossroads. While he was not certain, he thought that he and his horsemen had seen Federal infantry in his front as well.[13]

Lee realized that the presence of Union infantry meant that another race, such as the one for Spotsylvania Court House, was underway. That same afternoon Lee placed Hoke's four strong brigades under Richard Anderson, commander of the First Corps. With Pickett's division that had just been returned, Longstreet's aggressive old corps was almost at its former strength, and it was to be sent to perform a miracle.

Even before he received confirmation, Lee had sensed the threat to his left was reduced. It was now clear that while Grant was strung out on the roads converging from the north and west, his infantry was at its most vulnerable. The keys to Cold Harbor were held by tired cavalry. A decisive and aggressive blow delivered by refreshed well-led men might destroy the Union infantry in detail as it came southeastward. Anderson had therefore been ordered to pull out from behind the left protecting the approaches to Atlee, from the rear of Early's and Breckinridge's divisions. He was to move to the extreme right, joining Hoke's units between Old Cold Harbor and Gaines' Mill, and be ready at dawn to smash and roll up the Union left.

The two other corps commanders had already had their chances – Hill on the North Anna and Early at Bethesda Church – and now Anderson was to get his turn. It was to be the last great Southern offensive in the eastern theatre that could stop the Union juggernaut with hope of any strategic effect. Shortly after Fitz Lee's report, Anderson sent word to Lee that his corps was inserting itself into the right wing, connecting with Hoke's brigades on his right just south of Bethesda Church.

In a letter written at the end of May 1864, the Union surgeon, A. M. Stewart, described the feelings of many in his army:

> Much of this may never, can never be written; and were it, could not be understood by those not exercised therein. No matter; we are here on the south bank of the Pamunkey River, where we lately crossed on a pontoon bridge. Yes, here again on the Peninsula, although from another point than formerly approached. Again on this Peninsula, where, two years ago we endured so much, suffered so terribly, and from whence we retreated so ingloriously. The future will tell whether this latter coming will prove more successful than the first.[14]

Dr. Gaines' old house and four-story gristmill had stood on the narrow floor of a sharply hilled valley. Nearby the Powhite Creek spread into two large millponds and became Powhite Swamp. It was here almost two years before that Hill, Longstreet and Anderson had shattered Major General Fitz John Porter's corps in the final spasms of the Seven Days' battles. Sheridan's cavalry had torched the old mill and house on their recent return from the Yellow Tavern raid. On the north side of Cold Harbor road toward the battle line, on a gentle hillside above the mill's ruins, half a dozen weather-beaten tents, with faded "U.S." insignia still on the flaps made up the Army of Northern Virginia's headquarters.

Lee had moved there to be as close as possible to the assault at dawn on June 1. He was still too weak to ride horseback or perhaps he would have directed the proposed turning movement himself. However, he had confidence in Anderson and waited at his headquarters for reports to come in.

❋ ❋ ❋ ❋ ❋

Sheridan's cavalry spent a nervous night, bolstering their newly captured breastworks with fencewood and brush, expecting heavy counter-attacks at any moment. Grant's headquarters reported that at least once, well after midnight, a Confederate force charged the Michigan cavalry.[15] Sheridan sent courier after courier with frantic messages to Wright's VI Corps, which had not pulled out of the westward trenches until after 1 p.m. Smith's XVIII Corps was expected to soon begin arriving to help out as well.

Hoke's four brigades numbered almost 7,000 men, dug in just west of Cold Harbor. Along with Anderson's full divisions containing more than 12,000, Hoke was expected to take part in the general assault that would drive out the outnumbered cavalry and smash the Union infantry flowing down. As Alexander of the First Corps said:

> We arrived in front of Cold Harbor & formed a line of battle & connected with Hoke, by about sunrise...This morning luck seemed to be on our side & a great opportunity was offered us...So we had all the time we needed to work our sweet will upon Sheridan, & once we had gobbled him up the other corps, in their scattered condition, should have been easy prey. [16]

The following failure of Lee's plans was another example of the dismal leadership and inept handling of army units that by now seemed to set the standard for his corps commanders. Lee had assumed that Anderson had talked personally with Hoke about a coordinated assault. Instead, Brigadier General Johnson Hagood had informed Hoke second-hand that he was to move to the attack only after Anderson's assault developed against the Union flank. Lee also had thought that Anderson would by now have consolidated and reorganized his reinforcements, particularly the 20th South Carolina. That unit, just arrived from Charleston, numbered more than 1,100 men. They arrived, as August Dickert noted:

> Like all new troops they had overloaded themselves with baggage and thus being overloaded, straggling was universal...these troops had seen but little real service...They had all the courage of veteran troops, but lacked acclimation.[17]

The regiment's commander was its ranking colonel, Lawrence Keitt, a powerful orator, politician, secessionist, and friend of "Bully" Brooks who had caned Senator Charles Sumner of Massachusetts in 1856. Keitt's unit had been one of the more pampered of Beauregard's garrison forces around Charleston, and upon arrival, should have been placed under the control of one of Anderson's seasoned field veterans. Either Anderson did not dare make a change or else he had no interest, and not only was Keitt allowed to outrank Colonel John Henagan for command, but brigade commander Joseph Kershaw placed the untried unit in the vanguard of the attack force for early morning, June 1.

Sheridan's troopers numbered only about 6,500. The Michigan and Massachusetts men had barricaded all three roads into Cold Harbor. They drank coffee and sorted ammunition for their seven-shot Spencer carbines and Sharps breech-loaders. At about sunrise, shooting was heard in front of their piled timbers.

Kershaw's brigade had been pushed toward the line in a southeasterly direction before daybreak. They filled their cartridge boxes on the way, fixed bayonets, and closed their ranks. As soon as the line was properly formed the order was given to advance, without a skirmish line, the brigade led out by Keitt who was mounted on a grey charger. It was almost eight that morning as Dickert continued:

> Never before in our experience had the brigade been led in deliberate battle by its commander on horseback, and it was Colonel Keitt's want of experience that induced him to take this step. Across a large old field the brigade swept towards a dense piece of oak-land, studded with undergrowth, crowded and swaying in irregular lines, the enemy's skirmishers pounding away at us as we advanced. Col. Keitt was a fine target for the sharpshooters, and fell before troops reached the timber, a martyr to the inexorable laws of military rank.[18]

The brigade plunged on into the deep trees, many crawling through the brushy undergrowth until they could find the protection of larger trees from which to fire back. When the Union's dismounted cavalry advanced in solid column and attacked the wavering 20th South Carolina, its officers began to order a withdrawal back to Cold Harbor Road. Most of the brigade, under the cover of gun smoke hovering in the trees, were able to return to their starting point, repeating-rifle bullets stinging at them all the way. Colonel William Wallace of the South Carolina 2nd Regiment said:

> Our brigade, under the command of the lamented Colonel Keitt, was sent out to reconnoitre, and came upon the enemy in large force, strongly entrenched. Keitt was killed, and the brigade suffered severely. A few skirmishers thrown out would have accomplished the object of a reconnaissance, and would have saved the loss of many brave men. Our troops, finding the enemy entrenched, fell back and began to fortify.[19]

Robert Stiles, observing the tangle and dismal rout with his artillery battery nearby, said:

I have never seen any body of troops in such a condition of utter demoralization; they actually grovelled upon the ground and attempted to burrow under each other in holes and depressions.[20]

Hoke's division had not moved an inch in support of Anderson's lead units. Some of his brigadiers did not even realize that a Confederate attack had taken place. Clingman's North Carolinians, positioned hardly seventy-five yards from Kershaw to their left, supposed the noise to mean a Federal assault. Clingman wrote:

I then supposed that the enemy had made only a feint in that [Kershaw's] direction, whereas, in fact, as I have subsequently learned, this brigade fled precipitately from the field after discharging their muskets.[21]

He was referring to the scattering of Keitt's South Carolinians. Clingman certainly knew about running, as his men had lost the Cold Harbor crossroads the day before when Fitz Lee's cavalry had fallen back because of lack of infantry support. And, as preparations began for a second charge at Sheridan's positions, those same North Carolina brigades had not fully joined their line with the brigades to the left.

Clingman was assured that Hagood's brigade would be positioned to close a gap between Hoke's and Kershaw's divisions, created by a steep gully and stream. There was, then, a seam separating those units at the far right corner of the lines that would offer disaster to Hoke's forces later in the contest.

Artillery Chief Alexander wrote:

In carrying out the order to close upon Hoke's division one blunder was made which afterward proved serious. Between our right & Hoke's left a swampy thicket, along a small stream, was allowed to make a gap of perhaps fifty yards between Hoke & Kershaw's divs.[22]

Clingman's North Carolinians covered the Cold Harbor Road and Brigadier General William Wofford's brigade of Kershaw's division took up the line's formation north toward Bethesda Church. The separation in the otherwise solid defensive layout was judged by Porter Alexander to be impassable and no efforts were made to fuse the line. Considering the unsettling and recoiling that had been going on for most of the day, that minor situation received little attention. Anderson was as confused as ever and was intent on entrenching Pickett's and Field's divisions on an angled line with Hoke. The quick positioning of new units into an unsurveyed line led to one circumstance that would have enormous impact later.

Part Three
Aftermath of June 1

At about nine in the morning, Sheridan reported that Wright's lead division was coming into the line in his support. His dismounted cavalry had performed outstandingly, but he was more than agreeable to turning the defenses over to Wright and the soon-expected Smith before the next Confederate attack. At ten o'clock, a second half-hearted movement by Anderson's division was made against the solid Union breastworks. It fizzled away so quickly that artillery from Parker's batteries that had been positioned to move forward was left standing halfway from their protected positions, and was forced to dig in where they were under heavy fire.[23]

Lee had little time to be disappointed at that most recent failure, and as before, with Early, no recriminations were issued toward either Hoke or Anderson. Lee realized that while his army had squandered a vital opportunity, he would have to move quickly to keep Grant from pinning him against Richmond. He moved Breckinridge's small division to Cold Harbor to strengthen and extend his far right wing, and prepared to go there in person.[24]

There had been heavy skirmishing up and down the six-mile line at the same time that the flank assault failed. Early's units attacked the western part of Burnside's line and Warren's diminished Pennsylvania Reserves regiment. Warren had been ordered to move against the enemy in his section of line when Southern units crossed directly in front of the V Corps, but he failed to do more than fire his field guns. Brigadier General Henry Lockwood, Charles Dana reported, was ordered to take Warren's left-most division against the Confederates. Lockwood reportedly had "lost his way" and was subsequently cashiered by Grant.[25] Some distance south, Birney's division of the II Corps advanced almost 600 yards into the Southern line and displaced one of Breckinridge's brigades.[26] Both Heth and Breckinridge were forced to make brigade readjustments without informing Lee. There were weak places on the defensive line that could not be discovered until the North attacked.

Wright's VI Corps came into the lines by mid-morning and earnestly began to dig in. Little more than two weeks before, one of the corps' larger brigades, the 2nd Connecticut Heavy Artillery, was in the comfortable garrison of Washington. Never in combat, many of them wore bright blue uniforms issued before being shipped out. Their newness stood out among the worn-out clothes of the rest of the Army of the Potomac. They were placed within Russell's division of the VI Corps that had arrived first to bolster Sheridan. Within two hours, Smith's vanguard showed up, aching from a march of more than twenty miles. As they came in, the sleeping Connecticut men had to move over. When one soldier tugged at another to arouse him, telling him, "Jim, there's a pile of troops coming in. I guess there's going to be a fight." Jim blinked and replied, "I don't care a damn. I wish they'd shoot us and be done with it. I'd rather be shot than marched to death."[27]

They had lost many stragglers on the roads to Cold Harbor. Those two corps were too tired to respond quickly to any new action. The men had been walking all night and were too exhausted to eat when they finally arrived. They were placed using the Cold Harbor Road as a guideline for the movements to come, Wright's corps on the left and Smith's on the right. The units faced toward the rising ground where butternut infantry and artillery were waiting.

One of the brigades in the Third division of the VI Corps was the 10th Vermont, led by Colonel William Henry. It had been pulled out of the western part of the line at one that morning and was one of the first to relieve Sheridan's cavalry. Infantryman Edwin Haynes says that the troopers greeted them with wild demonstrations of joy. The Vermonters arrived to the sounds of Custer's band playing "Hail Columbia," and approached into the middle of what appeared to be a celebration. Haynes says;

> ...on the contrary, they had been roughly handled, and did not mean to let the enemy know it... Here we saw a sight which made the blood curdle, and at every thought of which the soul sickens and turns away. We had heard of the occurrence, but never had been so unfortunate as to behold it before. Right over the field where the battle had done its fiercest work, the fire had swept, and many a brave fellow, wounded and dying, unable to move from the place where he had fallen had the little remaining life drawn out of him by the flames, and his body burned to a crisp.[28]

Private Frank Wilkeson visited the scene of that morning's fighting, coming in with his battery that evening. He remembered:

> ...We heard considerable fighting in front of us, and towards evening we marched over ground where dead cavalrymen were

plentifully sprinkled. The blue and grey lay side by side, and their arms by them. With the Confederates lay muzzle-loading carbines, the ramrods of which worked upward on a swivel hinge fastened near the muzzle of the weapon. It was an awkward arm and far inferior to the Spencer carbine with which our cavalry was armed. There were ancient and ferocious-looking horse pistols, such as used to grace the Bowery stage, lying by the dead Confederates. The poverty of the South was plainly shown by the clothing and equipment of her dead. These dead men were hardly stiff when we saw them. All of their pockets had been turned inside out. That night, while searching for fresh, clean water, I found several dead cavalrymen in the woods, where they had probably crawled after being wounded. I struck a match so as to see one of these men plainly and was greatly shocked to see large black beetles eating the corpse. I looked at no more dead men that night.[29]

Lyman of Meade's staff explained that a heavy frontal attack against the Confederate line close to their Chickahominy anchor the afternoon of June 1 was necessary if Grant's assault scheduled for June 2 was to succeed. As soon as Smith's winded infantrymen came in behind Wright's corps, orders for that attack were given. Smith recounts whimsically that he was ordered to cover the three-mile section of line from Wright's flank to Bethesda Church, and since he could not fill the space to his standards, decided to join in the assault.[30] After a brief reconnaissance, it was decided that one division would hold the Mechanicsville and Shady Grove roads while two divisions would move against the Southerners, positioned in a wooded area fronting a wide field.

Smith sent urgent appeals to Meade for ammunition, reminding the army commander that there had been no supply train to meet the XVIII Corps at White House Landing. The messages for ammunition and concerning "precarious positions" continued until as Lyman tells it, Meade, already in his peak bad temper, roared, "Then, why the hell did he come at all for?"[31]

The attack began sometime before five in the afternoon, when two of Smith's divisions led by Brigadier General William Brooks and Brigadier General Charles Devens, Jr., crossed the hazardous field leading to the enemy's line. Smith said:

> Under severe fire, they crossed the open field, and entering the wood, made their way through slashings and inter-laced tree-tops, and carried the rifle-pits, capturing about 250 prisoners.[32]

Colonel Guy Henry's brigade on the extreme right carried the Confederate rifle pits on its front, but then ran against an elevated breastwork on its right flank. No fire could be effectively brought against that position which bore down on the 21st Connecticut and 40th Massachusetts, so they dropped back to the clearing. Another brigade, including the 98th New York, made it through the first woods and, crossing another field, ran into a second line of earthworks. As they worked to tear apart the obstacles of sharpened stakes and trees the Southerners erupted with a volley that almost melted the Union soldiers' front ranks. The attackers wavered and many withdrew into the captured pits behind them.

Brigadier General James Ricketts' division of primarily New York and Ohio units had joined in that first wave, and were out to prove themselves. They were the Milroy's Boys who had embarrassed themselves in the Wilderness. They were the unit that Hancock called "a weakly child" and "weary boys."[33] Ricketts had been their commander for a few weeks and had nursed them along. In a second assault in the face of heavy losses, those men climbed over the Southern works, taking scores of prisoners and driving the rest back. Elsewhere the Confederate lines held firm, and a furious fire fight developed as darkness began to deepen on the field.

The commander of the 2nd Connecticut Heavy Artillery was Colonel Elisha Kellogg, a big burly man who humiliated his officers and brutalized his men until they seemed on the brink of mutiny. He was intent on bringing some respect to his unit, characterized as a "brandbox regiment" by the hard veterans of Grant's infantry. He was given to flaming temper outbursts followed by unconventional kindness to his men, and they were devoted to him.

Adjutant Theodore Vaill said:

> The men who were cursing him one day for the most intolerable rigors of his discipline, would in twenty-four hours be throwing up their hats for him, or subscribing to buy him a new horse, or petitioning the Governor not to let him be jumped.

The 2nd Connecticut was drawn up near an old Federal breastwork on the right of the Cold Harbor-Richmond road. The regiment was so large that it was divided into three battalions. Colonel Kellogg drew a design of the Confederate works that he wanted taken and gave his battalion commanders instructions for the attack. The objective began with a line of rifle pits only 200 feet in their front; behind a thin belt of trees was another open field that adjoined the main rebel line.

MOVEMENTS UP TO 10:30 A.M. JUNE 1, 1864

MOVEMENTS FROM 10:30 A.M. TO MIDNIGHT JUNE 1, 1864

It was a fearsome array of trenches guarded in front by heavy abatis of brush, sharpened stakes, and pointed pine logs. Stretching for miles in both directions, the line was studded with artillery emplacements. Kellogg's would be operating as the lead regiment of Brigadier General Emory Upton's division, and their pride swelled to be involved with the hero of Spotsylvania. Colonel Kellogg stood on the breastwork logs and told the "Heavies":

> Now men, when you have the order to move, go in steady, keep cool, and keep still until I give you the order to charge, then go in arms a-port with a yell. You are not to fire a shot until we are in the enemy breastworks.[34]

The three battalions went forward at intervals of one hundred feet and with muskets uncapped. When Upton gave the order to advance, Kellogg led his men forward, his garrison cap on the tip of his uplifted sword, just after five that afternoon.

At close order, the first battalion swiftly reached the row of rifle pits to find them abandoned. They then moved through the scrub pines, down into a slight hollow, and up against the thickly laid abatis. Through gaps in the logs and brush some men caught a momentary glimpse of musket barrels and slouch hats just as they were trapped in a sheet of rifle flames "sudden as lightning and red as blood – so near it seemed to singe the men's faces."[35] Incredibly, that barrage was high and few of the Connecticut men were hit as they fell flattened to the ground. At Kellogg's command, those men leaped up to clear the abatis and the entire left Confederate line opened up on them, shooting down more than two hundred in minutes.

Kellogg, shot in the upper jaw, managed to shout, "About face!" as he was hit twice more in the head and fell dead on top of the abatis. "Wild and blind with wounds, bruises, noise, smoke, and conflicting orders, the men staggered in every direction, some of them falling upon the very top of the rebel parapet, where they were completely riddled with bullets," Vaill later reported.[36]

The 2nd Connecticut had followed the seam created by the gully and creek on the flank of Clingman's division that separated him from Anderson's corps. They had managed to get in front of the 51st North Carolina regiment before being observed. Captain Fred Blake, sighting the low ground in front and to the left, shouted, "Here they are, as thick as can be!" Within perhaps eight paces came a heavy Union column. Clingman wrote:

...They had on apparently new uniforms, and were marching at a quick step...From the fact that the column displayed four flags, I took it to consist of four regiments...As my men had been firing at objects elevated...I was apprehensive that they might fire too high. I therefore in a loud voice said: "Aim low and well!" As I did this a tall and uncommonly fine looking officer in the front rank of the enemy's column, hearing the order and looking me directly in the face, took off his cap and waving it about his head, cheered his men in words I could not catch...a soldier immediately on my right discharged his musket and the ball entered the upper part of his forehead, and he fell backward staggering the two men behind him.

The discharge from my line at once knocked down the front ranks of the column, while the oblique fire along the right and left cut down the men rapidly all along the column towards the rear. In a few moments the whole column...lay down. Nothing could have been more unfortunate for them. While they thus lay there, the men of my command continued to reload and discharge their pieces into the thick, dark mass. The officers fired their repeaters, while such as had none borrowed muskets from privates and discharged them at particular individuals. As the survivors lay still to avoid attracting attention, it was soon impossible to distinguish the living from the dead. After some fifteen or twenty rounds had been fired into the prostrate mass, I directed the firing to cease...A portion of the column, not more than a tenth, arose and fled to the rear; many of these, however, were shot down as they attempted to escape.[37]

Upton came among the terrified Connecticut soldiers and tried to rally the rear battalions. He grabbed a discarded infantry musket and began firing. "Men of Connecticut, stand by me! We must hold this line!" he shouted. The units had become intermeshed and officers seemed unable to exert control. But Upton managed to form a firing line even as dozens of Union men scampered out of the smoke and noise to surrender. When one of the disheartened officers ran up to report that his command, running low on ammunition, was unable to move the Confederates, Upton screamed at him, "If they come there, catch them on your bayonets and pitch them over your heads!"[38] Upton kept alive what was left of the first battalion and most of the other two from the heavy artillery regiment, forcing them to lie down as their line crowded forward.

Adjutant General Martin McMahon, amazed at the carnage, wrote:

> The second Connecticut Heavy Artillery...had joined us but a few days before the battle, its uniform was bright and fresh; therefore its dead were easily distinguished where they lay. They marked in a dotted line an obtuse angle, covering a wide front, with its apex toward the enemy, and there upon his face, still in death, with his head to the works, lay the Colonel, the brave and genial Colonel Elisha Kellogg.[39]

Even as the North Carolinians cheered their success with the 2nd Connecticut, more VI Corps soldiers, led by the 87th Pennsylvania, moved up into the gap between Clingman and the adjoining Georgian infantry under Brigadier General William Wofford of Kershaw's division. Clingman contended with a vigorous assault on the 61st North Carolina to his right which was repulsed after getting to within eighty or so yards from the lines. The undergrowth allowed units of some size to come close to both exposed flanks and even fifty or so yards into the rear of the lines. Camouflaged by heavy smoke and the thickness of the woods, the 151st New York delivered a shocking volley into the backs of Clingman's 8th Regiment. Almost the whole of the 51st North Carolina was taken prisoner by the 10th Vermont. Clingman afterward accused the Georgians and Wofford of abandoning their positions and leaving him to face Northern troops in front, rear, and flank. Wofford's men had in fact been holding strongly against Ricketts' brigades until they saw themselves trapped. Hundreds were taken captive as they ran into the troublesome gully.[40]

The Union division led by David Russell, farther to the left, was chopped up badly as it ran into inter-laced barriers of stakes and trees and felt the full effect of crossing artillery fires from Parker's and Huger's batteries. Russell's men were raked by terrible fire from front and flank, until ordered to lie down in whatever shallow ground they could burrow. The Southern fire hit especially hard the three New Jersey units in the first brigade. Russell was wounded, but stayed on the field to try to salvage what he could in the unrelenting flame and noise.

Anderson seemed to find his bearings at about the time Clingman's units were set to be devoured. The North Carolinians were formed into a new line at a right angle to the earlier one. From there the hard-pressed 8th and 51st made a stand and were soon assisted by Brigadier General Alfred Colquitt's Georgia brigade. Gregg was detached from Field's division, along with Brigadier General Eppa Hutton's brigade, to come to the rescue. Colonel William Wallace's 2nd Regiment of Kershaw's division was hurriedly pressed in against part of the Union brigade of Colonel William Barton. They succeeded in repelling the

48th and 112th New York regiments. Colquitt's five companies of the 27th Georgia Regiment helped Clingman mount a charge to reestablish part of the Southern trench line. Hutton and Clingman got into a sharp argument when the former ordered the North Carolinians to move back and allow Hutton's brigade to settle into the area that Wofford and Clingman had lost in Wright's attack.

It had been three hours since the action had started, and was pitch dark. Men still shot at each other by the light of burning powder as the last Federal troops were chased out of the gap. Doctor George Stevens, a surgeon recently returned to the VI Corps from Fredericksburg, wrote this account:

> The order for the charge was given, and our two commands, weary and exhausted...dashed impetuously forward...with shouts and cheers, making for the rebel works...Volleys rang out upon the evening air, crashing louder and still louder. The First and Third divisions of the Sixth Corps, in heavy column...cleared the abatis and seized the rebel works, while the Second division on the left, discovering a strong force of the enemy planting a battery on our flank, engaged them and forced them back. Smith's command...by a desperate charge was also largely successful. The whole line thundered with the incessant volleys of musketry, and the shot and shell of the artillery shrieked and howled like spirits of evil. The sun was sinking red in the west, and the clouds of dust and smoke almost obscured the terrible scene. Hundreds of our brave fellows were falling on every side...
>
> The First division, after a stern resistance...was forced to give up the line of works it had captured...Only the Third division held its ground. The others...in spite of most determined efforts, were forced to swing back.
>
> As darkness came, the conflict still raged, and sheets of flame rolled from one end of the line to the other...As the sound of the battle died away at nine o'clock, the advantages gained by us were held, and our men set to work to strengthen the works they had captured from the enemy, and to throw up new ones.[41]

The losses from the fighting on June 1, concentrated along the shallow front of the Southern line south of Bethesda Church only a mile from the Chickahominy River, were appalling.

Estimates made at the time have proved to be accurate: VI Corps, 1,200 killed, wounded, and missing; XVIII Corps, 1,100. Lee's forces also had substantial losses of approximately 1,800, with 750 or more taken captive from Hoke and Kershaw before the Federal breakthrough was halted.

Terrible and important events were beginning to take shape in the watershed of the old Chickahominy. The Army of the Potomac, never known for its speed under any circumstances, had moved rapidly and withheld nothing in its exertions to capture little more than an empty farming village. The Army of Northern Virginia had been equal to the task, with sacrifice and aggressiveness made sharper by desperation. The stage was set for one of the most amazing confrontations of the war.

Ulysses S. Grant at his headquarters at Cold Harbor.
By Brady & Co.

(B-36-National Archives)

Ulysses S. Grant and his staff of nine at Cold Harbor. Among those pictured are John Rawlins, Cyrus Comstock, and Ely Parker on the extreme right. By Brady & Co.

(B-2008-National Archives)

Horatio Wright
of the VI Corps soon
after Cold Harbor in
1864.
By Brady & Co.
(B-4198-National Archives)

Winfield S. Hancock with his II Corps divisional commanders, Barlow, Gibbon, and Birney, at Cold Harbor. By Brady & Co.

(B-21-National Archives)

William Farrar Smith of the XVIII Corps and his staff at Cold Harbor. By Brady & Co.

(B-39-National Archives)

Jubal A. Early
of the Second Corps,
taken soon after the
war.
(BA-2028-National Archives)

**Richard H.
Anderson,**
commander of the
First Corps.
(BA-1817-National Archives)

Ambrose P. Hill,
head of the
Third Corps.
(BA-1190-National Archives)

Robert E. Lee,
in one of the last
wartime photographs
for which he would
pose.
(BA-1186-National Archives)

Chapter Eight

Cold Harbor

Part One
June 2

"Grant has grown so enamored of his left flank that he will probably work his way down toward the James River, and we shall have another decisive battle of Cold Harbor..."
>- *Richmond Examiner*
>May 30, 1864

"We began to understand that Grant had taken hold of the problem of destroying the Confederate strength in the only way that the strength of such an army, so commanded, could be destroyed, and that he intended to continue the plodding work till the task could be accomplished..."
>- George Eggleston[1]
>Lamkin's Virginia Battery

"It was a bad place to settle down. They were now in the lowlands of the Chickahominy, a sluggish stream running in places through a kind of Dismal Swamp. The sun was hot. The mosquitoes were thick. The stench of hundreds of unburied horses and men at Cold Harbor blew over the country with every breeze. Water for the troops had to come almost entirely from surface drainage. Malarial ills, known as Chickahominy fever, began to be prevalent."
>- Private Theodore Gerrish[2]
>20th Maine

"The terrain was flat and the thin pine woods were sprinkled with numerous small clearings...The Confederate lines were unusually straight at Cold Harbor, because the flat ground did not dictate the lines to those laying them out as so often happened in broken country. The straight lines were well-suited to crossing fires of artillery, which could tear through the piney woods much farther than the eye could see."
>- Robert Krick[3] in
>*Parker's Virginia Battery*

In the evening and night of June 1, Lee tried to find out the condition of the Bermuda Hundred line from Beauregard. He had earlier repeated a rumor to Davis of a reported advance of an enemy force up the York River Railroad. Lee now wondered if Grant, checked on the Chickahominy, might be moving across the James River. Beauregard was sent warning about that possibility and Lee again suggested that "as two-thirds of Butler's forces has joined Grant, can you not leave sufficient guard to move with the balance of your command to the north side of James River and take command of the right wing of the army?"[4]

While that may or may not have been a wise plan, Grant was not finished with the situation north of the Chickahominy. Cold Harbor sat astride the Confederate flank, and while many Southern units were moving in that direction, it seemed doubtful to the Federal command that Lee could have built so formidable a defensive line there.

If there was any place on that six-mile line where a powerful assault might succeed, it would be at that corner of the Peninsula. The Chickahominy ran through the Confederate rear, and a breakthrough that would send an army in retreat across that river so close to Richmond might bring the war to a close. It was also the only method left, and either Grant made the most of Cold Harbor or he would have to develop a new campaign.[5] He took the sour news of the June 1 assaults with as much optimism as possible.

That evening Hancock received orders to draw the II Corps away from Warren's V Corps on the Union right wing and made a forced night march to reach Wright's left flank before dawn of June 2. Grant's massive assault upon Lee's right would begin at five that morning. Hancock's official report said:

> Every exertion was made, but the night was dark, the heat and dust oppressive, and the roads unknown. Still, we should have reached Cold Harbor in good season had not [our guide] Captain Paine unfortunately taken one of my divisions by a short cut where artillery could not follow, and so thrown my command into great confusion. My staff officers are entitled to great credit for reuniting the column and repairing the unfortunate mistake. The head of my column reached Cold Harbor at 6:30 a.m., June 2, but in such exhausted condition that a little time was required to allow the men to collect and to cook their rations...The attack ordered for this morning was postponed until 5 p.m.[6]

So another movement fell victim to the roads of Cold Harbor. What was meant to be a march of nine miles, hard enough on already tired soldiers, turned into a punishing hike of more than fifteen miles for some of Hancock's units. The profound darkness and poor maps added to the dense clouding of road dust to cause total confusion. The short-cut was narrower than had been assumed and cannons became stuck between thick trees, and Hancock's column piled up. Men on horses ran into tree limbs or sometimes fell down eroded embankments. Eventually a counter-march to another road was made. That most recent foul-up wore out the already foot-sore II Corps. Exhausted and hungry, Hancock was greeted with a surprisingly upbeat message from Meade when II Corps was in place:

> Every confidence is felt that your gallant corps of veterans will move with vigor and endure the necessary fatigue.

Charles Dana reported that "there joined this army yesterday ten old and new regiments, making an additional force of 3,727 reinforcements. The largest of these regiments were the 21st Pennsylvania [cavalry, dismounted], 950 men, 4th Delaware, 503 men, and the 4th New Hampshire, 500 men." He also mentioned, in his count of losses from the day's fighting, that one of Deven's brigades from XVIII Corps came out of the struggle with only three field officers left from the minimum of twenty-six.[7] Those replacements, particularly to fill lower level command, were needed.

※ ※ ※ ※ ※

Grant's headquarters staff tried to keep a positive attitude about the events of June 1. Porter noted that Grant was fully prepared and "eager as usual to push the advantage gained." A supply of oysters arrived at headquarters that day, and the staff at the evening meal was delighted to see their jovial commander attack the oysters with enthusiasm, along with his regular hard bread and roast beef.[8]

There seemed to be agreement that the fierce attacks on Lee's right end had accomplished some positive results. Meade had his jumping-off place for the next morning's frontal assault because of the ground won by Wright's divisions. There was hope that, finally, there was fighting ground between Lee and Richmond.

Both Grant's and Meade's headquarters followed II Corps into Cold Harbor later the morning of June 2. Lyman observed:

> Of all the wastes I have seen, the first sight of "Cool Arbor" was the most dreary! Fancy a baking sun to begin with; then a fore-

ground of breastworks; on the left, Kelly's wretched house; in the front, an open plain, trampled fetlock deep into fine, white dust and dotted with caissons, regiments of soldiers, and dead horses killed in the previous cavalry fight. On the sides and in the distance were pinewoods, some red with fires which had passed through them, some grey with the clouds of dust that rose high in the air. It was a Sahara intensified, and was called "Cool Arbor!"[9]

Lyman also described his commander, Meade, as having been in a particularly bad mood after the bedlam of June 1:

> Gen. Meade was in one of his irascible moods tonight, which are always founded in good reason though they spread themselves over a good deal of ground that is not always within the limits of the question. First he blamed Warren for pushing without orders; then he said each corps ought to act for itself and not always lean on him. Then he called Wright slow (a true proposition).[10]

Meade repeated his low opinion of William "Baldy" Smith. The two had never been friends and had previously had some personal difficulties. Meade tended to feel resentful toward all of the "Western-ers" that General Grant had brought with him into the Army of the Potomac, and it was evident that he still felt somewhat insulted by his status as "commander-yet-not-commander" of that army. Smith was at that time still a favorite of Grant from the old days who could never defer to the "hero of Gettysburg." Another problem was the politically powerful Burnside, whose corps was formally consolidated into the Army of the Potomac only on May 24. He testily refused to receive orders directly from the nominal head of the army. Meade also dis-liked and suspected Gouverneur Warren, disagreed in substance with Grant's sidling and assaulting strategies, and was on the whole an un-happy man by June of 1864. A letter to his wife on June 1 ended with the following:

> The weather is beginning to be hot, but I keep in the saddle during the day, and sleep soundly at night.
>
> The papers are giving Grant all the credit of what they call successes; I hope they will remember this if anything goes wrong.[11]

✳ ✳ ✳ ✳ ✳

Early that morning, Lee was able to ride horseback for the first time in ten days. He was still enfeebled, yet he made the trip to

Mechanicsville to look for Breckinridge and his three brigades who had not arrived as expected. They were to connect with Hoke's division on the far right to bolster that sensitive area for the attack that Lee expected any moment. Lee knew that Breckinridge had been engaged to some extent in yesterday's fighting and would need to rest after the eight miles march. A guide, the young Major Henry McClellan, was assigned to bring the vital reinforcements into the line. After some searching, Lee found Breckinridge eating a leisurely breakfast with his troops, still far from their assigned area. Major McClellan, having no maps and being as ignorant of the country as anyone else, had taken Breckinridge and his men on a round-about trek that made their arrival several hours late. Lee, composed as ever, said nothing in recrimination but urged Breckinridge to hasten his men down the line.[12]

At Mechanicsville, Lee learned that the Union II Corps had disappeared from his Third Corps front. Seeing the increase in troop concentrations toward Cold Harbor, Lee then ordered Hill's corps to split, sending Wilcox's and Mahone's divisions to take positions beyond Breckinridge, in the far gap between Old Cold Harbor and the Chickahominy River. He almost expected to hear the opening guns of a new assault before he made the ride back to Gaines' Mill.

Meanwhile, if Grant were shifting forces away from his right to his left, it would mean that the west flank might be weakened enough for a spirited attack from Early's forces on the far end. A strong turning there would upset Grant's general plans to some degree. Thus, while at Mechanicsville, Lee gave Early discretionary permission to move upon the Union if he found any favorable opening.[13]

In the early afternoon, Breckinridge moved into position. Special attention was given to the left anchor of his brigades' connection with Hoke's right, where a branch of Boatswain's Swamp created a steep-walled marsh. Union entrenchments were less than seventy-five yards in front, at the apex of Meade's "jump-off" wedge. Brigadier General Samuel McGowan's brigade and selected artillery were emplaced just behind Hoke's line, where the Federals might strike.

With Breckinridge's arrival, Major Henry McClellan was invited to come to Lee's tent. Having had less than success as a guide, the major was almost fearful of what was to come, and put the feelings in his own words many years later:

> With a sinking heart I obeyed. The General was seated on a camp stool in front of his tent, and open map spread out on his knees. When I was in position before him, he traced a road with his index finger, and quietly remarked, "Major, this is the road to Cold Harbor." "Yes, General," I replied. "I know it now."

Not another word was spoken, but that quiet reproof sunk deeper and cut more keenly than words of violent vituperation would have done.[14]

Wilcox and Mahone had their men digging into the line by three o'clock that afternoon. At the extreme of the Confederate right, with Mahone's five brigades in the rear of Breckinridge as the only reserve on the six-mile defensive line, Wilcox settled his division in, his right units on the north bank of the Chickahominy at the Grapevine Bridge. They took over from the remnants of Fitz Lee's cavalry that had held the area since May 30.

Even before those men had begun their first row of rifle pits, Lee needed one final adjustment. Two years before, a division commanded by Major General Daniel H. Hill had used a slight promontory south of Gaines' Mill to help split a Union corps. That elevation, less than a mile from the riverbank, known as Turkey Hill, had a dominating view of the Chickahominy bottom lands. At about three that afternoon, a detachment of Breckinridge's 23rd Battalion, with two of Wilcox's brigades assaulted the small force of Union soldiers that controlled Turkey Hill and drove them away. Well placed Union artillery gave one of Wilcox's brigades, led by Brigadier General Alfred Scales, substantial casualties. But with control of that high-ground, the Confederate right flank was fast becoming invulnerable.

Skirmishing went on up and down the line from dawn until late that evening of June 2. Breckinridge's troops were harassed all afternoon with sharpshooting and artillery fire. The real work of trench building went on and by the hour, Lee's positions taking on the features that would be remembered as the most cunning and elaborate of the war.[15]

※ ※ ※ ※ ※

Some of Early's pickets were able to count individual units on the Federal side, so closely had both forces moved their entrenchments. Every movement was discernible, and one soldier said that it was as dangerous in the flat areas to the rear as it was in the front rifle pits. The artillery kept busy moving and returning fire. For example, a morning attack on Anderson's positions was halted by Huger's and Haskell's batteries. There were a dozen minor back and forth actions which had little effect but made trench life miserable.[16]

Burnside's IX Corps held the far right and had a difficult time adjusting their lines due to sporadic probing and sharp-shooting by Early's opposite divisions. Brigadier General Thomas Crittenden's 1st Division of three full brigades had shuttled toward the southwest for about a half mile late on the evening of June 1. Early attacked it that evening, and only with the help of Warren's covering units did Crittenden avert serious damage. At around ten that same night, Grant ordered a general attack along the entire line, scheduled for dawn the next morning. Planing was continuing for further movements by the V and IX Corps when a counter-command arrived canceling that grand assault because of Hancock's troubles in reaching the lines at Cold Harbor.

Part Two
Settling In

Just after noon on June 2, the IX Corps withdrew to the southeast, away from the Totopotomoy. The 2nd Michigan covered the rear while the corps moved to a new position on the extreme Union right, closer to Bethesda Church. Warren's V Corps was set in one of the strongest forward positions in Grant's line. His divisions formed a compact, reinforced wedge about one mile south of Bethesda Church almost in the face of Ramseur's and Field's units. They were placed in an ideal defensive posture which had absolutely no bearing on the combat to come and would remain essentially inactive for the remainder of the Cold Harbor campaign.

At about two that afternoon, Heth's and Rodes' divisions vigorously attacked Burnside's far right skirmish line. Early had sensed those shifting movements and saw an opportunity to attack Crittenden's 1st division now left in the open. Supported by elements of Gordon's improvised division, Rodes moved in on the road from Hundley's Corner off to the west. Heth came into Crittenden's right flank in a wheeling movement, pivoting on an old farmhouse owned by the Johnson family. When Gordon's men suddenly pulled back through the artillery lines to the right of Old Church Road, Garber's battery opened up on the Union front with canister, sending them retreating in mass. Colonel Joseph Sundburg's 3rd Maryland brigade and the 2nd New York Rifles were pushed back from their entrenchments as Heth's men crashed in, cloaked in a torrential rain.

Burnside then arrived in the threatened area and personally formed his corps on open ground in three long lines of battle by division fronts. Crittenden's pummeled division was now joined by Potter's and Willcox's divisions. The batteries of the 7th Maine and 34th New York Artillery exchanged shells with Poague's guns while heavy fire erupted from both sides. Several hundred of the 1st Division were taken captive and hundreds more killed or wounded before darkness and the solidifying Union lines halted the action.[17]

John L. Smith of the 118th Regiment of Pennsylvania Volunteers, the Philadelphia "Corn Exchange Regiment" described their activities. His regiment was part of Griffin's division of Warren's V Corps, which was supposed to help cover Burnside's IX Corps movements:

Skirmishers from Bartlett's brigade held the extreme right of the 5th Corps. On their right were the skirmishers of the 9th Corps with whom they were supposed to unite. Between them...was a deep, thickly wooded ravine, which effectively concealed the two bodies from each of other...Having never seen Burnside's pickets...they [V Corps] were wholly unacquainted with the fact that it had been withdrawn.

Smith explained that when Burnside's men left, there was no way of slowing down Rode's division that plowed into them while the 118th's skirmishers dug gun pits and waited out the heavy rain. That detachment, only 160 men, was trying to fix a meal when:

The sweep was so sudden and in such force that there was but little resistance. The enemy went with rapid strokes from post to post. To the "drop your guns" were many unwilling affirmative responses, until eighty-six enlisted men became prisoners...two officers also captured...and four wounded...Just then a regiment made a splendid charge on the right, but after firing a volley, fell back.

The fight now seemed to grow warm in every direction. The little affair the 118th men had organized in their own behalf had assumed proportions they had not counted on. They were really in front of the firing line, and a big battle was now in progress...shots flew through like whirlwind, shells thundered through the branches.

The enemy now advanced, howling one of their terrific yells. The line...fell back to a line of entrenchments in the rear. The head of the advancing column was not seventy yards off. Their blankets were rolled, horse-collar fashion, over their shoulder. Their gray suits and slouched hats satisfied Smith...of their identity, and they went to work putting shot after shot into them. From the right came a cry, "For God's sake, stop firing, yelled Sweitzer's men, "Don't you see they are our own people?" "Our people be damned; look at their slouched hat and gray clothes! Give them hell, and we'll clear 'em out of this!" and Smith still pegged away. The men who insisted that the advancing soldiers were not Confederates could not be convinced of their error until it was too late and the enemy were so close that those who were not captured were forced in confusion to the rear.
Solid shot came plunging in from the right...Rodes, who had cleared everything that had interposed, now made a desperate charge along the whole line, but Ayres, Bartlett and Sweitzer were all in shape to receive him, and he was handsomely repulsed.[18]

Early's men had retaken the rifle pits and entrenchments beyond Sydnor's Mill and by the day's end were in a semi-circle along Shady Grove Church Road, cupping the north end of the battle line. Burnside's divisions were now at a right angle to Warren's V Corps and the two forces were as close together as possible. Crittenden's and Potter's men were trying to dig new breastworks in the mud and heavy rain while being peppered by small-arms fire. The soldiers' clothes were literally rotting while some had not received rations the entire day, and found fitful sleep only late in the night when the shooting finally stopped.

The assault by Early and the Second Corps effectively prevented any movement by Grant's right wing to support his three corps at Cold Harbor. Nine Federal divisions and their artillery were pinned in the upper corner of the Totopotomoy line by three Confederate divisions, and would not become involved in the terrible events of June 3. Early's corps suffered many losses in the effort; a sharpshooter killed Brigadier General George Doles of Rodes' division as the lines were readjusted.

Many years later, Captain William S. Long, commanding the 44th North Carolina, described the action that day against Burnside and remembered the clear weather after a "splendid night marred only by an artillery duel." His regiment belonged to Henry Heth's division of Hill's Third Corps that had been holding the hooking left of the Southern positions. Of all that fire and violence, Long was amazed at running so far without mishap, and the unforgotten sounds of combat:

> ...a sound...that sometimes brings further explanation of the surprise – horror – pain – anger – fury – you see the fire as the flash leaves the muzzle of the gun...you hear the smash of shrapnel – the hum of the minnie, the plunge of grape, the groan of the wounded, the agonizing shriek of terror from the mortally wounded...[19]

Meanwhile, late on the night of June 1, Baldy Smith had received Meade's order to join the attack against the right of Lee's army at first light the next morning. Smith promptly replied:

> Your order for an attack is received. I have endeavored to represent to you my condition...an attack by me would be simply preposterous – not only that, but an attack on the part of the enemy with any vigor would probably carry my lines more than half their length...I have called on Gen. Wright for 100,000 rounds of ammunition...Deserters report enemy massing on my right for an attack in the morning.[20]

Hancock, while keeping quiet about it, was still trying to locate his rear regiments at mid-morning. After a first-hand inspection of his II Corps was made, and downpours of rain began turning the powdery Chickahominy dirt into a quagmire, Grant and Meade concluded that their great assault should be postponed again until what Confederate Porter Alexander called, "Grant's favorite hour, 4:30 on the 3rd." As Grant told Meade:

> In view of the want of preparation for an attack this evening, and the heat and want of energy among the men from moving during the night last night, I think it advisable to postpone assault until early tomorrow morning. All changes of position already ordered should be completed today and a good night's rest given the men preparatory to an assault at, say, 4:30 in the morning.

Then as Meade notified his corps commanders of the postponement, with an additional order:

> Corps commanders will employ the interim in making examination of the ground in their fronts and perfecting their arrangements for the assault.[21]

Wright had warned late on the night of June 1 that Lee was heavily reinforcing his front. At that time, Meade had argued that any extra time given to Lee would cause problems for their planned attack. In his judgment, Lee had stretched his forces thin to hold against five corps on a long battle front, and there had to be weak points at either the far right or at the Cold Harbor end. As it turned out, events caused Warren to be held still and Burnside would do no more than go through hesitant motions. Therefore, whatever happened would be up to Hancock, Wright, and Smith. The entire outcome of the campaign depended on a quick, powerful assault such as Hancock's at Spotsylvania or Brigadier General George Thomas's advance upon the impossible Confederate position at Missionary Ridge the previous November. A drizzling rain started that lasted into the night, cooling the air and giving the tired Union divisions their first real rest in days.

The Army of Northern Virginia had been given an extra twenty-four hours to prepare. The defensive positions on the Confederate right flank were unlike anything yet constructed. From the swamps close to the Chickahominy to the hills and ravines on the Totopotomoy, every physical trait had been turned into an elaborate defensive puzzle. Small creeks, patches of thick shrubbery and briars, clumps of dwarfed pine trees, gullies and soggy black swamps were incorporated into the plan with skill that had by now reached amazing effectiveness for earthworks. Whole woods of ash, birch, and dogwood were chopped, layered, and left with branches pointing out as thick as wool and as enmeshing as barbed wire. In front of Breckinridge's and Hoke's lines the ground was particularly deceptive. There were uneven hills and slight rising areas that looked unimposing, yet possible lanes of approach would bring the unwary into natural funnels where crossfires covered every spot. The entrenchments overlapped and used each modulation to advantage. From across the empty lowlands, Union soldiers could have no idea of the inter-lacing ditches and abatis that awaited them, growing more challenging each hour. Even the skirmishers and pickets were dug in. To make it even more effective, the line from Anderson on the left to Hoke and Breckinridge going right was bowed slightly, so that advancing bodies of men would be drawn into approaches that could be hit front dead ahead and from both sides.

As Confederate engineer Colonel Jedediah Hotchkiss pointed out:

> Lee's veterans had by this time all become skillful military engineers. They threw up lines of defense abounding in salients whence heavy guns could send out searching cross-fires, at short range, against every portion of an attacking enemy. The infantry were well-provided with loopholes and crevices between logs, from which to fire, also at short range, with deliberate aim. Hunger but made them fiercer combatants.[22]

During the night of June 2, more artillery batteries were brought into Kershaw's line from Cabell's battalion to add to Huger's, Haskell's, and Lamkin's guns. Chief of Artillery Alexander supervised Anderson's artillery deployment. He took special care in covering the gap where the break had occurred between Kershaw and Hoke on June 1.

That location in the southern end of the trench line received repeated attention in the notes and memories of several Confederate observers. During the late fighting on June 1, a solitary gun from Cabell's battalion was placed in the rear of the gap and had helped stem the Federal advance there. That same gun fired all morning on June 2 to keep the swampy area clear.[23] After the first Federal assault there on June 1, Kershaw had put three regiments in to hold at what appeared as a precarious "thumb" of trench line.

Hardaway's, Cabell's, Haskell's, and Huger's artillery battalions were on the right wing of Anderson's First Corps. Their guns were pointed directly into the avenues of approach of Wright's VI Corps. Along with Cutshaw's battalion of field pieces, Huger's also had a clear field of fire into the approaches of Hancock's II Corps. In front of the divisions of

Field and Pickett, Huger had placed twenty-four guns. On the far right of the Southern line, there were six more artillery battalions set to create crossfires from Turkey Hill up to Gaines' Mill. More guns, including howitzers, were being added by the hour.[24]

Brigadier General Evander Law reinforced the line on his right between Kershaw's and Pickett's divisions with his own Alabama regiments, as well as Brigadier General George Anderson's Georgians on the morning of June 2. He was allowed to use his discretion as to wherever support was most needed and, after inspection, believed that the line held by Pickett's old division was firm enough. Kershaw's positions seemed as solid, except for that infamous joint where Union brigades had penetrated the evening before. According to Law:

> On examining the line I found it bent sharply back at almost a right angle, the point of which rested upon a body of heavy woods. The works were in open ground and ill-adapted to resist an attack. The right face of the angle ran along a slope with a small marshy stream behind and higher ground in front. The works had evidently been built just where the troops found themselves at the close of the fight the previous evening.
>
> Convinced that...our line could be broken at that point, I proposed to cut off the angle by building a new line across its base, which would throw the marshy ground in our front and give us a clear sweep across it with our fire from the slope on either side.[25]

That was the place identified by Alexander. Two brigades of Field's division, the 15th and 4th Alabama, were sent to occupy it, and all day was spent turning it into a true death trap. Artillery was placed at both ends of the new line, abreast of the infantry. Kershaw then withdrew that portion of the division which occupied the salient, the men having leveled the works as far as possible before leaving them. Whoever was responsible for the design, the effects of it would be unforgettable on the morning of June 3.

Farther down the line, just below New Cold Harbor crossroads, one of Breckinridge's regiments commanded by Lieutenant Colonel George Edgar sent a skirmish line of two companies out to reconnoitre the ground just to the front. Because of the continuous artillery fire in the area, he had thought to firm up his trenches. Those men of the 26th Battalion discovered that the front edge of their position was a salient, jutting out onto an old road and turning into a series of gullies covered with pine saplings. Edgar then appealed to Echol's brigade commander, Colonel George Patton, for permission to have the position leveled and the 23rd moved to the rear, or else to be reinforced by at least a brigade. Edgar felt certain that the projecting point would be heavily assaulted, as it was more exposed and advanced than other positions. But Breckinridge's headquarters had been moved that afternoon and nothing could be done. To add to that, Wilcox on Edgar's left ordered him to extend his line more to the left, thinning an already thin line. Apparently, one of Wilcox's brigadiers gave in to one North Carolina unit's appeals and allowed them to withdraw backward to better shelter from the rain. Their mistreatment at Turkey Hill earlier was perhaps the reason for the act of kindness given to them. It left, however, the 26th Battalion in more than an awkward state. Those 400 men were supported on the right by the Kanawha Rifles and the 22nd Virginia, amounting to perhaps fewer than 900 total to maintain the tantalizing salient. Edgar's men spent a fitful night, staying busy by digging to keep from concentrating on their fragile situation.[26]

※ ※ ※ ※ ※

Grant received word from Wilson that his operations against the Virginia Central Railroad had been successful, destroying two bridges over the South Anna and uprooting a considerable amount of track. Grant discounted the long-term effect, saying that, "Like us, the rebels had become experts at repairing such damage."[27] At almost the same time as that message arrived, Rosser and a detachment of cavalry caught one of Wilson's brigades off guard during its track burning and enjoyed the "rare fun" of chasing off Sheridan's horsemen.

Moving with his cannon, Frank Wilkeson wrote:

> On June 2nd the Second Corps moved from right to the left. We saw many wounded that day. We crossed or marched around a swamp, and the battery I belonged to parked in a ravine. There were some old houses on our line of march, but not a chicken or a sheep or a cow to be seen. The land was wretchedly poor. The night of June 2 was spent getting into battle-line. There was considerable confusion as the infantry marched in the darkness. In our front we could see tongues of flames dart forth from Confederate rifles fired in the direction of the noise they heard, and their bullets sang high over our heads. My battery went into position just back of a crest of a hill. Behind us was an alder swamp where good drinking water gushed forth from many springs. Before we slept we talked with some of the Seventh New York Heavy Artillery, and found that they were sad of heart. They knew that they were to go into the fight early in the morning, and they dreaded the work. The whole army seemed to be greatly depressed the night before the battle of Cold Harbor.[28]

MOVEMENTS UP TO 1:00 P.M. JUNE 2, 1864

Routinely, with no delusions or claims, individual soldiers made preparations. Captain John Anderson of the 57th Massachusetts Veteran Volunteers of Burnside's IX Corps wrote:

> The Massachusetts men had no way of knowing their fate...they said their prayers and they wrote what many believed were their last letters home. Most pinned pieces of paper to their coats that had their names and regiments written on them, so that their bodies could be identified when they were killed, as they were sure they would be.[29]

Porter said in his memoirs:

> In passing along on foot among the troops at the extreme front that evening while transmitting some of the final orders, I observed an incident which afforded a practical illustration of the deliberate and desperate courage of the men. As I came near one of the regiments which was making preparations for the next morning's assault, I noticed that many of the soldiers had taken off their coats, and seemed to be engaged in sewing up rents in them. This exhibition of tailoring seemed rather peculiar at such a moment, but upon closer examination it was found that the men were calmly writing their names and home addresses on slips of paper and pinning them on the backs of their coats, so that their dead bodies might be recognized upon the field, and their fate made known to their families at home. They were veterans who knew well from terrible experience the danger which awaited them, but their minds were not occupied with thoughts of shirking their duty, but with preparation for the desperate work of the coming morning. Such courage is more than heroic – it is sublime.[30]

Smith of XVIII Corps had received his order from Meade and had at once protested both the nature and timing of the assault set for the next morning. Smith later said:

> Such an order for battle as was developed in that circular – an attack along the whole line – is denounced by the standard writers on the art of war, and belongs to the first period in history after man had ceased to fight in unorganized masses. Giving up the few advantages belonging to the assailants, it increases largely the chances of successful defense, and would never be adopted by a trained general, except perhaps under certain peculiar conditions, where also the attacking force had an overwhelming superiority in numbers. Aghast at the reception of such an order, which proved conclusively the utter absence of any military plan, I sent a note to

General Wright, commanding the corps on my left, asking him to let me know what was to be his plan of attack, that I might conform to it, and thus have two corps acting in unison. General Wright replied that he was going to "pitch in." This left to me only the attack in front contemplated in the circular.[31]

The XVIII Corps commander described his dissatisfaction with his position in the Federal line as well as the frontage of attack given him against the Confederate line. Since Warren's V Corps had not been able to join with the XVIII Corps, Smith had to place a division to cover the open plain and various roads to prevent what he saw as a threat to his flank. At the center of the Confederate trenches Smith saw "earthworks like a curtain with a flanking arrangement at each end." There the right could be exposed to artillery from Smith's right and on the left, from guns in front of both his own corps and Wright's. That was the well-known seam in the Southerners' line where "a small stream with marshy sides" ran back toward the enemy lines, with a slight elevation on the right which Smith saw as possible shelter to any troops moving down that stream in the attack. His 2nd division under Brigadier General James Martindale would share that avenue of approach with Wright's brigades the next day.

No one, from Grant and Meade on down to division level, had made a detailed survey of the grounds that those three corps would cross over to get at Lee's earthworks. The fact that the Army of the Potomac contained many engineering officers in senior positions makes the oversight even more curious. Everyone assumed that headquarters in descending order would provide for making accurate field surveys. But such reconnaissance at corps level was not a given routine.

The commanders of the Army of the Potomac spent a dismal day wearing down their units with incessant shuffling while the Southern line was burrowed and quickened to devilish proportions. Lee's veterans, slow to fear even earlier, had by the summer of 1864 proved that when armed with good rifles, standing in well-built trenches and supported by adequate artillery, they could not be broken by frontal assault. In the disarray of early June 2, perhaps an all-powerful charge of three corps, nearly 48,000 men, might have met with some success. By dawn of June 3, it did not stand a chance.

Regimental commanders quietly notified their troops, word of the attack spreading down the web. The individual soldiers would survey their own small fragment of the scene as they passed over it in combat. They would have to deal with whatever they encountered on their own on the way toward Richmond on June 3. Charles Banes of the Philadelphia Brigade, II Corps, wrote:

Early in the evening a disagreeable drizzling rain set in, and the men who were not on picket duty at the front lay on the wet ground with knapsacks or cartridge boxes for pillows, and their faces covered with blankets, or, in the absence of these, with their caps or portions of garments, to prevent the pattering of rain from spoiling their rest. In this situation they fell asleep, in blissful ignorance of the storm of death to be encountered on the morrow.[32]

Chapter Nine

Cold Harbor

June 3, 4:30 to 6 a.m.

"Everyone felt that this was to be the final struggle. No further wheeling of corps from right to left, no further dusty marches."
- Colonel Martin McMahon[1]
VI Corps Staff

"This fight was near Gaines' Mill, a place made famous by a great battle fought by McClellan in 1862. The old soldiers among us recognize many familiar spots. It is a dreadful hole."
- Private John Haley[2]
17th Maine Regiment

"Another assault was ordered, but being deemed impracticable along our front, the charge was not made."
- Brigadier General Emory Upton[3]
VI Corps

"Marse Robert has all his men here, and old Grant has his whole army. We are going to get at it and have a graveyard fight sure enough, and you will see it."
- Sergeant George A. Woodrum[4]
26th Virginia Battalion

"Altogether this has been one of the most disastrous days the Army of the Potomac has ever seen, and the Second Corps has especially suffered."
- Brigadier General Francis Barlow[5]
II Corps

Grant's side-stepping through Virginia had gone on for thirty days. Never before had Lee's army been in such a prolonged engagement with the enemy. In 1862, McClellan had fought for a week on the Peninsula before being driven to escape at Harrison's Landing. Pope had required two weeks before he was back in Washington's outer protections after Second Manassas, and even Lee's grand movement into southern Pennsylvania — to Gettysburg and back — had taken only eighteen days.[6] Grant's hammering in the spring of 1864, accompanied by ghastly human costs, was unrelenting.

On May 31 and again on June 2, Lee appealed to his chief lieutenants:

> Send to the field hospitals, and have every man capable of performing the duties of a soldier returned to his command.[7]

The rain had a cooling and calming effect, but it also depressed the hungry Southerners, with their backs against Richmond. There they were, survivors of the scorched brambles of the Wilderness and the heated puncturing of the Spotsylvania defensive line. A heavy weariness had set in on them weeks ago, and yet they had never wavered as their commander daily planned some new stroke and they kept digging. In Richmond, the wife of George Pickett received a letter dated June 3 from her husband who was by then stationed with the rest of the First Corps close to New Cold Harbor:

> Here we are still, my Sallie...Over a crimson road both armies have returned to Cold Harbor. The Wilderness, alas, is one vast graveyard where sleep thousands of Grant's soldiers; but Grant, like our Stonewall, is fighting not to save lives, but country.
>
> ...I believe it was old Jube [Early] that gave Marse Robert the title of "Old-Spades-Lee," or "Old Ace of Spades," because of his incessant activity of throwing up defenses, trenches, breastworks, etc.[8]

The lines at Cold Harbor became a watershed. The wet, reddish clay that was shoveled up from entrenchments was remembered strikingly by soldiers of both sides. The Confederate line was between six and seven miles in length, stretched as thin and tight as a hatband.

From the extreme right, Fitz Lee and his small force of cavalry were posted across the Chickahominy to keep close watch on Sheridan and to report any movement towards the James River. Half a mile north of the muddy river was Wilcox's division, with Breckinridge on his left supported by Mahone, whose division was the only reserve on the Southern line. Beyond him, northward, was Hoke, with Hutton's brigade from Pickett's division extending to the ravine made unforgettable by the June 1 attack; brigades of Anderson, Law, and Gregg served as a second supporting line there near the gap. Kershaw, Pickett, then

Field took up the line going north. Ramseur commanded Early's old division, Gordon's next, then Rodes', and finally Heth's division forming a temporary arc at the extreme left.

The murky Chickahominy sprouted branches everywhere, as did the Totopotomoy behind the Union lines. At two junctures, water courses from the lower river cut into the Southern line. The junction of Breckinridge and Hoke's brigades just north of New Cold Harbor, a fetid branch called Boatswain's Creek, or Swamp, created what seemed like a sheltered pathway that Smith referred to in his rather superficial reconnaissance on June 2. It was a tentacle of Powhite Swamp reaching eastward that sliced the ground where Kershaw's units had been put into mayhem on June 1. Those innocent, scarcely observable rivulets, fed now by heavy downpours, would make hell out of the obvious advance routes from the Federal left.

Their line, running from the south, was anchored by the cavalry below Barkers Mill. Sheridan was supposed to use that position to fire on Lee's right flank during the engagements starting on June 1, but had hardly been heard from. Hancock's mighty II Corps held the Union left trenches, joined by Wright's VI Corps moving to the right. Near Bethesda Church, Smith's XVIII Corps formed next in line followed by Warren and Burnside. Those two right-most corps may as well have been camped a hundred miles away.[9]

❈ ❈ ❈ ❈ ❈

Just after midnight, early on the morning of June 3, the 19th Massachusetts was awakened, given two days' rations of coffee, hardtack, and sugar, then allowed to go back to sleep until daylight.[10] Part of the brigade led by Colonel Henry McKeen, also containing the 19th Maine, 15th and 20th Massachusetts and ten more regiments, those troops all belonged to Gibbon's division and were slated to move out behind a line of skirmishers at four-thirty that morning. Rawlins's official report made the time of the actual assault uncertain, saying that Gibbon's first brigades stepped off at around four forty-five. The II Corps was to attack on the extreme left, and Hancock began the assembly of his units in columns before daylight.

Gibbon and Barlow's were the primary assault divisions with the third, under Birney, held in reserve. Gershom Mott's old division had been reduced to a brigade of Birney's command but would not be brought into the battle, despite being full strength.

Gibbon's two lead brigades belonged to Colonel Thomas Smyth, formerly of the Irish Brigade, and Brigadier General Robert Tyler from the Corcoran Legion. They were to advance on the right and left, respectively, to be followed toward the enemy lines by the brigades of Colonel Henry McKeen and Brigadier General Josh "Paddy" Owen. Gibbon's brigades were in the more usual line deployment, with Tyler and Smyth abreast and with McKeen and Owen coming in close columns of regiments. The last were set to deliver fast crashing blows into the Southern barriers.

It was not an auspicious beginning that morning for II Corps. When Hancock's men formed up and saw the fortifications ahead of them that they were about to storm, many took a moment to scribble their names on pieces of paper and pin them to their blouses. The heady fragrance of swamp azalea and magnolia in the air gave a falsely calm setting to the day.[11]

Gibbon wrote of another episode just before the grand assault:

> I was up before daylight and riding to the front to see that the troops were all in position ready for the assault, at the hour named, in accordance with the orders issued the night before – I found one whole brigade, including its commander, still sound asleep. This brigade was to act as the support to the brigade making the assault on the left of my line. The troops were hurriedly awakened, formed and sent to the front.[12]

They were from Owen's 2nd brigade, made up of one New York regiment and four of Pennsylvanians. Owen had disappointed Gibbon before at Spotsylvania Court House, where his men failed to respond to an attack order on May 18 and instead sheltered themselves in rifle pits in the rear. For that and additional indiscretions to arise on June 3, Gibbon later recommended a court martial for Owen.[13]

Brigadier General Francis C. Barlow was considered one of the most aggressive field commanders in the army. Twenty-nine years old, Barlow wore his customary checkered shirt and thread-bare, bluish trousers, and old kepi. One journalist described him as looking "like a highly independent mounted newsboy."[14] He, as at Spotsylvania, would lead his men personally. His two leading brigades belonged to Colonel Nelson Miles, later made famous as a fighter against the Sioux and Cheyenne tribes, and Colonel John Brooke, whose regiments had broken the deadly Mule Shoe salient at Spotsylvania. Those regiments, primarily New Yorkers and Pennsylvanians, were Hancock's most effective shock troops. Each brigade contained a regiment of former heavy artillerymen who would find exceptional honor and horror that early morning. Behind were the Irish Brigade of Colonel Richard Byrnes and the 3rd brigade under Colonel Clinton MacDougall. Barlow deployed two lines of brigades. John Noonan was in the 69th New York Infantry of Barlow's Division. He remembered:

> The march of the night before had been a heavy one...we had no water, the dust was choking, and went astray for several miles. Some rested in an orchard, and so between fatigue and green apples several men were unfit for duty the morning of the 3rd...[15]

❋ ❋ ❋ ❋ ❋

Frank Wilkeson, stationed behind the II Corps assembly area, recorded:

> Before daybreak of June 3rd the light artillery men were aroused. We ate our scanty breakfast and took our positions around the guns. All of us were loath to go into action. In front of us we could hear the murmurs of infantry, but it was not sufficiently light to see them. We stood leaning against the cool guns, or resting easily on the ponderous wheels, and gazed intently into the darkness in the direction of the Confederate earthworks...Indistinctly we saw moving figures. Some on foot rearward bound, cowards hunting for safety; others on horseback riding to and fro near where we supposed the battle-lines to be; then orderlies and servants came in from the darkness and we knew that the regimental and brigade commanders were going into action on foot. The darkness faded slowly, one by one the stars went out, and then the Confederate pickets opened fire briskly; then we could see the Confederate earthworks, about six hundred yards ahead of us – and could just see them and no more. They were apparently deserted, not a man was to be seen behind them...We filled our sponge buckets with water and waited, the Confederate pickets firing briskly at us but doing no damage. Suddenly the Confederate works were manned. We could see a line of slouch hats above the parapet. Smoke in great puffs burst forth from their line, and shell began to howl by us. Their gunners were getting range. We sprang in and out from the three-inch guns and replied angrily. To our left, to our right, other batteries opened; and along the Confederate line cannon sent forth their balls searching for the range. Then their guns were silent. It was daylight...In our front were two lines of blue-coated infantry, one well in advance of the other, and both lying down. We were firing over them. The Confederate pickets sprang out of their rifle-pits and ran back to their main line of works. Then they turned and warmed the battery with long-range rifle practice...The Confederate infantry was always more effective than their artillery,

and the battery that got under the fire of their cool infantry always suffered severely. The air began to grow hazy with powder-smoke...Out of the smoke came an officer from the battle-lines of infantry. He told us to stop firing, as the soldiers were about to charge.[16]

Hancock's two divisions were to attack at what would prove to be the two most vulnerable and deadly places in Lee's whole defensive line. Gibbon, on the right, was about to move against Breckinridge's uneven connection with Hoke, where an unseen swamp seeped forward into the slightly rolling ground. Barlow's men, known as the Red Division, were getting ready to drive into the shallow road on Breckinridge's left where a regiment of Virginia skirmishers guarded a blunt salient.

John Day Smith of the 19th Maine wrote:

As soon as it began to grow light on the morning of June 3rd, the order to charge was given. It must be confessed that order was not received with much hilarity. It was the same order the troops had heard and obeyed almost daily for twenty-eight days. Except in the Battle of the Wilderness it had always been against strong entrenchments. If the Second Corps ever felt and showed its unwillingness to charge entrenchments, it was at Cold Harbor. There was some hooting at the brigade commanders by the soldiers, but when it was ascertained that these officers were going to lead the men, there was no further hesitation. The ground had not been looked over. There was no effort to examine the enemy's entrenchments to find a weak place in them, if there were any."[17]

Hancock gave the signal and his four brigades, giving a roar, rose up and began their charge. The country was rolling and open and hardly two hundred yards had been covered when Tyler and Smyth encountered a shallow swamp which widened back as they advanced. As the men pushed toward the Confederate trenches, they were close enough to see the red Virginia clay made slick from the recent rains. After their skirmishers had jumped from their pits back behind the protective earthworks, the Southern gunners began to rake the field. Men reported later that they saw no one in the enemy line to even shoot at. They also did not realize that their brigade had been split by the swamp as if the regiments had run upon a great wedge. Tyler's two infantry regiments, led by the 8th New York Heavy Artillery, slogged to the right into a ravine which stalled them in front of the Confederate trench wall. They overran an advance line and took more than two hundred prisoners as a sheet of fire hit them from three sides and wounded Tyler. Coming quickly behind were McKeen and the 19th Maine, whose orders were to lead the First brigade through the decimated wreck of Tyler's command. When McKeen's brigade came in, there was a carpet of dead and wounded before them. The 19th Maine and three Massachusetts infantry regiments began to desperately dig in on the spot, and having no shovels in hand, used bayonets and cups to scoop out a shallow earthwork in the face of the enemy.[18]

Colonel Thomas Smyth and his brigade had veered left along the rim of the brackish swamp. Led by the 14th Connecticut, they ran up a moderate ridge within a hundred yards of the entrenchments when they came under fire and their attack abruptly stalled. Tyler's 164th New York had become separated from their parent unit and had brushed to the right of Smyth on their way to the Southern earthworks. They were wearing colorful Zouave uniforms and, commanded by Colonel James McMahon, were the only large force to actually breach Breckinridge's left that morning. As his men crashed into the enemy parapet, McMahon ran to the front and pulled the regimental flag from a fallen color-bearer's hands. He managed to plant it atop the position as he was shot repeatedly in the head and chest. When his body was recovered, he was identified by his brother, Martin McMahon of the VI Corps, only by the special buttons on his sleeves.[19]

Colonel Henry McKeen rallied the second line and was met by the same metal storm from artillery and infantry that had destroyed Tyler's charge. McKeen himself was shot through the mid-section and writhed in great pain, begging his adjutant to shoot him. Colonel Frank Haskell of the 36th Wisconsin, a hero of Gettysburg, took command. Corporal Ernest Waitt of the 19th Massachusetts wrote about that strange scene:

> On they ran, over two lines of works, across the fields that were swept by a terrible fire of canister from the enemy's batteries, while the musketry volleyed terribly...The regimental colors fell but "Mike" Scannell of Co. I picked them up and carried them forward. When the line halted, Major Dunn said, "Mike, you keep the colors." "Not as corporal," said Mike, "Too many corporals have been killed already, carrying colors." "I make you a sergeant," responded the Major. "That's business," answered Mike, "I'll carry the colors."

> The severity of the fighting was such that there were numerous changes of brigade commanders. First one Colonel would receive a wound and then another, down the list, until finally a Lt. Colonel commanded a brigade. The awful fire caused the line to break and it was obliged to call a halt under the brow of a hill. The men immediately began to pass up rails from a fence nearby and these

were piled. Then, with dippers and plates, the dirt was thrown up until a good line of work was formed, so near to those of the enemy that a stone could be thrown into them, and a man could not show his head without being shot.[20]

Haskell, whose 36th Wisconsin had started the dawn attack in the rear of the brigade, was now on the advance line. He had hardly begun a survey of his predicament, warning the stiffened remnants of his command to lie low, when a rifle ball pierced his head and killed him instantly. His body joined the thick rows of dead and wounded, not twenty feet from the main breastwork. There, the 8th New York artillery lost 505 men, including their commander, Colonel Charles Porter. It had all taken no more than ten minutes.

On the other side of the swamp, Smyth's stunned force was pinned down by unmerciful enfilade fire as Owen's Second brigade of Pennsylvania troops came in behind them. Ever the innovator, Owen, instead of shouldering through the ranks of Smyth's stalled regiments, formed on that brigade's left. He ordered his regiments into a solid square formation and began to charge, parallel to the Southern battle line, while under fire. They came across the swamp at one point, ascending a little hill, and wheeled into a frontal charge that was hit by a veritable hailstorm of bullets. Charles Banes wrote:

> The Philadelphia Brigade, after enduring for a short time a heavy fire from the enemy, were ordered to hold a position within seventy-five yards of the Confederate works. Taking advantage of the ground, with surprising rapidity they protected themselves with a shallow rifle-pit, using for the purpose bayonets, knives, and tin-cups. At night entrenching tools were received, and the line was properly strengthened. The actual time that elapsed from the commencement of this assault until its failure was only twenty minutes.[21]

Gibbon's contribution to Grant's assault was finished. He reported that his division lost 65 officers and 1,032 men killed and wounded that morning, along with more than 500 missing. Private Ernest Waitt remembered:

> Lieutenant Col. Nelson Miles, who commanded a brigade under Barlow in this battle, is authority for the statement that on the night of June 2, these three officers, Colonels McKeen, Haskell, and McMahon, slept on the ground under the same blanket. They were talking together during the evening, and bantering one another as to which would be the first hit the next day. Within fifteen minutes

from the time Gibbon's line of battle started, the next morning, these three officers were lying dead on the battlefield.[22]

While Gibbon's brigades were caught by a swamp and Confederate fire, Barlow moved his men inexorably toward the sunken and pine-covered roadway that headed directly into the salient on the fringe of Breckinridge's right. Where Wilcox was to weld his Confederate brigades together and anchor the extreme flank, he had allowed the covering force for that point to be thinned to hardly more than two regiments. Led by Colonel Nelson Miles, Barlow's leading left brigade surged out of the woods and across a broad, open field and over the almost-hidden road.

Meanwhile, Colonel John L. Brooke took his men over the same road, on the right side, and up a slight hill. Brooke's brigade, led by the 2nd Delaware and the 7th New York Heavy Artillery, stumbled into segments of an old fence. The 7th "Heavies" had only recently been put into service, and numbered almost 1,600 men.

Frank Wilkeson witnessed the next events:

> Suddenly the foremost line of our troops, which were lying on the ground in front of us, sprang to their feet and dashed at the Confederate earthworks at a run. Instantly these works were manned. Cannon belched forth a torrent of canister, the works glowed brightly with musketry, a storm of lead and iron struck the blue line, cutting gaps in it. Still they pushed on and on. But how many of them fell! They drew near the earthworks, firing as they went and then with a cheer the Red Division of the Second Corps (Barlow's) swept over it.[23]

Despite the flailing fire from that small force, Miles' men were able to smash into the outer perimeter of the salient, coming into the left edge where the tiny force of Kanawha Rifles stood. The 26th Michigan of Captain James Lothian and 2nd New York Heavy Artillery led by Colonel Joseph Whistler made straight down the path of the washed roadway across a line of rifle pits, capturing the two cannon that had been opposing them, along with a number of prisoners. The ground in front of the 23rd Virginia Battalion, who were thinly holding to the right along with the Rifles, was becoming a muddy mire that slowed Miles's attack force.

On the other side of the Breckinridge salient, Edgar and his 26th Virginia were left to their fate. Brooke, his regiments spread out wider than Miles' strong column, cracked Edgar's outer protection and the

2nd Delaware and the 7th New York artillery stormed into the breach. Edgar's men gave them the warmest reception possible as he later said that "large groups of Federals fell, more than I ever saw on any other battle-field."[24] Outnumbered, Edgar men could do little more than fall back. Within perhaps five minutes of hand-to-hand combat, the 26th lost 219 men, or almost half of the battalion. Sergeant Arthur DuBois of the 7th New York was there, and later recorded:

> We had not long to wait in the woods. As we gained the other side of the woods this salient came to our view for the first time. At the command, double quick, it was but a few moments we were scrambling up its incline. So quick had been our movements only a few musket shots had been fired by the enemy...if anybody ever got a warm reception we did. The enemy bravely stood their ground, not waiting for us to come over their works, but meeting us on the parapet. They contested every inch. I remember as I reached the top of the works a brave fellow confronted us. Standing below he thrust his bayonet into the comrade by my side and was about to give me the same dose, but a charge from my gun changed his mind. It was a hand-to-hand fight to the finish. Clubbed muskets, bayonets, and even swords got in their deadly work.[25]

The Confederates battled with shovels, sticks of wood, bayonets, and clubbed musket stocks as they were pushed back by sheer numbers and the 7th New York climbed over the nearest parapet. The New Yorkers carried off two hundred prisoners, but Brooke, as he was about to reach the top of the parapet, was critically wounded by canister.

An embattled Edgar remembered seeing his adjutant, having taken two bullets, still fighting with his sword before being covered up by bluecoats. He saw Lieutenant William George receive a ball through the neck and a bayonet thrust through his side, the attacker clubbed to death by George's comrades, and the two disappear in the swarm. Color Sergeant George Woodrum stood beside his regimental flag and watched the wave of Federal infantry move in. Firing his last pistol shells, he declared, "they are going to run over us, but they will not take this flag until they have passed over my dead body." Witnesses said that Woodrum picked up the flagstaff, which had a sharp lance point on the end, and drove it into the chest of a Federal officer. Woodrum fell with two shots through the chest. Later, the flag was reported captured by Company D of the 7th. Edgar himself was bayoneted in the right shoulder and was about to be captured when he heard Brigadier General Joseph Finegan with the Florida brigade coming to his rescue.[26]

Confederate artillery had found Miles' flank with a deadly cross-fire, delivering canister and case shot at short range into men packed so deep that they could not raise their rifles. His own 5th New Hampshire regiment began to back out and once outside the captured lines, could not be slowed. They began to flow rapidly out of the pits and back over the sunken road.

At about that moment, supported by the veteran Maryland Line, Finegan's well-known, "ruffian" brigade came down on the Red Division. That Brigade was composed of two large regiments that had recently been on garrison duty in northern Florida. Lee had placed them in Mahone's reserve force behind the third great line of entrenchments. William Goldsborough of the Maryland Line wrote:

> It was midnight of the 2nd June when the battalion halted...They were tired, for they had marched many weary miles in the past few days, and the strain...had been fearful...they slept soundly, and their awakening was rude and unexpected. From where they lay wrapped in their blankets they were sheltered somewhat from the direct fire of the enemy owing to a rise in the ground on their front...where a body of Federal troops held a position of higher ground. Between the Second Maryland and the salient held by Echols' troops was a dwelling and outhouses which somewhat obscured their view of the salient, where eight pieces of artillery were in position. In the rear of the Marylanders, some three or four hundred yards, was Finegan's Brigade of Floridians, which had been engaged in throwing up a line of works to be used in case any disaster should occur at the first.

> General Breckinridge was not in error when on placing them where he did he should observe: "This is a most important position, and I feel I can intrust it to that Battalion." Before daylight on the morning of the 3rd the enemy began a skirmish fire, but this did not arouse the sleeping men. A few arose and folded their blankets, but the majority of them slept on...Through the dim mist they saw what appeared to be a heavy skirmish line of Echols' command running back on their left flank. A body of men came forward and...opened fire on the Marylanders still in their blankets, and many of them were thus shot while they slept...Private Buck' Weems, who was conspicuous for the big straw hat he wore that day, suddenly exclaimed: "I see the gridiron, Boys! Let's charge 'em!" and at the same time Captain John Torsch called out: "It is the enemy – charge!"...and without an instant's hesitation they dashed forward upon the enemy...Although in overwhelming numbers, these were quickly driven back, with heavy loss, by the furious onset of the

Marylanders...The conflict was brief, but terrible; it was hand to hand; the artillery was wrested from the Federals and they were driven out of the salient at point of bayonet.[27]

With the 1st and 2nd Maryland infantry in support, the Florida men came pounding in. That part of the struggle was remembered as cutthroat and dreadful, bayonets and short swords swinging. The positions of the over-crowded 7th, in some places pushed in by Pennsylvanians of the 145th and 148th regiments just entering the trenches, were raked and re-raked by close artillery fire and relentless driving from Finegan's battalions. Colonel Richard Byrnes and the Irish Brigade were coming up in support, and in seconds he and Colonel Orlando Morris of the 66th New York were shot down, along with hundreds of men who never even saw the Confederates because of the teeming smoke. Punished beyond sensibility, Barlow's brigades began to dig in with knives, tin cups, spoons, and their bare hands, hardly fifty yards from their recent successes.

Corporal John Hatton's 1st Maryland Battery had been assigned to Breckinridge's line that morning. Hatton recorded that on that cool morning, just as dawn lighted, their expectations of an attack were realized. As musket fire grew louder, a cry went up, "To your guns, boys, – bring the canister!" He wrote:

> ...as far as the eye could see left and right, came a blue map of desperate humanity, shouting, firing, with officers directing them with drawn swords and with the "Stars and Stripes" waving over their ranks, making a swift and determined charge on our lines...

The 1st Maryland was nervous about opening fire for fear of hitting their retreating butternut skirmishers. It fired salvo after salvo of grape into the advancing blue body as it came shrieking into Southern lines, thinned but powerful.

> Notwithstanding the terrible slaughter of our guns, they succeeded in breaking into our line...captured an artillery battery and began to establish a line and turn the captured guns on us...while this exciting and desperate struggle was in progress at the salient our battery was belching charges after charges of canister as fast as we could fire...the heavy charges of grape plunged into their ranks, scattering them...making them crowd to our left to avoid the deadly fire...Finally they paused and then wavered and then turned their backs in precipitated flight...My gun followed them with death-dealing work...they retreated over the field as they could, dropped

into the picket holes to save themselves from the extensive fire that furrowed them for eight hundred yards in front of my gun...[28]

New York artilleryman Frank Wilkeson continued:

> For once the several corps had delivered a simultaneous assault, and I knew it was going to be now or never. The powder-smoke curled lowly in thin clouds above the captured works. The tops of many battle-flags could be seen distinctly, and then there was a heavy and fierce yell, and the thrilling battle-cry of Confederate infantry floated over us. "Can our men withstand the charge?," I asked myself. Quickly I was answered. They came into sight, clambering over the parapet of the captured works. All organization was lost. They fled wildly for the protection of their second line and the Union guns, and they were shot by scores as they ran. The Confederate infantry appeared behind their works and nimbly climbed over, as though intent on following up their success, and their fire was as the fury of hell. We manned the guns and drove them to cover with bursting shell...Twenty minutes had not passed since the infantry had sprung to their feet, and ten thousand of our men lay dead or wounded on the ground. The men of the Seventh New York Heavy Artillery came back without their colonel...Men from many commands sought shelter behind the crest of the hill we were behind. They seemed to be dazed and utterly discouraged. They told of the strength of the Confederate earthworks and asserted that behind the line we see was another and a stronger line, and all the enlisted men insisted that they could not have taken the second line even if their supports had followed them...We drew the guns behind the crest of the hill, and lay down in the sand and waited.[29]

Winfield Scott Hancock was in great pain, as the leg wound that he had suffered at Gettysburg began to swell and small fragments of bone began to work toward the surface of his skin. He could not explain why his two divisions had attacked widely separate sections of the enemy line or why the 3rd division, largest of all in II Corps, had made no move to support the heroic breakthroughs of either Gibbon or Barlow. Hancock's casualty report after the assault at Cold Harbor read, for all divisions: men and officers killed, 490; wounded, 1,714; missing, 960; for an aggregate of 3,164. But those figures do not include losses by the 1st Delaware, 4th and 8th Ohio, and 14th Indiana of Smyth's command, which would add several hundred more to the total.[30] By the time the wounded left near the Southern positions could receive attention, which took more than four days, almost all were dead.

✷ ✷ ✷ ✷ ✷

True to his word, Wright's plan of attack was to "pitch in," and he attacked with all the power he had. The tested divisions of Ricketts and Russell had their brigades formed on one great line, and they began to move, and not for very long or far. Brigadier General Thomas Neill's brigades were placed on the right, in an "active reserve" role, with hopes of connecting with Smith's 2nd division against the broad right front of Anderson's line. But they were headed for the concave center of Anderson's immovable wall, and there would be little time for skillful maneuvers. Lyman, who was at the old Kelly house where Wright kept his command post, commented:

> At that moment the cannon opened, in various directions, and the Rebels replied vigorously. There has been no fight of which I have seen so little as this. The woods were so placed that the sound, even, of the musketry, was much kept away, and the fighting...was completely shut from view. All the warfare for us was an occasional round-shot, or shell, that would come about us from the Rebel batteries. In the direction of the 18th Corps the crash of the musketry was very loud, but elsewhere scarcely to be noticed.[31]

The VI Corps drove across much of the same ground that had been contested the evening of June 1. Charging from their trenches south of the old Grapevine Bridge Road, the objective was the same ravined and mushy ridge of intersecting and devious earthworks held by Hoke and Anderson's right almost eight hundred yards away. Success depended on coordination with Smith's XVIII Corps moving on the right of Neill. Wright's divisions were aimed at practically the same indentation where Hoke and Kershaw, of Anderson's corps, had been pounded in by Ricketts' brigades with heavy losses that evening of June 1.

That was the site where special care was taken in case another Federal assault again came in that direction. There Evander Law had placed his 4th and 15th Alabama with the 13th Mississippi, and Alexander had placed three artillery brigades from North Carolina and Virginia. Ricketts' 10th Vermont and 14th New Jersey were the first to test the firmness of those awesome fortifications. Long-range guns struck at both flanks of those three exposed divisions as the infantry stepped out. The swelled formation moved only a hundred yards before the thickets and gullies broke it into confusion. Groups of men fell or were knocked back before they could see the weapons that hit them. One of the brigades got as close as two hundred and fifty yards from the Confederates before the great assault wavered and collapsed within ten minutes of its beginning. Not a few VI Corps units stuck to the ground from the first moment and did not try to move against what one Maine soldier said was, "poured from the rebel lines, which we could not see, those volleys of hurtling death."[32] One of these still units was Upton's brigade, pinned down and reluctant to join the now bloated and blackened forms of their 2nd Connecticut comrades slaughtered on June 1.

The entire line was pinned down under crossfire from the onset. Desperate soldiers began to scoop out shallow rifle pits after an advance of no more than two hundred yards. One brigade commander later reported that he was supposed to have used the movements of the brigade on his right as a guide. When that unit failed to even stir, "for some reason the charge was not made."[33] The destruction of the densely grouped men who did churn on against Hoke and Kershaw was too amazing for easy words to recall.

Confederate artillery officer Robert Stiles, a witness to those brief minutes of fire and noise, wrote:

> Here, then, is the secret of the otherwise inexplicable and incredible butchery. A little after daylight on June 3, 1864, along the lines of Kershaw's salient, his infantry discharged their bullets and his artillery fired case-shot and double-shotted canister, at very short range, into a mass of men twenty-eight deep, who could neither advance or retreat, and the most of them could not even discharge their muskets at us.[34]

Dickert of Kershaw's division participated in the repulse of Wright's corps that morning. He recalled:

> Then the musketry began to roll along in a regular wave, coming nearer and nearer as new columns moved to the assault. Now it reaches our front, and the enemy moves steadily upon our works...As soon as their skirmish line made its appearance, followed by three lines of battle, our pickets in the front of us were relieved, but many fell before regaining our breastworks, and those who were killed had to lie during the day between the most murderous fire in the history of the war, and, sad to say, few survived. When near us the first line came with a rush at charge bayonets, and our officers had great difficulty in restraining the men from opening fire too soon. But when close enough, the word "fire" was given, and the men behind the works raised deliberately, resting their guns upon the works, and fired volley after volley into the rushing but disorganized ranks of the enemy. The first line reeled and attempted to fly the field, but were met by the next column, which halted the re-

treating troops with bayonet, butts of guns, and officers' swords, until a greater number were turned to the second assault. All this while our sharpshooters and men behind our works were pouring a galling fire into the tangled mass of advancing and retreating troops. The double column, like the first, came with a shout, a huzzah, and a charge. But our men had by this time re-loaded their pieces, and were only too eager awaiting the command "fire." But when it did come the result was telling – men falling on top of men, rear rank pushing forward the first rank, only to be swept away like chaff. Our batteries on the hills and rear of those mounted on our infantry line were raking the field, the former with shell and solid shot, the latter with grape and canister. Smoke settling on the ground soon rendered objects in front scarcely visible, but the steady flashing of the enemy's guns and the hail of bullets over our heads and against our works told plainly that the enemy were standing to their work with desperate courage. The third line of assault had now mingled with the first two, and all lying on the ground hidden by the dense smoke...[35]

The great thrust by VI Corps on June 3 was chopped to bits, and the men who had given their best efforts were left exposed to the merciless elements of trench warfare. Lyman remembered:

At six o'clock we got notice that Russell's division could not carry the line in their front. Ricketts, however, on the right of the VI Corps, got their first line, and so did the 18th Corps on his right; but the 18th people were pushed back, and this left Ricketts a good deal exposed to enfilade; but he held on. A singular thing about the whole attack...was that our men, when fire was too hot for them to advance and the works too strong, did not retreat as soldiers often do, but lay down where some small ridge offered a little cover, and there staid, at a distance from the enemy varying from forty to 250 yards.[36]

Coming in on the right of Russell, Neill moved his brigades of Wright's 1st division forward in column. They surged against Kershaw's left positions. Led by Brigadier General Frank Wheaton, Neill's leading brigade of Pennsylvanians and New Yorkers crashed against the outer defensive line like a battering ram, overpowering the advance enemy rifle pits. Advancing further than the companion units, Wheaton's regiments were subjected to a fiendish enfilade fire that chewed down the length of his front while taking heavy concentrations of Kershaw's artillery flush in front. Lewis Grant, in command of Neill's 2nd brigade, the famous Vermont Brigade, submitted this terse report:

Col. Seaver advanced the Third Regiment to the first line and relieved one of Gen. Wheaton's regiments. About this time I received orders to render General Wheaton all the aid he desired. He desired to be relieved entirely from the front line, and accordingly the Fifth Regiment moved forward.[37]

VI Corps made no further advances upon the Southern wall at Cold Harbor.

❆ ❆ ❆ ❆ ❆

Smith's XVIII Corps was depending on the questionable shelter of a stream bank for the success of their portion of the attack. The hollow ran some distance from the forward entrenchments into the Confederate lines in the center of Anderson's First Corps. Smith at least attempted to survey the ground over which his three divisions would pass before the assault. The value of his cursory examination can be measured by the hopelessness of the task given to the XVIII Corps. At the best his men would be protected somewhat from crossfire until they were closer to the enemy lines, with the embankment giving some cover from the Confederate guns homed in from the right. While Wright and Hancock had had some knowledge and luck in aiming at possible weak points near the right flank of Lee's more hasty improvements, Smith's divisions were to run against a solid trench line where Anderson had been given four days to prepare defenses.

Colonel Martin McMahon, adjutant on Wright's VI Corps staff, later explained that any success for Smith depended upon a cooperative movement with Wright that would help protect the exposed flanks of both. But all three Federal corps attacked on divergent avenues of approach, facing their immediate fronts, causing each to uncover more flank the farther they advanced. The simple principle, to McMahon, was that even solid and well-timed attacks tended to spread with more space covered, and that made the defenders' work easier and deadlier.[38]

Major General Charles Devens, Jr., who had had some success against Anderson's positions on June 1, placed his brigades, led by Colonel William Barton's New Yorkers, on the right flank of his assault force. Brigadier General James Martindale was to move down the stream bed into the enemy line, with Brigadier General William Brooks bringing up the left to make and keep contact with Neill's division from VI Corps. Smith began:

At precisely 4:30 on the morning of the 3rd of June Martindale's command moved down the stream, out of the woods, and against the earth-works. The first line reached the foot of the works but fell back, under the heavy front and cross fire, to the edge of the woods, but within short musket range of the line they had gallantly attempted to carry.[39]

Some of Smith's brigades were understrength. For all of his complaining to the irritable Meade about manpower and supplies, the fact was that for the hardest undertaking on that foul morning, the XVIII Corps had the fewest men who could be put into action, and many of those were in poor condition for combat. Many of his brigades were physically exhausted, and most of his regiments were headed by captains and majors.

At four forty-five in the morning, the 1st brigade of Martindale's division, led by Colonel Griffin Stedman, moved down the shallow ravine and came out of that barely sheltered approach almost directly in front of George Anderson's Georgia regiments. At that point in the First Corps defenses, the engineers had developed an inward bow, with thick gun emplacements at both edges and in front. It was nothing less than a killing field.

Stedman later wrote:

> We formed in the woods in solid columns. I gave the command, "Forward!" We started with unloaded muskets and fixed bayonets. I was the first to enter the open field and see the enemy's lines, – a curve. I bade farewell to all I loved. It seemed impossible to survive in that fire; I was spared, while the officers of my staff who followed me closely, were struck down. We reached a point within thirty yards of the enemy's main works; but the fire was too murderous, and my men were repulsed. We left the woods with two thousand men; in five minutes we returned, six hundred less.[40]

Major John Langley's 12th New Hampshire led Stedman's brigade into that circle of fire in columns of regiments ten deep. Asa Bartlett of the 12th observed:

> The One Hundred and Forty-eighth New York Regiment was sent forward as skirmishers, but never went farther than the outer line of entrenchments; the other regiments going over them as they made the charge. To advance a manned column of troops into such a semi-circle of destruction...with front and back flanks entirely exposed to the fire of eight or ten pieces of artillery and more than a half-mile sweep of battle-lined musketry, was something fearful

to even contemplate, but how much more so to actually experience none can tell save those who were there. No wonder that Captain Barker...when he saw the field covered with his own brave men
and heard the cries of the wounded, some less fortunate than the
dead...denounced in righteous wrath the general, high or low, who
was guilty of ordering such a murderous charge as that...He declared with an oath that he would not take his regiment into another such charge, if Jesus Christ himself should order it.[41]

Waving a rifle's ramrod instead of a sword, Stedman led four regiments into the impenetrable Southern line. The 12th New Hampshire
was followed by the 11th Connecticut, the 8th Maine, and the 2nd
New Hampshire. Bartlett says that "after less than ten minutes, there
was no brigade to be seen." Some of the fallen were within yards of the
Confederate works, and those not dead pretended to be so rather than
risk point-blank fire. Those, said Bartlett, "...were obliged to lie all
day...until night or death brought relief." He witnessed a man, shattered by a shell, end his own misery by cutting his throat with a jack-
knife. "To those exposed to the full force and fury of the dreadful storm
of lead and iron that met the charging column, it seemed more like a
volcanic blast than a battle and was about as destructive. The men
went down in rows..."
Sergeant Piper of Company B of the 12th New Hampshire Volunteers said:

> The men bent down as they pushed forward, as if trying to
> breast a tempest, and the files of men went down like rows or blocks
> or bricks pushed over by striking against others.[42]

One sergeant from another New Hampshire company said that he
dropped down among what he thought was a group of dead comrades, when they suddenly got up and advanced without him. Nearby,
however, an angry company commander tried to arouse several files
of prostrate men with his sword, when he discovered that, "...nothing
but the Almighty would ever bring those men upon their feet."
George Place, also of the 12th New Hampshire's Company B, offered this:

> Thus we stood, all ready for the charge...Finally the Colonel
> drew his sword, "Forward, march" and the regiment started. We
> had not gone ten feet when a rebel battery on our left flank opened
> fire...The guns were so arranged that the iron storm swept past us
> about two rods in front. How it crashed and howled through the

pinetrees. For a moment the regiment quailed and halted...He [Captain Barker] flung his sword above his head and shouted with a voice that seemed as if the rebels must have heard, – "Forward!"...There was no more halting after that, until, swept down in killed and wounded, it lost all semblance of order, and could do no otherwise than fall back. That artillery discharge was immediately followed by the opening of musketry...we immediately enter an open field. It is bare of vegetation...A line of breastworks runs zig-zag; one in front, the other on the left. We cannot see a man in these works, for a dense cloud of battle-smoke rests all along the line. From the works in front, and the works on our left, arose a musketry fire so heavy, it seemed almost like one continual crash of thunder, while artillery on our left poured in the shells. Just as we entered the field, a shell plunged into the ground...and burst...Some small missile struck me just under the left eye...

James Rollins was at my left, Charles Marden next to him, and the next beyond, Charles Bunker. Soon after we got into the field, Rollins threw both hands, uttered a yell, and soon fell on his face...A bullet had gone through both his calves. I looked for Marden and Bunker to "dress" by, but they were missing; indeed there was such a wide gap on my left that I thought I had fallen behind my column, and hastened to catch up...only to find myself in the front column. We were now so near the breastworks that I could see the flash of the musketry quivering through the bank of smoke that lay above them, like lightning through a cloud...I was thinking of the hand-to-hand struggle that was to come when we reached the breastworks, when a bullet went through my right arm...About this time, the regiment began to fall back. Just before I re-entered the woods a bullet grazed my back...as I received the third blow, that old expression, "hit" im agin, blue jacket, he's got no friends', passed across my mind.[43]

The 12th and 2nd New Hampshire staggered on through the dead and wounded. As the 12th disintegrated, the 2nd arrived suddenly at the earthworks facing the 4th Alabama and the 15th Alabama of Law's brigade and the 13th Mississippi regiment from Brigadier General Benjamin Humphreys' division. They had closed the gap near Kershaw's section of the line and had spent the night angling their works into a hedgehog of artillery placements and abatis. As Colonel William Oates of the 15th Alabama wrote:

None of us slept any. The men worked all night and by day had an excellent line of defensive works completed. When day came details were sent to the rear to fill canteens...They had returned, and just before I could see the sun, I heard a volley in the woods, saw the major running up the ravine in the direction of Anderson's brigade, which lay to the right of Law's, and the skirmishers running in, pursued by a column of the enemy ten lines deep, with arms at a trail, yelling "Huzzah! Huzzah!" I ordered my men to take arms and fix bayonets. Just then I remembered that not a gun in the regiment was loaded. I ordered the men to load and the officers each to take an ax and stand to the works. I was apprehensive that the enemy would be at our works before the men could load.

As Capt. Noah Feagin and his skirmishers crawled over the works I thought of my piece of artillery. I called out: "Sergeant, give them double-charges of canister; fire, men, fire!" The order was obeyed with alacrity. The enemy was within thirty steps. They halted and began to dodge, lie down, and recoil. The fire was terrific from my regiment, the Fourth Alabama on my immediate right, and the 13th Mississippi on my left...The blaze of fire...went right into the ranks of our assailants and made frightful gaps through the dense mass of men. They endure it but for one or two minutes, when they retreated, leaving the ground covered with their dead and dying...[44]

The whole Confederate line continued the carnage, firing as fast as they could load and discharge. A busy Law, operating north of Kershaw, said that his line was held by fewer than a thousand men, and they saw line after line of Union men coming until their front was a writhing mass of humanity. The firing of his gunners became so heavy that Law feared they would exhaust their ammunition before that attack ceased. One officer saw the canister making contact at a hundred yards, mowing away whole lines and sending limbs high in the air.

The guns of the Richmond Howitzers were among those in Kershaw's line that morning. Manning one of those, artilleryman William Dame wrote:

...Up and down our battle line the fierce musketry broke out. To left and right it ran crashing and rolling like the sound of heavy hail, magnified a thousand times...with cannon like claps of thunder...into that storm of death the blue columns made their way. Straight in on our front the mass was advanced and we were hurling case-shot through their ranks...when we saw another column rush out of the woods to our right. It was almost upon us not 45 yards...we turned upon them with double-canister! Two or three shots doubled up the head of that column into a formless crowd that stood stubbornly for three or four minutes at pistol range, and the infantry and our Napoleon guns tore them to pieces. It was bloody work! They were a helpless mob...falling in rows...a mass simply melting away under the fury of our fire.[45]

Smith witnessed the first repulse of his men, and then went down to Martindale's position to take charge. He planned a second assault, but insisted that it could succeed only with cooperation with Wright's VI Corps. Messages to Meade and Grant were sent that only confused the army headquarters. Smith ordered Martindale to bring up Brooks, and to stay under cover until Wright was contacted. He actually expected an imperiled Brooks to implement his coordination with the VI Corps and make a combined assault with Neill's weak division on the other side of the woods. Smith added:

> While General Brooks was forming his column, so heavy a fire from the right came in on his troops that I at once ordered him not to move, but to keep his men sheltered until the cross-fire slackened. Going back to the right to ascertain the cause of the firing, I found that Martindale had anticipated matters, and that under his orders Stannard's brigade had made three assaults, having been repulsed in all with severe loss.

The attack by Brigadier General George Stannard's 1st brigade of XVIII Corps offers particularly dismaying scenes of men rushing into a death trap with small chances of achieving victory. Samuel Putnam, with a regiment of that second wave, the 25th Massachusetts Volunteers, wrote a first-hand description. His unit was made up of only 300 men, and the entire brigade of four regiments, the 23rd, 25th and 27th Massachusetts, and 55th Pennsylvania, contained hardly more than 1,500 men altogether. They were the well-known "Star Brigade" that had been hooted as "Parlor Soldiers" by Wright's hardened veterans upon their arrival on June 1. Putnam wrote:

> We were in close column by divisions this time – that is, a front of two companies in a division – five divisions. We heard loud cheering on our left, and artillery firing rapidly...An officer passed by and reported Hancock successful. "Forward!" The hour had come. We moved slowly up the slight elevation, beyond which a thousand deaths awaited us. No man faltered, and only the wounded ones fell out; for we were under fire all the time while lying under the trees. We gained the front...We were at once under a murderous fire. The enemy's works were directly in front. Colonel Pickett was marching at the head of the Regiment and at this moment waved his sword over his head, and shouted his orders: "Come on Boys; forward double-quick. Charge!" We dashed forward with a cheer.

The enemy's earthworks in our front, perhaps twenty rods distant, were enveloped in smoke and flame, and volley after volley of musketry sent bullets through our ranks like hail. At the same moment we received an enfilading fire of artillery on both right and left flanks...The slaughter was fearful.[(46)]

Like so many others that morning, those of the 25th Massachusetts still capable of it dropped to the wet ground and began the by now customary, feverish digging. They tossed up a low bank of Virginia soil, using anything available to provide some measure of physical protection. Along with the 25th regiment in the first assault was the 27th Massachusetts commanded by Major William Walker. As they were about to advance, an aide-de-camp to Stannard, Captain E. K. Wilcox, insisted, against protests from the enlisted men, that he join their regiment's advance. Then the 27th and the 55th Pennsylvania of Captain George Hill formed and moved out of that now-familiar ravine. As William Derby wrote:

> The brigade with a shout sprang up the hill, over the crest and the first line of rifle-pits, into the riven field. Forward, struggling like maddened billows against breakers – mown down by scores, – but onward until the second line of rifle-pits was reached...again they struggle to breast the iron hail, crouching to escape its fury, for that brigade had never learned to acknowledge defeat...Conceive the fierce onslaught, midst deafening volleys of musketry, thundering of artillery, and the wild, mad yell of battle...the ranks mown down as they contend for every inch they advance, until the lines crumble and break...

> It was almost impossible to move and live, the lifting of a head or hand being a signal for volleys of musketry. Many lay surrounded by the dead, which they arranged to make defenses...The surface of the field seemed like a boiling cauldron, from the incessant pattering and ploughing of shot, which raised the dirt in geysers of spitting sand. Some of the wounded attempted to work back to the ravine during the day, but only a few succeeded...Major Walker and Capt. Wilcox were instantly killed as the passed the last line of rifle-pits, the first by a rifle-ball through his neck, the latter pierced by several fatal shots...So thick were the dead..that one of our men lay a considerable time without knowing all around him were dead...[(47)]

The First brigade mounted another charge after a brief pause. The 23rd Massachusetts and the remainder of the 25th drove in for another try, as Oates observed:

JUNE 3, 1864 FROM MIDNIGHT UNTIL NOON

The charging column, which aimed to strike the Fourth Alabama, received the most destructive fire I ever saw. They were subjected to a front and fire from the infantry, at short range, while my piece of artillery poured double-charges of canister into them. The Georgians [Col. Bryan's 4 regiments] loaded for the Alabamians to fire. I could see the dust fog out of a man's clothing in two or three places at once where as many balls would strike him at once. In two minutes not a man was left standing...[48]

Derby and a few others of the Star Brigade were able to withdraw after darkness that evening, and when they passed the VI Corps survivors, they were welcomed into the army as equals. "From then," said Derby, "we heard nothing more of 'parlor soldiers'."

The 3rd brigade of Brooks division had gone into the third wave of attacks on the Confederate line that morning, a few minutes behind Martindale's and Stannard's brigade. They deployed along the heavy woods where they had met such furious resistance on June 1. One regiment, the 98th New York under Colonel Fred Wead, passed by the bodies of men from their unit that had been left two days before. The brigade commander, Brigadier General Gilman Marston, tried twice to bring his men over the Confederate breastworks. Twice repelled with enormous losses, he was left hugging rifle pits in front of Kershaw's and Law's cross-firing batteries. His companion brigade of Colonel Guy Henry did not even leave the woods and still received brutal treatment from the Southern cannon. Colonel William Kreutzer of the 98th New York wrote:

The enemy's shells, solid shot and rifle-balls all the while showered upon them, and hit every limb and twig about or above them. Nothing saved us but a slight elevation of the ground in front...Colonel Wead rose to his feet an instant on the captured line when a rifle-ball pierced his neck...he was carried to the barn beside the road, where he died the next day...[49]

The entire grand assault of June 3 was launched and smashed in less than twenty minutes. For many of the Confederates on the line, it seemed unbelievable that any assault had happened. It was over so quickly that many Southerners did not realize that their day's business was finished. Johnson Hagood of South Carolina, in line with Hoke's division just right of Hutton and Kershaw, said later that he was not aware at any time of any serious assault having been made.[50]

The enormous numbers of bodies left all over the frontage of the breastworks awed some. Law said:

On reaching the trenches, I found the men in fine spirits, laughing and talking as they fired. There, too, I could see more plainly the terrible havoc made in the ranks of the assaulting column. I had seen the dreadful carnage in front of Marye's Heights at Fredericksburg, and on the old railway cut which Jackson held at Second Manassas; but I had seen nothing to exceed this. It was not war; it was murder.[51]

Northern survivors shared the disbelief. Private John S. Graham of the 140th Pennsylvania Regiment wrote:

Where are they gone now, poor fellows, 176 left of 487, some to their long homes, the rest wounded. You ask me how I felt going into the charge and how I felt in and after I came out. I felt just as cool as I do now; I felt like I could take Richmond by myself. After I came out and was looking over the field and saw hundreds killed and others wounded...it was then that I thought about it...[52]

Edwin Forbes' sketch of the fighting at Bethesda Church on May 30, showing the repulse of Early's attack on Crawford's position.

(Library of Congress)

Leslie's Weekly illustrator Edwin Forbes' depiction of the June 1 assault by XVIII Corps at Cold Harbor.
(Library of Congress)

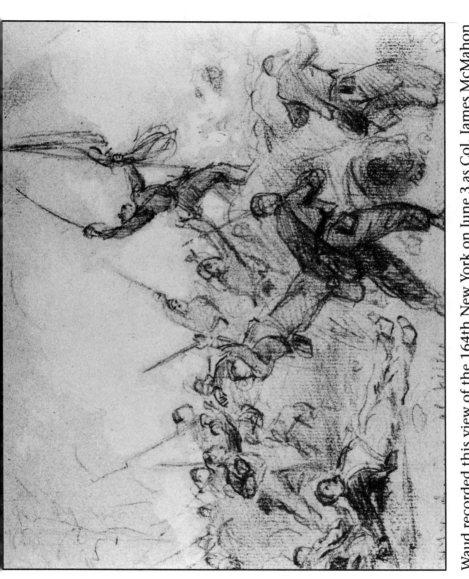

Waud recorded this view of the 164th New York on June 3 as Col. James McMahon placed the colors atop the Confederate earthworks and was shot repeatedly.

(Library of Congress)

Eyewitness to the assault by II Corps on June 3, _Harper's Weekly_ artist A. A. Waud drew this scene of the break-through by the 8th New York Heavy Artillery. Confederate prisoners are gathered in the foreground.

(Library of Congress)

Chapter Ten

Cold Harbor

Part One
June 3 and After

"They soon brought in the colonel who led the charge, and about one hundred prisoners. The Colonel was a brave man. He said he had been in many places, but that was the worst."
- Colonel William Oates[1]
15th Alabama

"A rebel major, while reviewing the carnage of the field...remarked to Surgeon Fish of the Twenty-Seventh, 'It was one of the bravest and most useless charges I ever witnessed'."
- Private William Derby[2]
27th Massachusetts Volunteers

"It is very interesting to revisit the battlefields of the war, but I never heard any one who was engaged there express a wish to see Cold Harbor."
- Brigadier General Thomas Hyde[3]
VI Corps

"It was perhaps the easiest victory ever granted to Confederate arms by the folly of Federal commanders."
- Colonel Charles Venable[4]
Lee's Staff

"Before 8 o'clock a.m. on the 3rd of June the battle of Cold Harbor was over, and with it Grant's 'overland campaign' against Richmond."
- Brigadier General Evander Law[5]
First Corps

By six o'clock the morning of the third, the noises of heavy fire began to slacken. Lee, at Gaines' Mill, sent staff officers for reports from his line commanders. A few shells had fallen near his headquarters camp, but other than that, the most he knew was from the incredible noise of the battle. Perhaps a half hour later, Lee and his staff had a picture of the grand assault's effects. The first news came from Hoke's section, reporting to Taylor of Lee's headquarters that they had not lost a single man in the line.[6] Wilcox's trenches, at the deep end near the Chickahominy, had not even been approached during the attack. Lee was informed of the breakthrough at Breckinridge's position and the losses sustained before the II Corps regiments were ousted, but the "Old Maryland" battalion was restoring the line even then. A. P. Hill had shown a courier the dead piled on top of one another in front of his emplacements, and said with a sweep of hand, "Tell General Lee that it is the same all along my front."[7]

"Baldy" Smith had witnessed the destruction of two of his three divisions and began sending messages frantically:

> General Martindale got into so hot a place that he was forced to assault the works without the assistance of the column of General Brooks. The assault was made three times, and each time repulsed...the enfilading fire of the enemy was so heavy as to force me to order Gen. Brooks not to attempt to advance his column until the fire was slackened...I have nothing but artillery fire to use against it...My troops are very much cut up, and I have no hopes of being able to carry the works in my front unless a movement of the Sixth Corps, on my left, may relieve at least one of my flanks from this galling fire.[8]

Other messages came into Grant's headquarters where Major General Andrew Humphreys, Chief-of-Staff of Operations and rapidly overshadowing both Meade and Rawlins in responsibilities, was trying to sort out priorities. For example, just after six o'clock Wright reported:

> I am in advance of everything else. If I advance my right further, without a corresponding advance by the 18th Corps, I am, from the form of the enemy's line, taken in flank and reverse...I think I can carry the enemy's main line opposite my center, but...my flanks cannot move without a corresponding movement by the corps on my right and left. My losses will show that there has been no hanging back on the part of the Sixth Corps...[9]

Meade, becoming more demoralized by the minute, then sent to Smith:

> General Wright had been given the order to assault and to continue without reference to your advance, and the commanding general directs that your assault be continued without reference to

General Wright's. Wright has...reported that he was waiting your advance to enable him to assault.

As Smith and Wright were sending their unhelpful messages, their men were trying to stay alive. Smith's next message to Meade was another excuse for delay and a plea for artillery ammunition, and defense of himself from charges that he had been extravagant with his supplies. Neither man knew that Martindale's division had been almost annihilated. Meade sent a terse reply:

> I am sorry to hear that Martindale is unable to assault. I have just heard from Warren, who is forcing the enemy on his right. I have ordered him to push forward his left in order to relieve the attack you are able to make.

Next, Smith asked for two batteries of field artillery without which he would not attempt another attack with Warren. Then, after eight o'clock, Smith received the third verbal order to attack. He said simply, "...That order I refused to obey...I had carefully examined the entire front of my line, and was convinced that no assault could succeed that did not embrace a portion of my works on the right, where I was powerless to attack...An assault under such conditions I looked on as involving a wanton waste of life."[10]

Meade had issued an order at seven o'clock for a renewal of the attacks by all three corps on the left, after clearing it with Grant. Grant added:

> The moment it becomes certain that an assault cannot succeed, suspend the offensive; but when one does succeed, push it vigorously, and if necessary pile in troops at the successful point from wherever they can be taken.[11]

Contradictory and confused messages came in over the telegraph. One of Grant's young staff colonels and an advocate for the frontal-assault offensive so evident in the Wilderness campaign and at Cold Harbor, Colonel Cyrus Comstock, was sent to review Smith's position with the engineers.

Comstock and his group spent nearly an hour at the front, then left without revealing their opinions to a mystified Smith. Their report for Meade described the XVIII Corps front as solid, even though Comstock spoke of a personal interview with Martindale, whose huddled remnant of a division was still burrowing in less than two hundred yards from Anderson's First Corps trench walls.[12] Major James

Franklin of Colonel Pinckney D. Bowles' 4th Alabama told of the XVIII Corps' last charge that morning:

> Line after line came out of the opposite woods, only to melt away under our continuous fire, until, with the last line, which went the way of the others, came a tall color-bearer...who bore his charge high in the air, as with steady tread he confidently advanced, looking only to the front...Amazed at his persistence, our men withheld their fire and called him to go back. But he did not hear, or if perchance he did, he did not take his orders from our side...our men in grey mounted the works, waved their hats to attract his attention, and fairly shrieked, "Go back! Go back! We do not want to kill you!"...This man of iron halted, looked carefully to his right hand...then as carefully to his left – not a man of his regiment in sight! It would have been no disgrace to have dropped or hurried back as fast he could...He did neither...He took his flagstaff from its socket, rolled up his color with provoking deliberateness in our faces...and when done, touched his hat to us in grateful appreciation. A right-shoulder shift an about-face, and then he began his march back to his own lines with a step as steady as had been his advance...[13]

The reports coming into Meade's headquarters were not promising. Word came that Burnside and Warren were on the move against Early on the Old Church Road and were hitting hard. In truth, Warren was not moving at all, and Hancock had been asked to send him Birney's division just to help him hold where he was. Burnside's first reports to Warren and the V Corps caused that false optimism.

Burnside had made it seem that he was operating as a wing of V Corps. He had sent forward one brigade, led by Colonel John Curtin, into the Confederate skirmish lines and had "blown up two of their caissons." Colonel John Hartranft's brigade of Brigadier General Orlando Willcox's division had actually reached the main line before being stopped by heavy enfilading fire. Burnside even had Wilson's 3rd Cavalry division come down from the upper Totopotomoy for a planned attack that never happened. In actuality, artillery fire from Cutshaw's and Hardaway's battalions cut Burnside's attempted advance to ribbons.[14]

With six battalions of well-emplaced guns operating, the Southerners were able to enfilade the entire attack zone from right and left. Confederate artillery officer Jennings Wise contended that most of the Union casualties were caused by their artillery fire that morning. By five o'clock a.m., any offensive efforts on the extreme right of Grant's line were over.

At about eight forty-five, Meade told his corps commanders to renew the assault. To Hancock, he sent:

> It is of the greatest importance no effort should be spared to succeed. Wright and Smith are both going to try again, and unless you consider it hopeless I would like you to do the same.[15]

That third order for attack was given through channels from corps level to divisions to brigades, losing credibility until it was clear that every unit was on its own discretion as to try to stand up and charge once more. Not a single regiment made an organized attempt. As Lieutenant Colonel Martin McMahon said, "To move that army further, except by regular approaches, was a simple and absolute impossibility, known to be such by every officer and man of the three corps engaged. The order was obeyed by simply renewing the fire from the men as they lay in position."[16]

The terrified, amazed, and physically exhausted men of the three corps lay in their make-shift ditches and fired in the general direction of the Confederate positions. In all reported actions after eight-thirty, this was the fullest extent of the continuance of any offensive at Cold Harbor on June 3. One of those shots hit Evander Law in the head, giving him a minor but painful wound, and making him the highest-ranking Confederate casualty of the day. Breckinridge had a horse knocked out from under him later that day, leaving him dizzy and faint, but not incapacitated.

At eleven o'clock, Grant himself rode out along his lines. He had received unclear suggestions of possible movements from several of his commanders, but the final comment was Hancock's: "the position on my front cannot be taken." At twelve-thirty, Grant sent to Meade:

> The opinion of the corps commanders not being sanguine of success in case an assault is ordered, you may direct a suspension of farther advance for the present. Hold our most advanced positions, and strengthen them...[17]

General Meade distributed a circular at one-thirty:

> Orders. For the present all further operations will be suspended. Corps commanders will at once entrench the positions they now hold, including their advance positions, and will cause reconnaissances to be made with a view to holding against the enemy's works by regular approaches.

One of the most enduring controversies associated with Cold Harbor has been the belief that the refusal by Federal units to renew the charges against the Confederate lines after the initial catastrophe amounted to mutiny. Many northern eyewitness accounts and official reports support that impression. The strongest voices that disclaim such a general disobedience came from Southern sources.[18] New Yorker Frank Wilkeson, among many, gave one account:

> By noon the stragglers were mostly gathered up and had rejoined their regiments, and columns of troops began to move to and fro in our rear in the little valley...I saw a puff of smoke between the marchers and myself, heard the report of a bursting shell, and twelve of that column were knocked on the earth. Their officers shouted "Close up! Close up!" The uninjured men hurriedly closed the gap and marched on. The dead and wounded lay on the ground, with their rifles scattered among them. Soon some soldiers came out of the woods and carried the wounded men off, but left the dead where they fell. We buried them that night. Then, as the day wore away...I saw staff officers ride along the lines, and then I saw the regimental commanders getting their men in line. About four o'clock in the afternoon I heard the charging commands given. With many an oath at the military stupidity which would again send good troops to useless slaughter, I sprang to my feet to watch the doomed infantry. Men, whom I knew well, stood rifle in hand not more than thirty feet from me, and I am happy to state that they continued to stand. Not a man stirred from his place. The army to a man refused to obey the order, presumedly from General Grant himself, to renew the assault. I heard the order given, and I saw it disobeyed.[19]

Brigadier General Cullen Battle of Hoke's division later wrote:

> The carnage on the Federals' side was awful. I well recall having received a report from Gen'l Hoke after the assault. The ground in his entire front, over which the enemy had charged, was literally covered with dead and wounded, Hoke not losing a single man. No wonder that the command was given to renew the assault, the Federal soldiers sullenly and silently declined. The order was issued through the officers to sub-ordinate command, and from then descended through wanted channels, but no man stirred, the immobile lines pronounced a verdict, silent but emphatic, against any further slaughter...[20]

It would take some time before Grant and Meade were able to grasp the extent of their losses on June 3. Even as late as three o'clock, Grant wired Halleck in Washington that the day had not been decisive and that Confederate losses were about the same as his own. South Carolinian Dickert could have showed him easily enough:

> Men lay in places like hogs in a pen – some side by side, some across each other, some two deep, while others with their heads lying across the heads and body of their dead comrades...[21]

XVIII Corps' losses that day would finally be counted at 3,019 men killed, wounded, and missing.[22] Wright's VI Corps' losses are set at 1,170. Not even on the cold December battlefield in front of Fredericksburg in 1862 had the Army of the Potomac seen such a day, and with as little gained from it.

❋ ❋ ❋ ❋ ❋

Before dark on June 3, Lieutenant Colonel David McIntosh was ordered to relieve the batteries of an artillery unit in support of Gregg's section of the line. The position was near the edge of the infamous salient that Barlow's division had pierced. The ground behind the line was a network of deep trenches and ditches that made moving heavy artillery in and out difficult. McIntosh remembered that many of the trenches were filled with bodies, and his guns passed over them as they were wheeled into formation. The work was so slow that darkness overtook the harassed gunners before they had three guns in place, and William Mahone, the division commander, blamed the battery commander who was being pulled out. McIntosh seemed delighted as Mahone, a short, emaciated man in a red flannel shirt, got ready to fist-fight a blond giant gunner named McLaughlin.[23]

❋ ❋ ❋ ❋ ❋

The wounded and dead, said Law, covered at least five acres in front of Field and Kershaw's divisions. Alexander said that the ground in front of the ingeniously reshaped ravine between Kershaw and Hoke was piled with bodies: "where the efforts of the enemy were most concentrated prolonged, and where their loss was the heaviest."[24] Great numbers of the bodies that went down in that hour before six were still living, many shattered, and many hardly wounded at all but being shot if they made any move to show it. The flat grounds offered no protection, and those that were not able to crawl or hobble to their own lines were left to the slim mercy of Southern marksmen in the lines. Many were shot if any life signs were revealed; many were fired at even if they were dead already. Bartlett of the 12th New Hampshire wrote:

So worse than savages...and malicious were some of these heart-less fiends in human shape, that they not only shot at those who showed any signs of life, but amused themselves by making targets of the bodies of those that were dead. A number of the Twelfth received their death wounds from these cowardly miscreants...[25]

Smith later noted:

At the close of the battle General Martindale was less than two hundred yards from the enemy's line, and in the open space be-tween were many dead and wounded. For three days no cessation of hostilities was asked for and common rumor gave as a reason that there was a fear of refusal, as there were no dead or wounded of the enemy between the lines to be cared for. Some of our wounded were brought in by men who risked their lives in the act, and some were rescued by digging trenches to them. The groans of such as could not be reached grew fainter and fainter until they ceased.[26]

Witnesses told of scenes of breath-taking courage as men after dark-ness attempted to bring in those still breathing. But the day's heat had finished the work of bullets in many cases. Many who were reached could do no more than grasp a hand and give a few words before dy-ing. Some of those brought in lived only for a few moments after be-ing taken to field hospitals. Slit trenches were run out to check on those with strength enough to moan, and it looked like gopher bur-rows radiating from the lines held by the Federal forward units. George Stevens said:

The whole plain was dug over...One is reminded of the colo-nies of prairie dogs with their burrows and mounds.[27]

With whispers and soft crawling, brave individuals tried to locate those still alive. After listening for faint breathing or moaning, they would take blankets and lift the wounded man up and noiselessly make their escape. In many cases, enlisted men would take special risks to locate the bodies of particular officers. Many of the dead were pulled back, at great risk, rather than be left on that field. A 12th New Hamp-shire sergeant told that twenty of their regiment were brought in for burial on the night of the third, and twenty-eight the next night. Sol-diers searched for comrades among the dead, risking their own lives by lighting matches to identify those men on the ground. McMahon wrote:

When night came on, the groans and moaning of the wounded, all our own, who were lying between the lines, were heart-rending. Some were brought in by volunteers from our entrenchments, but many remained uncared for beneath the summer suns and the unrefreshing dews of the sultry summer nights.[28]

As difficult to interpret as anything concerning the events at Cold Harbor are the strange accounts of the "Truce." The accounts of Union veterans of that assault of June 3 were bitter at Lee for not agreeing quickly to a cease-fire to allow aid to be given to the unfortunate men left to blister and die. Southern accounts were more objective, as there were few, if any, of their own comrades left unprotected and suffering. To them, the possibility of further attacks was very real, and they were concerned with the large numbers of Federals dug in close to their defenses. The sharp-shooting, detested by all but practiced by both sides up and down the battlefront, made any movement a life-and-death decision. Lee expected Grant to make a formal appeal for a truce. To the thousands of crippled and bleeding from the three Federal corps, questions of courtesy did not hold for much. In some cases there were informal overtures made by the corps staffs to ask for time to remove and bury the dead, all to no avail. On June 5, for example, a note from an officer named Auger – possibly from Hancock's II Corps – was passed to a staff officer of First Corps, asking for a six hour armistice to bury the dead. When the message was delivered to Lee, his reply was, "I did not know that Gen. Auger was commander of the Army of the Potomac."[29]

Hancock was the first of the senior commanders to request that Grant take action. The hope of saving many of the wounded had passed by the morning of June 4, but the other concern was that the dead, many of whom had been lying on the field since June 1, had to be interred. William Oates of Alabama said:

The stench from the dead between our lines and theirs was sickening. It was so nauseating that it was almost unendurable; but we had the advantage, in that the wind carried it away from us to them.[30]

William Derby of the 27th Massachusetts wrote:

Four days of sun and rain, with the severe heat of summer, had passed over our slain, and the air was laden with insufferable putrescence. We breathed it in every breath, tasted it in the food we ate and the water we drank. What seemed intolerable to us was doubly so to the enemy, from their nearness to the dead, and from the fact that the revailing winds...carried the fumes directly to them.[31]

Both sides suffered while arrangements were made. Some Union officers felt that an official request for a truce could be considered an acceptance of defeat. The Southern command made it apparent that they awaited the formality of such a request, and it was not to be soon forthcoming.

Part Two
Maneuvers

"I had immediate and entire command of the field all day, the Lieutenant General honoring the field with his presence only about an hour in the middle of the day," Meade wrote his wife the following morning.[32] His credibility in the Army of the Potomac by evening on that day had reached bottom level. Meade directed that, since the Confederates had been firing massed artillery at their forward positions in hopes of driving those men back to their original lines, corps commanders should open all guns up at midnight and continue the barrage until daylight. Meade added that each corps commander could determine that, if he feared this would bring on return fire from the Southerners against the vulnerable troops in the front, that he could be exempt from the order. Twelve o'clock came, and not a shot was fired from any of the three corps on the Union left.[33]

There were many other indicators that morale in the command in the Army of the Potomac was unraveling by the afternoon of June 3. Lyman was sent to locate Warren of V Corps, and could not find him along the lines to the right of Smith and XVIII Corps. But Lyman found himself a target for any of several weapons as he perched on horseback and looked for a reclusive corps commander. Upon finally seeing Warren, Lyman related:

> Warren looks care-worn. Some people say he is a selfish man, but he is certainly the most tender-hearted of our commanders...Warren feels it a great deal, and that the responsibility, and many things of course not going to suit him, all tend to make him haggard. He said: "For thirty days now, it has been one funeral procession, past me; and it is too much! To-day I saw a man burying a comrade, and, within an hour, he himself was brought in and buried beside him. The men need some rest..."[34]

Smith was for all purposes taken out of the command chain. He and Meade would not speak again, even through routine circulars. Hancock, the most respected military officer in the army, was confused, exhausted, and in great physical pain. Wright of the VI Corps was a sphinx, not responding to either messages or personal visits by several of Meade's staff.

At one point, Grant took a small entourage to visit the camps of his corps leaders, and one observer found that no one wanted to speak to one another in that military icicle.[35]

The Northerners, at the company level, took matters into their own hands as much as possible. Entrenching tools were delivered to the front so that "rabbit holes" could be shoveled out under the barrels of the Confederates. The shooting was more or less continuous all along the six-mile line and would remain so until the armies moved.

Several Federal sources reported a Confederate attack in the evening of that awful day, against Barlow's burrowing division in front of Breckinridge. There was never a complete quiet, and the Southerners were as prickly and nervous as their enemies. Charles Dana reported to Halleck that a Confederate assault was made on the fronts of all three Federal corps on the night of June 4, though Alexander assures that no night attacks were ever made at Cold Harbor. Oates wrote that there was an attack on his Alabama troops every evening after June 4.[36] The sporadic volleying and artillery fire were routine, but most hated of all was the insidious work of the sharp-shooters. Confederate artillery officer Major Robert Stiles wrote:

> Sharpshooting at best...is a fearful thing. The regular sharp-shooter often seemed to me to be little better than a human tiger lying in wait for blood. His rifle is frequently trained and made fast bearing upon a particular spot – for example, where the head of a gunner must of necessity appear when sighting his piece – and the instant that object appears and, as it were, "darkens the hole," crash goes a bullet through his brain.[37]

A Connecticut private wrote in a letter home:

> Our life in the trenches is like this: first, the trench is a long passage, as the name indicates, running in a direction with reference to the enemy's works. The earth is thrown toward the enemy; and this, with the trench or ditch, forms a protection some eight feet high. The trench is eight or ten feet wide: in this space the troops remain, unable to leave it on account of the enemy's sharpshooters. The officers dig holes in rear of the trench, in which our spare time is passed. Like a rabbit, the soldier burrows deeper and deeper as danger increases. At least one-third of the troops are constantly on duty; at night they are all on the alert.[38]

❋ ❋ ❋ ❋ ❋

June 3 was the birthday of President Jefferson Davis. At around five in the morning, he could hear the sustained roar of distant artillery and like many in Richmond, said that the window panes rattled from the tremors of massed fire just nine miles to the northeast.

At seven, his three children and his pregnant wife greeted Davis with a rendition of "Happy Birthday." He looked and felt every minute of his fifty-six years. His grief over the loss of his son, Joseph, and the frustration over his war efforts had combined to age him considerably. He had not received any news from Lee of the great battle that he knew had come. There were no reserves, and nothing between Lee and the city of Richmond. Shortly after one that afternoon, Davis received a short dispatch from Lee, which read:

> So far every attack of the enemy has been repulsed. His assaults began early this morning, and continued until about 9 o'clock...the only impression made on our line was at a salient of Gen'l Breckinridge's position, where they broke through and captured part of a battalion. He was immediately driven out with heavy loss...[39]

A more detailed report was delivered by Colonel William Johnston, Davis's personal aide, which contained descriptions of Grant's massive frontal assault, in which, "the enemy came twenty-six men deep and extending the length of the lines, lasted hardly a quarter of an hour. Ten thousand men in blue dropped to the ground."[40] Cheered at the news, Davis arranged to leave at once to personally see the field where Lee had again checked the Union army.

John B. Jones of the War Department in Richmond wrote:

> June 3D. – Raining, gently and cool.
> As early as 4 a.m. there was an incessant roar of artillery, the vibrations of which could be felt in the houses. It could be heard distinctly in all parts of the city. And ever and anon could be distinguished great clashes of musketry, as if whole divisions of infantry were firing at the word of command. It continued until 11 o'clock a.m. when it ceased. A dispatch from Lee stated that his line had been repeatedly assaulted, and every time the enemy was repulsed...No doubt the slaughter has been great![41]

Lee was at his headquarters at about eleven that morning when he was visited by Postmaster General John H. Reagan. That official had brought with him two state judges from Richmond to view the scenes of the great battle that had everyone in the city on edge. They had ridden up through Mechanicsville and passed a few hundred yards behind the Confederate lines until they reached Gaines' Mill and Lee's headquarters. They saw shells falling here and there in the command area, and were afraid to ride in further. Reagan himself entered the headquarters as a group of Federal prisoners was hurried through. He found Lee alone except for a single orderly. Later, Reagan described his extraordinary visit:

> I said to him it seemed that a great deal of artillery was being used. "Yes," he replied, "more than usual on both sides." He added, "That does not do much harm here." Then, waving his hand toward the front, where the rattle of musketry made a noise like the tearing of a sheet, he observed: "It is that that kills men." He then remarked that General Grant was hurling columns from six to ten deep against his lines at three places for the purpose of breaking them. "General," I said to him, "if he breaks your line, what reserve have you?"

> "Not a regiment," he replied. "And," he added, "that has been my condition ever since the fighting commenced on the Rappahannock. If I shorten my lines to provide a reserve he will turn me; if I weaken my lines to provide a reserve, he will break them."[42]

Lee told Reagan how fatigued his veterans were, and how the want of good food had cost more casualties than the enemy's bullets. He asked the Postmaster General to urge the commissary-general in Richmond to send them all available potatoes and onions, because scurvy was breaking out among his men. As soon as Reagan had left, Lee asked President Davis's office for any available troops. Lee had intelligence, in the form of scores of prisoners, confirming the presence of the XVIII Corps on his field. Therefore, "no time should be lost if reinforcements can be had," which meant that any troops still held by Beauregard should be sent northward to him now. Within hours, Brigadier General Matthew Ransom's brigade was on its way to his army. The fresh unit was soon at Bolton's Bridge on the Chickahominy, along with three companies of artillery, to keep an eye on Grant's possible movements across the Chickahominy toward Richmond.

At mid-afternoon Davis arrived at Lee's headquarters, along with the Chief of Ordnance, Colonel Josiah Gorgas. Gorgas had been instrumental in producing munitions in a region where little industry had previously existed, and had become heroic for using everything from blockade running to domestic production to keep Lee's army supplied with weaponry, when his commissariat could not even feed the soldiers. Davis and Gorgas were amazed at the slaughter in front of the Confederate main lines. By now it was obvious that Grant had stopped his general assaults, but Lee's grim Confederates were hardly relaxed behind their triple lines of expertly devised breastworks. Davis mentioned that the Richmond newspapers had derided Lee frequently about his "spade-work." As they were talking, Gorgas rode up, dressed in his finest uniform and wearing a bright blue cape. Lee quickly and courteously begged Gorgas to dismount and move back from sight of the line. "With that blue cloth, you are a target for either side." Then, with a smile, Lee added that he would rather the Ordnance Chief return to Richmond and send him more ammunition.[43]

By evening, lines of skirmishers had been reestablished in the fronts of Breckinridge and Finegan, and their wounded taken away for such care as could be afforded. At eight forty-five that evening, Lee sent the Secretary of War, James Seddon, the only statement on Cold Harbor that he would ever make:

> Our loss today has been small, and our success, under the blessing of God, all that we could expect.[44]

✳ ✳ ✳ ✳ ✳

The fighting was by no means over. There was constant probing by both sides, and on Saturday, June 4, a heavy attack was made on Finegan's piece of the breastworks, none of which amounted to much. The Confederates also attempted to dislodge elements of the Federal II Corps that were within talking distance, with little good result. Those men were trapped too closely to the bristling enemy defenses to try to organize a withdrawal, and greeted any probing by the Southerners with blasting fire. Charles Banes of the Philadelphia Brigade told:

> Several times during the day attempts were made by the enemy to dislodge them [elements of a division of the II Corps], and their officers could be heard urging their men to "advance and capture the few hundred Yankees"; but each assault met a deadly repulse.[45]

A few had been able to sneak away from the dangerous front. One of those was George E. Place from XVIII Corps' 12th New Hampshire. He wrote:

> I reached the field hospital, and sat down among a group of wounded men, so as to get my wounds dressed. As I raised my eyes,

I saw that I was seated near an amputating table. The spectacle was too harrowing, and I arose to go away, but immediately grew faint, and had to sit down again. I was compelled to sit there nearly an hour before my condition would allow me to go away. Twice during the time I was there, a load of arms, legs, hands, and feet were carried off on a shelter tent and dumped into a ravine.[46]

Despite Hancock's appeals, Grant made no official attempt to secure a halt to the hostilities until Sunday, June 5. No clear explanation has ever been given for that delay. Lyman of Meade's staff said that Meade sent for him at three that afternoon and said that he wanted the Colonel to take a letter from Grant under a flag of truce to the Confederate lines and that Hancock would give him the directions. Lyman's story continued:

I received the order as if my employment had been that from early youth, and proceeded at once to array myself in "store" clothes, sash, white gloves, and all other possible finery. After searching in vain for a bugler who could blow a "parley," I set forth with only a personable and well-dressed cavalry sergeant, and found the gallant Hancock reposing on his cot. "Well, Colonel," says H., "now you can't carry it out on my front. It's too hot there. Your best bet is to go to the left, where there are only pickets, and the officers there will get it out." So the ever-laborious Major Mitchell was summoned and told to provide some whiskey for the Rebs and a flag...there seemed to be nothing white about, except the General's shirt, but at last he found a pillow case which was ripped and put on a staff...then we made our way towards the left and found General Birney's men moving that way, who furnished us information about the road and a guide, Colonel Hapgood of the 5th New Hampshire, corps officer of the day....He was ornamented with a bullet hole through his hat, another through the trousers, and a third on his sword scabbard. We rode till we struck the breastwork at Miles's Headquarters...

There, in a maze of tunnels and cellars, officers lounged about writing and talking. One, identified as Colonel R. Hamyl, asked Lyman if he knew where he was going. He was then guided through some trees and cautioned about the sharp-shooting from the tallest grove. They swiftly rode at a gallop to a place where enemy pickets could be seen barely a hundred yards away. A Federal lieutenant called out and got one of the Southerners to come over. Word was sent down each picket-line that a flag of truce was going in.

Then we left our horses and went forward, the sergeant carrying the flag...we came upon their party, standing some paces off. It
was exactly like a scene in an opera...On the road stood a couple of
Rebel officers, each in his grey overcoat, and just behind, a group of
some twenty soldiers – the most gipsy-looking men imaginable; in
their blue-grey jackets and slouched hats; each with his rusty musket and well-filled cartridge-box. I...was introduced to Major Wooten
of the 14th North Carolina sharpshooters, belonging to A. P. Hill's
Corps...I am free to confess that the bearing of the few Rebel officers I have met is superior to the average of our own. They have a
slight reserve and an absence of all flippancy...They get this I think
partly from the great hardships they suffer, or, still more, the hardships of those at home, and from a sense of ruin if their cause fails.
We attack, and our people live in great plenty, with no one to make
them afraid; it makes a great difference...

Lyman then had to wait while the Confederate officer took his
message away. He was amazed to see the pickets of both sides begin a
truce of their own, meeting and talking until an officer broke up the
sudden friendliness. Just then, someone shot a rifle, and there was a
blaze and roar of musketry reverberating down the line. Now officers
from both sides began to yell, cautioning their men to hold fire. The
whole procedure took until after ten at night, when a Confederate
major returned and sent Lyman away, telling him that an answer to
the message would come through the pickets later. He wrote on his
return to II Corps headquarters:

So we shook hands with the Rebs and retreated from the unsa-
vory position...I kept on to camp, where the General greeted me
with: "Hullo, Lyman, I thought perhaps the Rebs had gobbled you
during that attack."[47]

※ ※ ※ ※ ※

The first message sent to Lee from Grant read:

Cold Harbor
June 5, 1864

General R. E. Lee
Commanding Confederate Army.

It is reported to me that there are wounded men, probably of
both armies, now lying exposed and suffering between the lines

occupied respectively by the two armies. Humanity would dictate that some provision should be made to provide against such hardships. I would propose, therefore, that hereafter, when no battle is raging, either party be authorized to send to any point between the pickets or skirmish lines, unarmed men bearing litters to pick up their dead and wounded, without being fired upon by either party. Any other method, equally fair to both parties, you may propose for meeting the end desired will be accepted by me.

U. S. Grant,[48]
Lieut. - General

Lee's answer came through the picket lines several minutes after midnight:

Gen. U. S. Grant:

I fear that such an arrangement will lead to misunderstanding and difficulty. I propose therefore, instead, that when either party desires to remove their dead or wounded, a flag of truce be sent, as is customary. It will always afford me pleasure to comply with such a request as far as circumstances will permit.

Gen. R. E. Lee[49]

The Confederate commander was not about to agree to a suggestion that did not follow normal procedure. McMahon said that: "A commander who sends a flag of truce asking permission to bury his dead and bring in his wounded has lost the battle. Hence the resistance on our part to ask for a flag of truce." Hancock's Chief-of-Staff accused both men for delay "based on something akin to points of etiquette." Conditions were becoming more horrendous every hour. On June 6, John B. Jones in Richmond wrote:

Yesterday, I learn, both sides buried the dead, with the exception of some Federals piled up in front of Lee's breastworks. A deserter says that Grant intends to stink Lee out of his position, if nothing else will suffice.[50]

Grant tried again the next day:

Your communication of yesterday's date is received. I will send immediately, as you propose, to collect the dead and wounded between the lines of both armies, and will instruct that you be allowed to do the same. I propose...between the hours of 12 p.m. and 3 p.m. to-day. I will direct all parties going out to bear a white flag, and not attempt to go beyond where we have dead or wounded, and not beyond or on ground occupied by your troops.[51]

Lee's answer showed that reaching an agreement was not going to be easy. "I regret that I did not make myself understood in my communication...," Lee began, refusing for a second time this informal gathering of the dead and wounded in some gentlemen's agreement. A flag of truce must be requested, in the usual way. Lee added that any parties that Grant sent out would be turned back. Grant tried again that evening, writing:

> The knowledge that wounded men are now suffering from want of attention, between the two armies, compels me to ask for a suspension of hostilities for sufficient time to collect them in, say, two hours...[52]

The Confederate commander received the more suitably worded request at about seven that evening. He suggested that the truce period be set at between six and ten o'clock, but his message did not get to Grant before midnight. After continued fumbling, during which a group of North Carolina men were captured after going in to look for some of their own officers lost on June 1, the deal was struck. The formal suspension of hostilities was set at the hours between six and eight o'clock in the evening of June 7, a full six days since the 2nd Connecticut Heavy Artillery had been slaughtered against the Southern earthworks. Their bright blue uniforms still distinguished their blackened and swollen bodies.

✷ ✷ ✷ ✷ ✷

The nine Confederates who had been taken captive on the evening of June 6 were ordered by Meade to be taken back at once under a flag of truce. The risky task of returning those men of the 8th and 25th North Carolina to their comrades in the dark night fell to later Brigadier General Thomas Hyde of the 7th Maine regiment. He told:

> How to make a flag of truce visible I did not know, but the order was imperative, so I took them to our first division, General Russell's...Russell said there was no way to get them over, but I pushed them on to the first line, the Jersey brigade under Penrose. They were lying down and firing as hard as they could at the enemy's

pits in the dark some two hundred yards off and the enemy was returning the fire with interest. Indeed the same thing was going on for some three miles, and it would have been impossible for anything to live between those rows of breastworks. I asked Penrose to stop his fire and see if the rebels would stop, and sure enough in a little while they did...At last I climbed over the works and stepped out into the unknown darkness beyond. Penrose came too, and when we had groped some hundred yards I sang out, "I want to see the commander of the rebel line!" "Say Confederate, for God's sake," said Penrose. I repeated my call and it was answered, "What do you want?" I told the reason of my coming, and they said, "wait till we communicate with General Lee." Now there was nothing to do but wait...If any irresponsible party fired his gun...there would be no chance whatever for me. So I crouched in a half-filled grave and waited, despite the stench and horror of it all. It seemed like hours before anyone came...and all the time black forms seemed to be encircling me in the blacker darkness...At last two of these black forms proved real, and were the colonel and his adjutant of a Mississippi regiment commanding the brigade just in front. I soon told my story, and we sat down on the ground and exchanged supplies and stories for a time. Then I went back for my nine rebels, and we had to put them out by force over the rifle-pits, they so dreaded the chance of the fire beginning. Right glad I was to see the last of them, as at two o'clock in the morning I wended my way through the zig-zags to a dusty resting place beside the standard of the 6th Corps. The roar of musketry was going on everywhere else as far as I could see, but Penrose's front was quite still, according to the arrangement with the Mississippi colonel.[53]

The Southern line officers had received the word from Lee that they were to allow Federal burial crews to work unmolested under their white flags. His circular order specified the hours from six to eight in the evening and warned against any fraternization with the enemy units. That part of the specifics was promptly violated, as men from both sides climbed over the breastworks unrestrained. Soldiers from Georgia units traded tobacco for knives and coffee, the latter being one of the more precious and unavailable items for a Confederate anywhere. Edwin Haynes of the 10th Vermont said:

> Many officers of these contending armies sprang over the high entrenchments to witness the bloody work they had done. Enemies met as friends. There was no boasting, no brandying of words – the event was too solemn for jokes between those who had fought with such stern bravery so long. No one can adequately describe the scene here presented. Hundreds of dead men, and many wounded

and helpless...lay stretched along between these lines that were in some places not more than one hundred and twenty yards apart, reaching from Totopotomoy Creek to the Chickahominy River. Some had lain here dead since they fell, six days before, but now swollen and torn by the leaden and iron tempest that had swept over and beaten around them...so that as to be scarcely recognizable by friends who eagerly sought them. There were some wounded, who yet survived all the shocks that meted death to so many others...The dead were hastily buried or taken away; then the sublime hour, an hour of peace, when the earth was calm and the air so still that the gods of war slept – was at an end, friends were enemies again, and they hurried back to renew the carnage.[54]

A II Corps officer described one poor man who said he had survived by sucking the dew from and eating the grass that he was able to pull close by him. There were very few fallen men still alive by now. A soldier from the 19th Massachusetts was brought in with six bullet wounds; he had been out there in the field of dead for four days. The great numbers of decaying bodies required fast remedy, and most were interred right where they had fallen. Hagood of Hoke's division wrote:

> The burial parties were in most instances unable to handle the dead, corruption had extended so far, and contented themselves with covering as it lay each body with a slight mound of earth.[55]

Derby of the 27th Massachusetts offered:

> The granting of the truce was a necessity rather than a virtue. Along the lines white flags were flying, and the enemy, with little else to do, were lounging about, with coarse and unfeeling jokes, such as, "You uns got it right smart, I reckon'....The ground was strewn with bloated and discolored forms, every feature so distorted that recognition from this source was impossible... The recognition of the private soldiers was almost impossible from the similarity of uniforms, excessive decomposition, and the great haste required. Unless papers or ornaments on their persons revealed their identity, they were buried as "Unknown." Now and then some poor wounded one was found, in all the horrors of a living death. For four long days and nights they had remained upon that field, with ghastly wounds, without food, water or care, and surrounded by remains exuding a stifling stench...So the work was chiefly with the dead. Long trenches were dug, in which they were laid side by side, with such winding sheets as their blankets afforded. As the sepulchral work progressed, the notes of a dirge, unutterably mournful and sad, came floating over the field from the bands within our

lines. This requiem was our only service for the dead. The utmost haste failed to entomb the immense mass of our slain, before a signal-gun gave notice that the "truce had expired." At the next gun the dogs of war would be let loose upon any remaining in the field, and hence our burial detail hastily retired. A few moments later we were again engaged in the deadly fray. Those comrades participating in the burial were so overcome by the stench as to be unfit for duty for several days.[56]

As soon as the signal was given that the truce period was over, the troops from both armies that had relaxed and mingled on the burial ground made quick escape over their respective fortifications. Many witnesses said that the atmosphere of the truce continued on into the night, and that firing along the fronts was subdued. However, Private Lewis Bissell of the 2nd Connecticut observed:

> This afternoon a flag of truce was ordered up between the Rebs and us. Our men went halfway, shook hands with the Rebs and exchanged bacon for papers. A rebel sharpshooter and one of our own shook hands but just as soon as they returned to their trenches, they began to fire at each other...[57]

Chapter Eleven

Part One
The Departure

"The 8th of June was a beautiful day, but very hot and severe for the boys in the rifle-pits. At night the military bands of both armies played. The Union bands played The Star Spangled Banner, Red, White, and Blue, and Yankee Doodle, while the Rebel bands gave us Dixie and The Bonnie Blue Flag."

- Private Samuel Putnam[1]
25th Massachusetts

"June 4, Saturday. Many delegates to the Convention in town. Some attempts by members of Congress to influence them...There has been continued fighting, though represented as unimportant. Still there is heavy loss, but we are becoming accustomed to the sacrifice. Grant has not great regard for human life."

- Gideon Welles[2]
U.S. Secretary of the Navy

"The fat bacon and onions brought in at that time from Nassau were very cheering to the flesh, and the almost prodigal charity with which several brigades contributed their rations to the suffering poor of Richmond was a striking tale...but there was a somber tinge to the soldier wit in our thin ranks which expressed itself in the homely phrase, 'What is the use of killing these Yankees? it is like killing mosquitoes - two come for every one you kill'."

- Colonel Charles Venable[3]
Staff Officer

"I think that Grant has had his eyes opened, and is willing to admit now that Virginia and Lee's army is not Tennessee and Bragg's army."

- Major General George Meade[4]
Army of the Potomac

"My Dear Father...June 5, Everything is going on gloriously for us and I think this campaign will virtually close the war. Yesterday the Yanks charged our works six times and were repulsed with a loss of about 8,000 killed and wounded to our only 500. At such odds I think we should exterminate them instead of their exterminating us..."

- Private James Bryant[5]
13th Virginia Cavalry

The armies remained in their tentative battle positions for nearly two weeks after the fateful assault at Cold Harbor. There was to be very little relief from the drudgeries of trench life in all that time. The general truce on June 7 had allowed some troops to stand without flinching and shake out their insect-infested blankets. The filth and fatigue was heavy upon the Union men who had taken the worst beating of the war, and were captive in the ditches around what had become a vast cemetery. One soldier from the 115th New York Infantry wrote, "A fellow sufferer very truly remarked that we are in a very bad state - the state of Virginia."[6] Brigadier General Lysander Cutler's division of the V Corps was taken out of the line for some respite on that quiet front and the commander said that he himself had not had a decent night's sleep nor a change of clothes since May 5.

The men dug deeper into the clay until they could live virtually underground, and the deeper they went the more useless those burrows became for any offensive action. Their trenches were in places so close together to the opposing combatants that they could eavesdrop on each other's conversations. The survival-minded built passageways to add protection from the unmerciful sniping while they traveled from one line to another. Lewis Bissell of the 2nd Connecticut Heavy Artillery wrote on June 4:

> Our troops are at work digging out the rebels. They are entrenched in woods in rather swampy ground. If we should have a long rain and the Chickahominy should rise, it would drown them out. Yesterday our troops were so close to them that they threw stones at each other, but when they get the chance, they shoot.[7]

The boredom ranked beside sniping as the worst aspect of trench life. A Virginia soldier, Gustavus A. Myers, on June 6 wrote in a letter to his father in Richmond:

> Much fagged by the campaign...the line here is by far the most harrassing of the war. We have had a brisk fight on our lines this morning (3rd) and repulsed the enemy after they had driven us partially back...send me my mail and some postage stamps. Send me something to read...I am safe so far. Please send three bottles of whiskey.[8]

At night, life on the fronts was more active than in the deadly daytime. Digging and clearing went on as the breastworks were improved. There were frequent volleys of musket fire and throbbing cannon salvos that did very little damage but made rest impossible. One detested new weapon was the Coehorn mortar. Those were squat tubs of iron, introduced during the fighting around Spotsylvania, that shot projectiles at high arcs that could come down anywhere on the line. The defenders had no warning of smoke or noise.

The days were records of meaningless deaths from sniper fire and accidents. A Massachusetts regiment lost thirteen men to a misfired artillery charge.[9] And of course, the sharp-shooting never ceased. Captain John Anderson of the 57th Massachusetts wrote of one encounter:

> One Confederate sentry was particularly annoying; he kept busy all the time loading and firing from behind a tree. I [Anderson] shot him, and after he fell others thought that he was just "playing possum" and began shooting at him...He was found riddled with bullets. After the first shot, it little reckoned to him whether it be one or a million. He had passed beyond being an enemy.[10]

Chief of Artillery Alexander told of an attempt to see John Gregg of Field's division:

> Within 100 yards of the tree I began to stoop and got within 50 when I stopped awhile to rest...to decide whether to crawl the distance or make dash...I made the dash successfully, not being fired on that I was aware of, I jumped headlong into the hole. I landed between two dead Texans, each shot through the head, a third one, alive and well, was squatted in a corner. He did not change his attitude, but smiled and said sociably, "By Gosh! You has to be mighty careful how you shows a head around here, or they'll get you certain! Thar's two they got this morning!"[11]

On the far left of Lee's positions, there was some effort to push at Burnside and Warren coming from Ramseur of Early's corps. On the 6th and again on the 7th of June, an attempt was made to turn the IX Corps flank by crossing a branch called the Matadequin Creek. Both movements were called to a halt when the swampy terrain prevented reinforcements from coming up from Field's division. On June 9, another attempt was made to dislodge Colonel William Truex's brigade of Ricketts' division, but nothing came of that effort either.

For Lee's veterans, the great job had been accomplished. They were given improved rations and were content to wait, as they had been, for the Federals to make the next fatal move. There were reports of Union infiltration towards the fords on the Chickahominy. Journalist William Swinton told:

When a rebel newsman suggested that Grant might move down the Chickahominy to try crossing at White Oak Swamp, Lee's veterans were exultant in the thought of the earthwork defenses that the Union troops would have to assail.[12]

The behavior seemed entirely uninspired on the parts of both forces. There was very little left of that warriors' spirit that had carried the Army of the Potomac the fifty-five miles from Brandy Station to the Peninsula. The Union men would not again risk themselves hopelessly, at least not here at Cold Harbor.

Emory Upton spoke for many when he wrote:

Headquarters Second Brigade
June 5, 1864

My Dear Sister:
    We are now at Cold Harbor, where we have been since June 1st. On that day we made a murderous engagement. I say murderous, because we were recklessly ordered to assault the enemy's entrenchments, knowing neither their strength nor position. Our loss was very heavy, and to no purpose. Our men are brave, but cannot accomplish impossibilities. My brigade lost about three hundred men. My horse was killed, but I escaped unharmed. Since June 1st we have been behind rifle-pits, about three hundred yards from the enemy. A constant fusillade from both sides has been kept up, and, though little damage has been done, it is, nevertheless, very annoying.

    I am very sorry to say I have seen but little generalship during the campaign. Some of our corps commanders are not fit to be corporals. Lazy and indolent, they will not even ride along their lines; yet, without hesitancy, they will order us to attack the enemy, no matter what their position or numbers. Twenty thousand of our killed and wounded should be today in our ranks. But I will cease fault-finding, and express the hope that mere numbers will yet enable us to enter Richmond.[13]

Brigadier General James Harrison Wilson commanded one of Sheridan's cavalry divisions and had been posted at the far right of the Federal army since June 2. His troopers had been tearing up railroad tracks to the west and had arrived to hook up with Burnside on the Totopotomoy flank. Wilson had been an aide to McClellan on the ill-fated campaign in the area two years before. He had served on Grant's staff at both Vicksburg and Chattanooga as an engineer. He was a young, impatient West-Pointer who had known some glory and would find more to come. He would be the cavalry commander to finally defeat Nathan B. Forrest the next year and would personally capture the fleeing Jefferson Davis in April of 1865. He came into Grant's headquarters camp on June 7 and was stunned to see the disarray in command. He first met Meade who was swatting his boots with a crop and pacing in front of the command tent. Meade came over to Wilson and stared into his face, looking uneasy and unsure. He then asked without any explanation, "Wilson, when is Grant going to take Richmond?" The young cavalry officer had a startled response for the field commander of the mighty Army of the Potomac. "Whenever the generals and troops in this theater all work together to that end," was all he could find to say.

Wilson went on toward Grant's headquarters. In the privacy of his tent, Grant asked the young trooper:

> "Wilson, what is the matter with this army?" Wilson responded, "Sir, there is a good deal the matter - so much that it would hardly do to go into detail - but I can suggest a good remedy. Take Parker, the Indian, [Col. Ely Parker of Grant's staff] and give Parker a scalping knife and a tomahawk, fill him up with the worst commissary whiskey available, and send him to bring in the scalps of a number of major generals." "Which ones?" Grant asked laughingly. "That did not matter much," said Wilson, "Just tell Parker to attack the first ones he comes to and not quit til he's scalped at least half a dozen. After that you will have a better army."[14]

That same Colonel Parker would later in life become the Commissioner on Indian Affairs under President Grant, and there exists no record of his scalping activities at Cold Harbor.

Grant's staff was relatively small, numbering about twelve on average. His old friend and mentor was Colonel John Rawlins, a tee-totaller who tried to keep Grant sober and often won and lost the battle. Wilson had once said that Rawlins was the one most indispensable man in Grant's entourage. Even he did not know at the time that Rawlins had developed fatal tuberculosis that was sapping away his energies. Grant's friend from the early days was beginning to lose his influence by now, superseded by other young hard-liners such as the domineering Comstock. Wilson was told by both Rawlins and Charles Dana that that young officer was a harsh influence on Grant and a man who had an insatiable appetite for desperate charges against heavily fortified entrenchments.[15]

By the second week of June 1864, the most reliable and balanced hand in the high echelon of Grant's command was Meade's Chief-of-Staff, Andrew Humphreys. That officer would succeed to command of Hancock's II Corps in a few months when fatigue and aggravation of his old wound would force even that warrior to step aside. Humphreys gave a succinct view of what some Federal commanders, Gibbon included, said were the hardest of the entire campaign:

> The daily skirmishing during this time was sharp and caused severe loss in some divisions; during the nights there was heavy artillery firing, and sometimes heavy musketry. The labor in making the approaches and strengthening the intrenchments was hard. The men in the advanced part of the lines, which were some miles in length, had to lie close in narrow trenches with no water except a little to drink, and that being the worst kind, being from surface drainage; they were exposed to great heat during the day; they had but little sleep; their cooking was of the rudest character. For over a month the army had had no vegetables and the beef used was from cattle exhausted by the long march through a country scantily provided with forage. Dead horses and mules and offal were scattered over the country, and between the lines were many dead bodies of both parties lying unburied in a burning sun. The country was low and marshy in character. The exhausting effect of all this began to show itself and sickness of malaria increased largely. Every effort was made to correct this; large quantities of vegetables were brought up to the army, and a more stringent police enforced...At the close of day on June 3rd, there were many of our wounded lying between the lines, very near the enemy's entrenchments, completely covered by the fire of his pickets and sharpshooters. But our men made extraordinary efforts by night to get in their wounded comrades, and so far succeeded that very few were left. There were many dead of both sides lying there unburied, and Gen. Grant proposed an arrangement for bringing in the wounded and burying the dead. This proposition was made on the afternoon of the 5th, but no cessation of hostilities took place for that purpose until the afternoon of the 7th, when a truce was agreed upon from 6 to 8 in the evening. Very few wounded were collected. Of those not brought in at night by their comrades, the greater number had died of their wounds and exposure. The dead were buried where they lay.[16]

✵ ✵ ✵ ✵ ✵

Andrews, like his fellow commanders, was still grimly hopeful that the horrific losses of the Army of the Potomac were somehow matched by the Southern army. Casualty figures at Cold Harbor are difficult to determine accurately even for the better-documented Northern forces. No trustworthy estimation of Confederate losses had ever been calculated until Alfred Young computed figures using the *Official Records and Dyer's Compendium*. The total of General Lee's losses from June 1 to June 12 was: 3,765 killed and wounded and 1,082 captured or missing, adding up to 4,847.

Losses for the Army of the Potomac have been calculated by several reliable historians. The most reasonable are given by Hancock's biographer, Glenn Tucker. Tucker's figures from June 1 to June 12 were: killed and wounded, 10,971, and 1,816 missing, totaling 12,787. In comparison, Hancock's losses from II Corps at Gettysburg had been 4,194 while at Cold Harbor the corps had sustained 3,510. Of that number, six colonels and forty-six officers of lower rank died of wounds in battle.[17] The story of loss was repeated with heartbreaking regularity from corps down to individual regiments. Private Samuel Putnam said of the 25th Massachusetts:

> The Twenty-Fifth landed at Bermuda Hundred on the 5th of May with seven hundred splendid veterans. One month's fighting in the rear of Richmond reduced this number to a trifle over three hundred; and the morning after the Battle of Cold Harbor (June 4th) there were only one hundred men fit for duty. "The Gallant six hundred," where were they? Killed, wounded, in hospital, and down in Southern prisons. This war and its deplorable results...[18]

Even units that had been spared the suffering of June 3 had much to lament. Lieutenant Colonel Stephen Weld of V Corps wrote about his 56th Massachusetts regiment:

> Our men are pretty used up by this campaign. Officers as well as men need rest, and I hope we shall get it before long. A great many of our men are without shoes and most all of them are in rags... I never knew before what campaigning was. I think, though, that all this army have a pretty fair idea of it now. We have had to march all day and all night, ford rivers, bivouac without blankets or covering during rain and sunshine, and a good deal of the time have been half-starved. I know that no one staying at home can have any idea of what this army has been through... We have lost 300 men killed, wounded, and missing since the beginning of the campaign. The missing amount to about 30 or 40 men, many of them killed and wounded. I have but 250 men for duty now, rather a contrast to the size of the regiment when we left...[19]

The 27th Massachusetts regiment was on the line throughout the ordeal of Cold Harbor. On June 9, one man said that their position was within pistol-shot of the enemy and that shells from both sides grazed their heads. They were detailed as sharp-shooters, and made quick work of pin-pointing their Confederate counterparts in the trees. There at least they were doing something visible toward the effort, and were soon themselves in the trees and picking off any rebel unwise enough to show his head. William Derby wrote:

> To narrate the experiences of each day would be to repeat the story of marchings and counter-marchings from front to rear, and from right to left, subjected to a fire which was hardly less annoying at the rear than at the front. "Spent balls" at the rear were glancing and ricocheting in every direction, and the "mortar shells" dropping where and when least expected; from neither of which could we find full protection. At the front the shots came direct, and, with watchfulness, the rifle-pits were effective against them. There is no doubt that our terrible repulse had given Gen'l Lee's army new courage and prestige. Flaming telegrams and dispatches were constantly being sent to Richmond, recounting the courage and victories of their troops, with the terrible carnage suffered by the Yankees. On the evening of June 9th, a rebel band in Longstreet's corps came to the front, and in a tantalizing way discoursed their national airs, which were responded to by Union bands with our national airs and "Rally Round the Flag." This music was as good as medicine to our worn troops...[20]

※ ※ ※ ※ ※

On the evening of June 3, Grant had actually announced at his staff meeting:

> I regret this assault more than any one I ever ordered. I regarded it as a stern necessity, and believed that it would bring compensating results; but, as it has been proved, no advantages have been gained sufficient to justify the heavy losses suffered...[21]

While encamped on the dreary Peninsula, the counting of losses from the last thirty days of fighting was more than enough to depress the Union commanders and their private soldiers equally. While the men in the line buried friends one at a time, Grant and Meade had done the undertaking for many thousands since crossing the Rapidan. Researcher Bryce Suderow estimates that total Federal losses for Grant's Virginia campaign before Petersburg, based on Dyer's *Compendium of*

The War of the Rebellion, as well as tables offered by individual commanders in the *Official Records*, at just less than 55,000.[22] William Swinton, the Confederacy's favorite Northern historian, concluded the total to be closer to 62,000. Since he was out to embarrass Grant whenever possible, few trust his enumeration. Brigadier General Richard Drum, Adjutant-General of the Army of the Potomac, based on incomplete records gathered soon after the war, arrived at the figure of 54,929.[23] The hard marching and combat, at a disgusting rate of attrition of nearly 2,000 men a day, had taken Grant's army to the wasteland at Cold Harbor so close to Richmond but still decidedly outside.

Several Federal units whose terms of service were finished were due to muster out while they crouched in the trenches. The Pennsylvania Reserves, 9th Massachusetts, 4th Ohio, 14th Indiana, 3rd Maine, 2nd Rhode Island Artillery – all had been sent out, more than a few scuttling from the entrenchments on their hands and knees – by June 8. More fresh regiments were coming in. While the burial details were shoveling in a race with the clock on June 7, Grant received a message from Halleck in Washington that sounded like a bill coming past due:

> I inclose a list of troops forwarded from this department to the Army of the Potomac since the campaign opened – 48,265 men. I shall send you a few regiments more, when all resources will be exhausted till another draft is made.[24]

That official message was disappointing if not embarrassing for Grant. He had been receiving conscripts to replace his veterans and was now running low on both. Halleck was bringing him to task that his campaigning had been costly beyond consideration to the War Department and President Lincoln for whom a new "draft-call" would be equally embarrassing so close to election time.

Undaunted by numbers, Grant was already writing his orders and developing his next schemes. He sent Sheridan and two cavalry divisions toward Charlottesville to link up with Brigadier General David Hunter. That officer had taken over from the disgraced Sigel after his setback at New Market. With troops brought in with George Crook, Hunter had defeated a small force of Confederates near Staunton, Virginia, on June 5 and had killed Lee's old friend, Brigadier General William "Grumble" Jones.

For Grant, it was time to leave the great cemetery of Cold Harbor behind and get back to business. Colonel Cyrus Comstock of the headquarters staff sulked that Grant's army was only wasting time at Cold Harbor. Amazing in his power of concentration, Grant ordered Meade to begin construction of an inner line to assist in the movements of Warren's V Corps to the left toward the Chickahominy. A fleet of transports was arriving at White House Landing and another fleet of barges and warships was assembled at Fort Monroe with a large supply of pontoons in readiness. The more he sat in his tent amid the stench and rubble of Cold Harbor, the more convinced Grant was that another movement and a new campaign would bring desired results. The alternative would be to stay put, and was not agreeable to the Federal field command whatsoever. He sent Halleck the sketch of his next plan, which called for yet another side-movement across the Chickahominy and the colossal task of moving at least William F. Smith's corps and perhaps some units from Meade's army across the great James River itself to combine with Butler. They would then mount an assault to envelope the port city of Petersburg. Grant did not discuss the fact that had a real general been in command of Butler's forces earlier, that "gateway" to Richmond would already be taken and the Confederate capital shut off from access to the Carolinas and Georgia. Grant wrote the War Department on June 5:

> My idea from the start has been to beat Lee's army, if possible, north of Richmond. After thirty days of trial I have decided that without greater sacrifice of human life than I am willing to make, all cannot be accomplished that I had designed outside of that city...[25]

Halleck was against the whole idea. The President's military Chief-of-Staff took to heart Meade's warning that another brutal loss would render the Army of the Potomac unfit for any effective use. "Old Brains" was looking over the balance sheets of human power and becoming more concerned than ever. He much preferred the less risky, methodical investment of Richmond from the Federal positions north of that city. Halleck could not rationalize the enormous costs of the previous month's maneuvering by seeing Grant withdraw and expose his army to the threat of being caught in mid-crossing on the James. As well, the one saving grace of Grant's positioning had been to keep his mighty force between Lee and Washington. It would be unsettling to allow Lee to shift strategy again and threaten the national capital in the middle of Lincoln's reelection efforts. Many of the previous defenders of Washington's barricades, the unfortunate "heavy artillery" regiments, were at that moment being put to rest under Virginia soil.

Ulysses S. Grant had made his mind up. He called in two of his devoted, reliable aides, Porter and Comstock, and sent them south toward the old battleground at Malvern Hill to reconnoitre the region. Both of those young men had made that journey with McClellan in 1862. Grant sought their assistance as engineers in deciding on crossing points a safe distance down on the Chickahominy and also in designating the site for a pontoon bridge across the broad James River. They were to take orders to Butler at Bermuda Hundred to begin operations against Petersburg as soon as the Army of the Potomac began to make its withdrawal from Cold Harbor. Great motions were being touched into life as the "New Campaign."

✳ ✳ ✳ ✳ ✳

George Meade had never had very warm relations with the press. He was rarely satisfied that he was being treated with fairness. Since the botched offensive at Mine Run the previous autumn, his military sense had been the subject of many editorials in New York and in his native Philadelphia. Meade's temper was legendary; he was quite sensitive about the perceptions in the North of his position in command, or sub-command, of the army with Grant. By June 7 he was in a manic state of nerves and depression. Whatever Grant was about to do, Meade was not taken into confidence. "Baldy" Smith said years later that Meade actually told him that every single movement from the Rapidan onward had been his own doing, and that he was tired of the papers talking only of "Grant's army" and that he would be happy to allow Grant to plan his own battles.[26] In such a fretful mood, Meade read a copy of *The Philadelphia Inquirer* from June 2.

Correspondent Edward Crapsey, who had been with the army all through Cold Harbor, had written an editorial letter to the *Inquirer* in which he attempted to set the public straight on the relationship between Meade and Grant. In his introductory notes Crapsey wrote:

> Let me break the narrative again, and say a word of Meade's position. He is as much the commander of the Army of the Potomac as he ever was. Grant plans and exercises a supervisory control over the army, but to Meade belongs everything of detail...in a word, he commands the army. General Grant is here only because he deems the present campaign the vital one of the war...History will record, but newspapers cannot, that on one eventful night during the present campaign Grant's presence saved the army, and the nation too; not that General Meade was on the point of committing a blunder unwittingly, but his devotion to his country made him loathe to risk her last army on what he deemed a chance. Grant assumed the responsibility, and we are still on to Richmond.[27]

Meade reacted quickly and called Crapsey to his tent, demanding an explanation. Crapsey repeated the story to Meade's face, a story that had followed the army through Virginia the last month and had been repeated countless times: Meade, after the second day in the Wilderness, with both flanks splintered and having barely escaped a total wrecking from Anderson's charge that evening, had recommended the withdrawal of the Federal army back across the Rapidan. Only General Grant had maintained the course and continued the war. "It was simply the talk of the camp," said Crapsey. Meade grew angrier with each word. He ordered the arrest of the news reporter and wrote up a general order that Crapsey be tossed out of the camp with all due discourtesy.

Provost Marshall General Marsena Patrick was ordered the next day to place Crapsey on muleback, backwards and with a placard around his neck that read, "Libeler of the Press." With loud cheering by all witnesses, the unfortunate reporter was driven out of the Federal sanctuary. He went straight to Washington and began to present his case to his newspaper friends, who were shocked and fearful about such treatment to one of their own. An agreement was struck that Meade's name would be omitted from all news dispatches by any newspaper correspondent unless he was associated with a defeat. Whitelaw Reid of *The Cincinnati Gazette* said that, "Meade is as leprous with moral cowardice as the brute who kicks a helpless cripple on the street...He does not care to grapple with newspapers that hint at the truth about him...that had Gen. Grant permitted him to control the motions of the Army of the Potomac, it would have retreated across the Rapidan after the battles of the Wilderness..."[28] Sylvanus Cadwallader of *The New York Herald* wrote:

> It was soon returned that Gen. Meade's name was never again to appear if it could be omitted, and that any official or general order important enough to be publicly reported would have Meade's signature left off, and the name of Gen. Grant substituted...Meade was quite as much unknown, by any correspondence from the army, as any dead hero of antiquity. [29]

The man who eleven months before was known as the hero of Gettysburg and who had even been mentioned as a possible candidate for President, would never recover politically. His military reputation rests primarily on his contributions in early July 1863 and fairly or not, the rest is merely supposition.

President Lincoln had in all appearances abdicated his role as commander-in-chief with pleasure. Still, he was kept personally informed of the fate of his army at Cold Harbor by Henry Wing of *The New York Tribune*. After the terrible assault of June 3, Wing came to

Washington to deliver his dispatches and resign from war service. His old wound from Fredericksburg had left him partially a cripple, and the pain was excruciating. As well, Wing was dazed from what he had witnessed at Cold Harbor, and tried to avoid telling Lincoln anything about it. He was called in by Lincoln while at the bureau, and reluctantly made a visit.

It had been three weeks since Lincoln had kissed Henry Wing for bringing word from the Wilderness. There were no such informalities as Lincoln met with Wing alone one evening. The newsman decided to spill everything that censorship would have forbidden putting in writing. He told the President of the assaulting that amounted to sheer murder. He grimly told of the struggles to shift blame and the petty quarreling among high command while men rotted on the field. He told Lincoln of his walking among the dead, looking for Connecticut boys that he knew that could be identified for notice back home, and he explained in graphic terms the marching and digging and dying that the Union army was enduring.[30]

So, Lincoln knew as much as any objective observer of what had occurred at Cold Harbor. He never expressed his opinion of what had been done or not done, but in a speech three weeks later in Philadelphia, Lincoln alluded to the fighting at Spotsylvania and at Cold Harbor. He repeated his often-stated admission of the war's terrible carnage and duration. He also used Grant's famous line to his own advantage:

> Speaking of the present campaign General Grant is reported to have said: I am going through on this line if it takes all summer...I say we are going through on this line if it takes three years more.[31]

Part Two
Toward the James

On June 7, Warren's V Corps had begun to shift, pulling out from behind their entrenchments and sliding across the rear of the three other corps until the forward regiments had gone five miles. The 118th Pennsylvania was nestled against Sumner's lower bridge on the Chickahominy. Here, there was little firing and soldiers had a chance to look at themselves and try to get cleaned up in the swampy water. John L. Smith of the Corn Exchange Regiment wrote:

> In the constant hard usage of the campaign the clothing was worn almost threadbare; the shoes went through to the ground. Shirts, drawers, and stockings, forlorn and dirty, were mostly beyond washing, and if change was to be made at all, a new issue was essentially necessary. [32]

The quartermasters found those V Corps units, and soon men were bathing in the river and putting on new clothes under and over. At one place, the 118th Pennsylvania troops were directly across the Chickahominy from members of the 35th North Carolina infantry. Smith continued:

> War may arouse bitter antipathies on occasions of actual combat, but when both sides speak the same language...hatred and antagonisms melt...Lone fishermen sat upon either end of the bridge, dangling their lines resultlessly and chatting complacently. In the absence of a mutually acceptable medium of exchange...coffee went for tobacco and hard-tack went for corn-bread. [33]

Things began that last week which would determine the course of the war. While Meade prosecuted journalists and Grant attempted to recover his martial attitude, Abraham Lincoln was renominated by the Republican party as their candidate for the fall elections. He was assured that the election was to be a bitter political struggle, a presidential contest in the midst of a civil war. His managers had joined him to a Southern Unionist, Andrew Johnson, in an appeal to finish the war upon something more than what purely Northern ideals could furnish. No president had won a second term in office since Andrew Jackson in 1832, and there was pitifully little for the candidates to brag about for the race of 1864.

After he learned sadly about the work of Hunter against Staunton, Lee also began to move his pieces around. He informed Breckinridge that he and his two battered brigades were to head toward the next-threatened western city of Lynchburg. The Kentuckian would gather together the survivors of Confederate forces in the Valley and, with his 2,100 men, attempt to check Hunter. Breckinridge agreed, still a bit groggy from a bad fall he'd taken on June 3 when his horse was killed under him.

Before Lee could begin to worry about cutting his line-force by two brigades, he learned that Sheridan and two divisions were also gone toward the Blue Ridge. Lee had nothing but rumors to work with, and on June 8 was told that Hunter's army was doubled by the arrival of Federal forces under Crook and Brigadier General William Averell. He would have to send a larger military force if he hoped to save the Valley and his food supplies; he would also need to send a mobile force to delay Sheridan's troopers.

On the morning of June 9, Wade Hampton and Fitz Lee took almost the entire cavalry component of the Southern army and went after the Union horsemen. Sheridan's mounted columns thundered north and west in a long arc, to Gordonsville and down to Amelia Courthouse. Hampton would strike out directly and catch the larger Federal force at a place called Trevilian Station. In a two-day battle, one of the hottest cavalry engagements of the war, Hampton's riders would solidly out-perform Sheridan and disperse any remaining ghost of Jeb Stuart. Custer's brigade was especially punished. He lost 800 horses his Michiganders had previously captured and even his personal baggage. On June 12, the Federal force would withdraw to the protection of gunboats on the Pamunkey, having lost nearly 1,600 troopers, twice the losses of Sheridan's raid on Richmond.

It was almost at that same time that word reached Lee concerning Major General Nathan B. Forrest's smashing victory at Brices Cross Roads in Mississippi on June 10 and 11. Lee now had some cheerful news to bolster him. However, he was about to lose the Army of the Potomac.

On June 9, alarms were received from Beauregard. An attack had been launched against Petersburg, on schedule, by the still-potent Army of the James. Beauregard had an effective army of fewer than 8,000, and was supplemented by inmates of local jails, over-aged veterans of a retired militia battalion, and the personnel and patients from

Petersburg Hospital. In the "Battle of the Patients and Penitents," Beauregard held out as Brigadier General James Dearing's cavalry units came in and drove off Butler's irresolute assault. Beauregard appealed to the War Department to send back his brigades from Lee's army. He insisted that the enemy's movement had been only the reconnaissance for future operations by Grant's whole army on Petersburg, and he was absolutely right.

On June 10, Lee was informed that Hunter had moved his 20,000 men into Lexington, Virginia, and had committed a wide variety of lootings and burnings of prominent buildings, including Washington College and the Virginia Military Institute. Hunter paid a reverent visit to the grave of "Stonewall" Jackson and promptly burned the nearby home of former Governor John Letcher.

※ ※ ※ ※ ※

While cripples and old men stood holding warm muskets and Hampton's troopers were smashing Custer's cavalry brigade, Lee arrived at one of the most difficult decisions he ever made. On Sunday, June 12, Lee held a short interview with the scraggly, often tempestuous Early. "Old Jube" was told that he would be taking his three divisions of infantry and two of artillery and following Breckinridge to the Shenandoah Valley at daylight the next day. The Army of the Valley would be resurrected, at the cost of one-fourth of Lee's Army of Northern Virginia.

That army had suffered casualties amounting to almost 27,000 since the opening encounter with Federal corps on the Orange Turnpike those first May days. Its commander understood their depleted condition. Lee's officer cadre had been demolished; of 58 general officers in field command on May 4, 23 had gone down into battle, and hardest hit of all was Jackson's old Second Corps that Early was taking back to the Valley. At Spotsylvania the "Dependables" had lost almost an entire division, and now stood at barely 8,000 men, half its original component. The same was true throughout. Of the 12 brigadiers that had been with the Army of Northern Virginia in the first week of May 1864, only one – Cullen Battle of Rodes' division – remained now with the same troops. Two had been promoted to fill vacancies above brigade level, and all the rest had been killed, captured, or grievously wounded. The fifty-five miles through the Wilderness to Cold Harbor had been a graveyard for his most essential, veteran infantry. As well, the month-long defense of the Confederate capital had been the funeral of the Southern high command.[34]

*****

Early's men prepared to leave the Cold Harbor line and be gone from that wretched place before the enemy could detect their movements. Others were also getting ready to leave. On June 12, Grant's two reconnaissance men, Porter and Comstock, returned with the news that a good site for the great pontoon bridge over the James could be found about ten miles downriver from City Point, on a point just beyond Charles City Court House. Grant nervously puffed his cigar while he listened to their report. Horace Porter wrote:

> We could hardly get the words out of our mouths fast enough to suit him, and the numerous questions he asked were uttered with much greater rapidity than usual...At the close of the interview, he informed us that he would begin the movement that night.[35]

At a site called Long Bridge, where the bridge had been burned and the debris was hanging from the banks, Grant and Meade took their staffs and made camp. The site was about ten miles from the far Union left, where the Chickahominy ran shallow and where Wilson began assembling a pontoon bridge for the V Corps, the second section of the Army of the Potomac to leave Cold Harbor. On the evening of June 12, Warren and his corps began their march from the secured battlelines held by VI and II Corps. Those two bodies were kept in a sharp war-footing in case Lee suddenly discovered the shifting of units. For some reason, the leaders in both armies were terrified of a night attack, although there was little evidence that Lee ever tried such a thing. Things along the front had been remarkably quiet for the last several days. Rawlins's official report of June 11 said:

> To-day the silence is more marked than before. The sound of a musket has scarcely been heard along the entire line. A few blurts of artillery, and the explosion of a shell or two over the trees, about the center of the line, have been the only reminders this afternoon of the enemy's presence.[36]

Burnside's IX Corps and Smith's XVIII Corps were pulled back at the same time, soon after dusk. Smith's men were marched backward to White House Landing, where they boarded transports and made haste for Port Walthall, near Petersburg. IX Corps followed him until, perhaps three miles from the Landing, Burnside's force turned and took a wide-arcing road down to the Chickahominy at Jones Bridge.

Once Warren's corps was across the river, after midnight Wright and Hancock took their units out of their entrenchments. Wright's divisions drew straight back and moved beside IX Corps toward Jones Bridge while II Corps followed Warren's men over the pontoons. Warren had orders to turn toward Richmond along the fringes of White Oak Swamp in what appeared to be a threat of advance on the city.

John L. Smith of V Corps wrote a poetic note:

> A few days more rolled leisurely away. Gradually, as if weary of fight, if it were for slaughter only, the gunnery subsided, until at last it seemed to cease entirely. As bright a moon as ever shadowed a Virginia landscape lit the heavens on the night of 12th of June, 1864. Guided by the light of its brilliant radiance, ere the midnight hour had gone, the far-reaching lines from the Matadaquin to the Chickahominy were all abandoned, and, stretching itself towards the James, the old Potomac Army, stiff and doughty as afore, was off for its lengthy grapple on the Appomattox.[37]

By dawn of June 13, the Federal trenches at Cold Harbor were empty. The rear regiments of Wright's VI Corps, the last to leave, left behind the silent rifle-pits and earthworks that men had been shoveling and fortifying up to the final moments. Confederate skirmishers ventured across and into the empty entrenchments. They found an enormous amount of refuse and discarded material that they promptly liberated before telling their commander that they were alone at Cold Harbor. Lee wrote to Secretary Seddon:

> At daybreak this morning it was discovered that the army of Genl Grant had left our front. Our skirmishers were advanced between one and two miles, but failing to discover the enemy were withdrawn, and the army was moved to conform to the route taken by him. He advanced a body of cavalry and some infantry from Long Bridge to Riddle's Shop, which were driven back this evening nearly two miles, after some sharp skirmishing.[38]

Confederate artillery officer Robert Stiles wrote:

> Thus far during the campaign, whenever the enemy was missing, we knew where – that is, in what direction and upon what line to look for him; he was certainly making for a point between us and Richmond. Not so now. Even Marse Robert, who knew everything knowable, did not appear to know what his old enemy proposed to do, or where he was most likely to find him.[39]

By all accounts, Lee had been left without a clue, and much was made by Northern chroniclers of Grant's "stealing a march" on the old man who managed the Confederate efforts. However, Lee was in close touch with Beauregard and with Bragg in Richmond and by the morning of June 14 knew that Grant was taking his forces toward the James precisely where they were to cross. His messages to various commanders made it clear that his only course of action would be to cover Richmond from possible assault and to help organize the defenses at Petersburg. On June 13, Anderson's corps, with Pickett's division attached, was on the Charles City road. As soon as some certainty formed as to Grant's real intentions, by late on June 14, General Lee sent Hoke's division to cross at Drewry's Bluff and rejoin Beauregard.

Alexander wrote:

> On Monday morning, Jun. 13...we waked and found the enemy gone. We were now only two corps; ours, under Anderson, and A. P. Hill's; Early having started after Hunter but the night before. Our corps at that time was about 12,000 strong Hill's probably about 11,000.

> I don't think Grant's movement was anticipated, nor was it discovered until after daylight. But by eight o'clock, I think, we were all in motion to cross the Chickahominy. Hoke's division, which was considered a part of Beauregard's army, was directed to go to Drury's Bluff on the James where we had a pontoon bridge, some ten or twelve miles from Cold Harbor...

Lee was fooled, perhaps to some degree. He had a weary army that amounted to less than one-third the strength of Grant's. Also, he faced Warren's V Corps that seemed to threaten Richmond, not knowing it was isolated and offered to Lee like some apple to pick while the rest of the Federal army moved against Petersburg. Alexander was convinced that failure to crush Warren at Riddle's Shop and the worrying over the feints toward Richmond cost Lee the war. Of Petersburg, he wrote:

> Could our single corps march behind those admirable breastworks our veteran artillery unlimber our guns on those platforms...the repulse of the enemy could not fail to be far more complete disastrous than it was at Cold Harbor...For Cold Harbor was but an accidental field, held by scratch works made in a few hours. But here [Petersburg] would have been a field skillfully chosen and fortified and prepared long in advance...It was requisite to repeat the bloody blow given at Cold Harbor...[40]

He mourned the fact that Lee was not in the fortifications at Petersburg to greet the Army of the Potomac, but he need not have worried. There would soon be much opportunity there in what would one of the most incredible sieges in modern military history, to see how little had been learned at Cold Harbor.

The Army of Northern Virginia moved south sending scouts ahead to try to detect the enemy's location. Grant and his corps were moving fast, toward the wide James and the most ambitious river-crossing of the war. Lee could not realize that he was leaving the scenes of his last victory in the field.

✳ ✳ ✳ ✳ ✳

The six miles of tunnels and ditches that ran in dozens of lines, interlaced and radiating until it appeared that the sand and red clay of the entire Peninsula had been churned up, were empty of living men after June 13. Dusty and trampled woods and fields went back to the undistinguished status known since McClellan's withdrawal two years earlier. That quiet, rubric corner of Virginia, its disturbed soil dampened by torrents of both blood and fearful perspiration, had lost any importance in the plans of the conquerors. It would scarcely be touched by history again.

The finishing words are from General Grant's memoirs:

> I have always regretted that the last assault at Cold Harbor was ever made. I may say the same thing of the assault of the 22nd May, 1863, at Vicksburg. At Cold Harbor no advantage whatever was gained to compensate for the heavy loss we sustained. Indeed, the advantages other than those of relative losses, were on the Confederate side. Before that, the Army of Northern Virginia seemed to have acquired a wholesome regard for the courage, endurance, and soldierly qualities generally of the Army of the Potomac. They no longer wanted to fight them "one Confederate to five Yanks." Indeed, they seemed to have given up any idea of gaining any advantage of their antagonist in the open field. They had come to much prefer breastworks in their front to the Army of the Potomac. This charge seemed to revive their hopes temporarily; but it was of short duration. The effect upon the Army of the Potomac was the reverse. When we reached the James, however, all effects of the Battle of Cold Harbor seemed to have disappeared.[41]

Within three days the scene would be set for the beginning of a new epoch in modern savagery – the assaults and investment at Petersburg. By June 15 the Petersburg defenders, numbering about 2,200 men of all arms under Brigadier General Henry Wise, were being assaulted by William F. Smith's freshly arrived divisions. A series of sharp frontal advances with heavy losses would set the tone of the Union tactical approach. Their commanders had learned little more from the Wilderness Campaign than that "human waves" eventually have an effect, if there was no limit to the number of troops available. Smith's soldiers, by then including an untested division of black troops, bent their heads forward into the maw of exquisitely fortified artillery. The "new campaign" would mark the end of mobile warfare in the east and would last for more than nine dismal months.

The final words were from Brigadier General Thomas Hyde, whose 7th Maine had seen its share of horror with Wright's VI Corps:

> It is very interesting to visit the battlefields of the war, but I never heard any one who was engaged there express a wish to see Cold Harbor again. Its vast upheavals of earth in fort and rifle-pit, in traverse and covered way, may now have yielded to the sun, the rain, and the plough, but it remains in memory the Golgotha of American history. Gladly we turned our backs upon it."[42]

Part three
Epitaph

The armed presence along the Chickahominy quickly dissipated. What was left by the troops would be picked over by the few hungry civilians in the Mechanicsville area. More than a few Southern voices told that the gaunt soldiers shared their rations of salt pork and potatoes with the local populace before the races to Petersburg and the Valley began. The Peninsular country, never prosperous, had been chewed down to the roots by tens of thousands of warriors and horses and then left to the patient elements. It had humbly given up its opportunities to all takers.

Two tired and changed armies moved away for further battles to the south, so quickly that there was scant space for reflections on what had just occurred at Cold Harbor. Those filthy and flayed veterans had been through more than thirty days of unrelenting and unequalled decimation. Clever plans and notebook tactics had given way to the conduct of nothing less than a gigantic brawl that had stretched over fifty miles of rugged country. The cooking fires still glowed as soldiers made travel to their next test of human will and gunfire at Petersburg.

There are perhaps no classic lessons of the genius of war-making to be gathered from what occurred at Cold Harbor; there might be little more for posterity than the understanding of the capabilities of desperate men. A modern observer is left with the sense of the immediacy that must have sparked these soldiers, a sense of the senselessness of presence without hope. The true order of the day was to live through the horrible moment at hand until the next ditch could be reached.

The Cold Harbor battlefield today, seen in the filtered sunlight, quietly trembles with the images of city boys and field hands crying and scraping a meager sanctuary in the featureless dirt. The badges of paper upon which were scrawled the messages of earthly ties can be imagined there in the nettles and leaves. It is possible to visualize a blood-stained diary found in the trampled debris and opened to the last entry – "I died at Cold Harbor." One can feel the hunger and heat of those who did the killing until all the passions had left them, except that for their own small place in the deep veins of earthworks. The roar of guns becomes sharply individualized when one can now stand between the long-gone combatants' positions and slowly look both ways, in this place of shelter without fire.

In 1866 an Act of Congress established a series of cemeteries that offer mute and eloquent testament to the struggles in the vicinity of the capital of the Confederacy. The Cold Harbor National Cemetery, placed within the actual grounds of two terrific battles, holds the remains of 2,008 Union soldiers within its low walls. In what was described at the time as "an intense search" of a twenty-two mile area, the hastily buried dead were brought there for proper interment, 1,313 of which are marked as unknown. In 1877, a large white sarcophagus was erected in tribute to the nameless. The inscription reads:

> Near this stone rest the remains of 889 Union soldiers gathered from the battlefields of Mechanicsville, Savage Station, Gaines' Mill, and the vicinity of Cold Harbor.

APPENDIX

The Organization of the Armies at Cold Harbor

Introduction

The organization of command and the placement of units at Second Cold Harbor has been difficult for historians to visualize and report accurately. Authorities from Buel and Underwood's (*Battles & Leaders, 1888*) to Douglas Southall Freeman have lamented that no definitive picture of officers and men, particularly for the Southern forces, has ever been developed for the period of operations on the Chickahominy in early 1864. Even modern researchers have had problems determining the composition of the two armies as of June 1. Organizational charts showing the armies before the battles in the Wilderness or even Spotsylvania are almost useless because of the substantial command changes required after those clashes. Also previous troop charts depicting the better-documented circumstances along the Petersburg arena, developing only days afterward, fail to explain many crucial events and processes that are necessary to evaluate the combat situation at Cold Harbor. The armies, Grant's almost as much as Lee's, underwent transformations and reorganization on a dynamic scale. Little documentation was done at the time to explain the additions and placements of units as they arrived or departed the fluctuating frontage along the Chickahominy. For example, little attention has been given to the forces that came with Pickett from the Bermuda Hundred to join Lee by the end of May 1864, or to explain the maze of movements made by some Federal units, particularly the XVIII Corps. At times, divisions came into the fighting zone without their chain of command making record, and dozens of Federal units were actually discharged during the confrontations.

These organizational charts are my attempt to clarify the order of units and command at Cold Harbor as of June 1, 1864. A comparison of those arrangements with any chart of both armies on May 4 dramatically illustrates the chilling costs of the Wilderness campaign.

Many of the command revisions shown had not been formalized by June 1, but all were in position at that time. Lee had more bureaucracy to deal with than did Grant when it came to naming replacements and giving promotions. For example, Lee's recommendations for promoting Dodson Ramseur and William Mahone to major generals were made on May 17 and not issued as certified until June 4.

I hope that the information supplied herein will assist the reader in better visualizing the character of the armies that met in the life and death embrace of Second Cold Harbor.

R. Wayne Maney

Organization of the Army of the Potomac

COLD HARBOR
JUNE 1, 1864

Lieutenant General Ulysses S. Grant – General-in-Chief, United States Armies in the Field
Colonel John A. Rawlins – Headquarters Chief-of-Staff
Major General George G. Meade – Commander, Army of the Potomac
Major General Andrew A. Humphreys – Army Chief-of-Staff
Brigadier General Henry Hunt – Chief of Artillery
Brigadier General Henry Bentham – Chief of Engineers
Brigadier General Marsena Patrick – Provost Marshal General (1st Mass. Cavalry, 80th N.Y., 3rd Pa. Cavalry, 68th Pa., 114th Pa.)
Captain Daniel Mann – Provost Guards and Orderlies

Army II Corps

Major General Winfield S. Hancock

1st Division, Brigadier General Francis Barlow
 1st Brigade, Colonel Nelson Miles
  (26th Mich., 2nd N.Y. Artillery, 61st N.Y., 81st, 140th & 183rd Pa.)
 2nd Brigade, Colonel Richard Byrnes
  (28th Mass., 63rd, 69th & 88th N.Y., 116th Pa.)
 3rd Brigade, Colonel Clinton MacDougall
  (39th, 52nd, 111th, 125th & 126th N.Y.)
 4th Brigade, Colonel John Brooke
  (2nd Del., 7th N.Y. Artillery, 64th & 66th N.Y., 53rd, 145th & 148th Pa.)

2nd Division, Brigadier General John Gibbon
 1st Brigade, Colonel Henry McKeen
  (19th Me., 15th, 19th, & 20th Mass., 1st Mass. Sharpshooters, 7th Mich., 42nd, 59th & 82nd N.Y., 184th Pa., 36th Wisc.)
 2nd Brigade, Brigadier General Joshua Owen
  (152nd N.Y., 69th, 71st, 72nd & 106th Pa.)
 3rd Brigade, Colonel Thomas Smyth
  (14th Conn., 1st Del., 14th Ind., 12th N.J., 10th & 108th N.Y., 4th & 8th Ohio, 7th W.Va.)
 4th Brigade, Brigadier General Robert Tyler
  (8th N.Y. Artillery, 164th, 170th & 182nd N.Y.)

3rd Division, Major General David Birney
  1st Brigade, Colonel Thomas Egan
    (20th Ind., 3rd Me., 40th, 86th & 124th N.Y., 99th, 110th & 141st Pa., 2nd
    U.S. Sharpshooters)
  2nd Brigade, Colonel Thomas Tannant
    (4th & 17th Me., 1st Mass. Artillery, 3rd & 5th Mich., 93rd N.Y., 57th, 63rd
    & 105th Pa., 1st U.S. Sharpshooters)
  3rd Brigade, Brig. General Gersham Mott
    (1st Me. Artillery, 16th Mass., 5th, 6th, 7th, 8th & 11th N.J., 115th Pa.)
  4th Brigade, Colonel William Brewster
    (11th Mass., 70th, 71st, 73rd & 120th N.Y with 3 co.'s of 72nd N.Y. attached,
    84th Pa.)

Artillery Brigade, Colonel John Tidball
    (6th Me., 10th Mass., 1st N.H., 2nd N.J., 1st, 11th, & 12th N.Y., 1st N.Y
    Heavy, 7 batts. of 1st Pa., 1st R.I., 4th & 5th U.S.)

Notes: Byrnes replaced Colonel Smyth of the 2nd Brigade in 1st Division, when
Smyth moved to 3rd Brigade, 2nd Division as Colonel Samuel Carroll was
wounded, then promoted on May 13; MacDougall replaced Colonel Hiram
Brown, 3rd Brigade, 1st Division, who was captured on May 12; McKeen replaced Brigadier General Alexander Webb, 1st Brigade, 2nd Division when that
officer was wounded on May 12; the 4th Brigade, 2nd Division was added to
General Gibbon's division when heavy artillery units were brought from Washington, D.C., on May 22; Brigadier General Hobart Ward, 1st Brigade, 3rd Division, was demoted for "misbehavior and intoxication" on May 12 and replaced
by Egan; Brigadier General Hays, 2nd Brigade, 3rd Division was killed May 5 and
replaced by Webb; what had been originally fourth division of the II Corps was
dismantled and redistributed after the miserable performance at Spotsylvania,
with Mott demoted and sent with Brewster into the 3rd Division.

Army V Corps

Major General Gouverneur K. Warren

1st Division, Brigadier General Charles Griffin
  1st Brigade, Brigadier General Romeyn Ayres
    (140th & 146th N.Y., 91st & 155th Pa., mixed units of 2nd, 11th, 12th, 14th
    & 17th U.S.)
  2nd Brigade, Colonel Jacob Sweitzer
    (9th, 22nd & 32nd Mass., 4th Mich., 62nd Pa.)
  3rd Brigade, Brigadier General Joseph Bartlett
    (20th Me., 18th & 29th Mass., 1st and 16th Mich., 44th N.Y., 83rd & 118th
    Pa.)

2nd Division, Brigadier General Henry Lockwood
  1st Brigade, Colonel Peter Lyle
    (16th Me., 13th & 39th Mass., 94th & 104th N.Y., 90th & 107th Pa.)

2nd Brigade, Colonel James Bates
   (12th Mass., 83rd & 97th N.Y., 11th & 88th Pa.)
3rd Brigade, Colonel Nathan Dushane
   (1st, 4th, 7th & 8th Maryland, the Purnell [Md.] Legion attached)

3rd Division, Brigadier General Samuel Crawford
Veteran Reserve Brigade, Major William Hartshorne
   (190th & 191st Pa.)
Independent Brigade, Colonel J. Howard Kitching
   (6th & 15th N.Y. Heavy Artillery)

4th Division, Brigadier General Lysander Cutler
1st Brigade, Colonel William Robinson
   (7th & 19th Ind., 24th Mich., 1st Battalion N.Y. Sharpshooters, 6th & 7th
   Wisc.)
2nd Brigade, Colonel J. William Hoffman
   (3rd Del., 46th, 76th, 95th & 147th N.Y., 56th Pa.)
3rd Brigade, Colonel Edward Bragg
   (121st, 142nd, 143rd, 149th & 150th Pa.)

Artillery Brigade, Colonel Charles Wainwright
   (3rd, 5th & 9th Mass., 9 batt.'s 1st N.Y., 15th N.Y., 1st Pa., 4th U.S., 5th U.S.)

Notes: General John Robinson and two of his three brigade commanders of
the original 2nd Division were wounded on May 8; this division was disbanded
as of May 9 due to losses of men and officers and a new 2nd Division was
created after substantial reinforcements were brought in by the end of May;
Cutler replaced Brigadier General James Wadsworth, who died May 8, as commander of the 4th Division; Robinson took the 1st Brigade, Hoffman took over
for Colonel Roy Stone, and Bragg for Colonel James Rice, both being severely
wounded on May 5 – all from the 3rd Division; Crawford's Pennsylvania Reserves left service on June 1, and he then took over 2nd Division from Lockwood
effective June 2.

Army VI Corps

Major General Horatio Wright

1st Division, Brigadier General David Russell
1st Brigade, Colonel William Penrose
   (1st, 2nd, 3rd, 4th, 10th & 15th N.J.)
2nd Brigade, Colonel Emory Upton
   (2nd Conn. Artillery, 5th Me., 121st N.Y., 95th & 96th Pa.)
3rd Brigade, Brigadier General Henry Eustis
   (6th Me., 49th & 119th Pa., 5th Wisc.)
4th Brigade, Colonel Nelson Cross
   (65th, 67th & 122nd N.Y., 23rd & 82nd Pa.)

2nd Division, Brigadier General Thomas Neill
  1st Brigade, Brigadier General Frank Wheaton
    (62nd N.Y., 93rd, 98th, 102nd & 139th Pa.)
  2nd Brigade, Brigadier General Lewis Grant
    (2nd, 3rd, 4th, 5th, 6th & 11th [Heavy Artillery] Vt.)
  3rd Brigade, Colonel Daniel Bidwell
    (7th Me., 43rd, 49th & 77th N.Y., 61st Pa.)
  4th Brigade, Colonel Oliver Edwards
    (7th, 10th & 37th Mass., 2nd R.I.)

3rd Division, Brigadier General James Ricketts
  1st Brigade, Colonel William Truex
    (14th N.J., 106th & 151st N.Y., 87th Pa., 10th Vt.)
  2nd Brigade, Colonel Benjamin Smith
    (6th Md., 9th N.Y., 110th, 12th, 126th Ohio, 67th & 138th Pa.)

Artillery Brigade, Colonel Charles Tompkins
  (4th & 5th Me., 1st Mass., 1st N.J., 1st & 3rd N.Y., 9th N.Y. Heavy,
  6 batt.s of 1st Ohio, 1st R.I., 5th U.S.)

Notes: Wright replaced Sedgwick as corps commander when Sedgwick was killed May 9; Penrose replaced Colonel Henry Brown after the 1st Brigade, 2nd Division, was destroyed on May 12; Upton was awarded a field promotion to brigadier general on May 17 but was not confirmed until later in the summer; Lewis Grant was made brigadier general later, but was officially granted rank dating back to April, 1864, and is thus denoted; Neill replaced Brigadier General Getty who was wounded on May 6, as commander, 2nd Division, as Neill was replaced in 3rd Brigade, 2nd Division by Bidwell; Cross took over for Brigadier General Alexander Shaler, 4th Brigade, 1st Division, who was captured on May 6; Edwards took command from Brigadier General Henry Eustis, 4th Brigade, 2nd Division, who was accused of drunkenness on May 6 but later headed 3rd Brigade, 1st Division; William Truex replaced Colonel Truman Seymour of the 2nd Brigade, 3rd Division, captured May 6 and Benjamin Smith replaced Colonel William Morris of that division's 1st Brigade, who was wounded on May 9.

Army IX Corps

Major General Ambrose E. Burnside

1st Division, Major General Thomas Crittenden
  1st Brigade, Brigadier General James Ledlie
    (56th, 57th & 59th Mass., 4th & 10th U.S.)
  2nd Brigade, Colonel Joseph Sudsburg
    (3rd Md., 21st Mass., 100th Pa.)
  Provisional Brigade, Colonel Elisha Marshall
    (2nd Mounted Rifles [dismounted], N.Y., 14th N.Y. Artillery, 24th N.Y. Cav.
    [dismounted], 2nd Pa. Provisional Artillery)
  Engineers, Captain Edward Park (35th Mass.)
  Artillery, Captain Alfred Thomas (3rd Me.), Captain Joseph Wright
    (14th Mass.)

2nd Division, Brigadier General Robert Potter
  1st Brigade, Colonel John Curtin
    (36th & 58th Mass., 45th & 48th Pa., 7th R.I.)
  2nd Brigade, Colonel Simon Griffin
    (2nd Md., 31st & 32nd Me., 6th, 9th & 11th N.H., 17th Vt.)
  Engineers, Captain George Whitman (51st N.Y.)
  Artillery, Captain Edward Rogers (11th Mass., 19th N.Y.)

3rd Division, Brigadier General Orlando Willcox
  1st Brigade, Colonel John Hartranft
    (2nd, 8th, & 27th Mich., 109th N.Y., 51st Pa.)
  2nd Brigade, Colonel Benjamin Christ
    (1st Mich. Sharpshooters, 20th Mich., 60th Ohio, 50th Pa.)
  Engineers, Colonel Constance Luce
  Artillery, Captain Adelbert Twitchell (7th Me.) & Captain Jacob Roemer (34th
    N.Y.)

4th Division, Brigadier General Edward Ferrero
  1st Brigade, Colonel Joshua Sigfried
    (27th, 30th, 39th & 43rd U.S. Colored Troops)
  2nd Brigade, Colonel Henry Thomas
    (19th, 23rd & 31st U.S., Colored Troops)
  Artillery, Captain Romeo Start, 3rd Vt., Pa. Independent Battery)
  Reserve Artillery, Captain John Edwards, Jr. (27th N.Y., 3 batt.s 1st R.I., 2nd
    U.S.)

Notes: IX Corps was organized independently of the Army of the Potomac and therefore had engineers and artillery at division level; Crittenden replaced Brigadier General Thomas Stevenson, killed by a sniper on May 10, as 1st Division commander; Ledlie took 1st Brigade, 1st Division for Colonel Samuel Carruth, wounded May 13; Sudsburg took command of 2nd Brigade, 1st Division from Colonel Daniel Leasure and Curtin did same from Colonel Zenas Bliss, 1st Brigade, 2nd Division, on May 24 when IX Corps was incorporated under Meade's command.

Army XVIII Corps

Major General William Farrar Smith

1st Division, Brigadier General William Brooks
  1st Brigade, Brigadier General Gilman Marston
    (81st, 96th, 98th, & 139th N.Y.)
  2nd Brigade, Brigadier General Hiram Burnham
    (8th Conn., 10th & 13th N.H., 118th N.Y.)
  3rd Brigade, Colonel Guy Henry
    (21st Conn., 40th Mass., 92nd N.Y., 58th & 188th Pa.)

2nd Division, Brigadier General James Martindale
  1st Brigade, George Stannard
    (23rd, 25th, & 27th Mass., 9th N.J., 89th N.Y., 55th Pa.)

2nd Brigade, Colonel Griffin Stedman
   (11th Conn., 8th Me., 2nd & 12th N.H., 148th N.Y.)

3rd Division, Brigadier General Charles Devens, Jr.
   1st Brigade, Colonel William Barton
   (47th, 48th & 115th N.Y., 76th Pa.)
   2nd Brigade, Colonel Jeremiah Drake
   (13th Ind., 9th Me., 112th & 169th N.Y.)
   3rd Brigade, Brigadier General Adelbert Ames
   (4th N.H., 3rd, 117th & 142nd N.Y., 97th Pa.)
   Artillery Brigade, Captain Samuel Elder
   (3 batt.s 1st U.S., 4th U.S., 5th U.S.)

Cavalry Corps

Major General Philip Sheridan

1st Division, Brigadier General Alfred Torbert
   1st Brigade, Brigadier General George Custer
   (1st, 5th, 6th & 7th Mich.)
   2nd Brigade, Colonel Thomas Devin
   (4th, 6th & 9th N.Y., 17th Pa.)
   Reserve Brigade, Brigadier General Wesley Merritt
   (19th N.Y. [1st Dragoons], 6th Pa., 1st, 2nd & 5th U.S.)

2nd Division, Brigadier General David Gregg
   1st Brigade, Brigadier General Henry Davies
   (1st Mass., 1st. N.J., 10th N.Y., 6th Ohio, 1st Pa.)
   2nd Brigade, Colonel J. Irvin Gregg
   (1st Me., 2nd, 4th, 8th, 13th & 16th Pa.)

3rd Division, Brigadier General James Wilson
   1st Brigade, Colonel John McIntosh
   (1st Conn., 3rd N.J., 2nd & 5th N.Y., 2nd Ohio, 18th Pa.)
   2nd Brigade, Colonel George Chapman
   (3rd Ind., 8th N.Y., 1st Vt.)

Horse Artillery
   1st Brigade, Captain James Robertson
   (6th N.Y., 7 batt.s 2nd U.S., 4th U.S.)
   2nd Brigade, Captain Dubar Ransom
   (9 batt.s 1st U.S., 2nd U.S., 3rd U.S., 15th N.Y.)

Organization of the Army of Northern Virginia

COLD HARBOR
JUNE 1, 1864

General Robert E. Lee - Commanding General
Major General Martin L. Smith - Chief of Engineers
Brigadier General William Pendleton - Chief of Artillery

First Army Corps

Lieutenant General Richard H. Anderson

Kershaw's Division, Major General Joseph Kershaw
  Kershaw's Brigade, Colonel John Henagan
    (2nd, 3rd, 7th, 8th, 15th & 20th, S.C., 3rd, S.C. Battalion)
  Humphrey's Brigade, Brigadier General Benjamin Humphreys
    (13th, 17th, 18th & 21st, Miss.)
  Wofford's Brigade, Brigadier General William T. Wofford
    (16th, 18th & 24th, Ga., Cobb's Ga. Legion, Phillips' Ga. Legion, 3rd Ga.
    Battalion Sharpshooters)
  Bryan's Brigade, Brigadier General Goode Bryan
    (10th, 50th, 51st & 53rd, Ga.)

Field's Division, Major General Charles Field
  Jenkins' Brigade, Colonel John Bratton
    (1st, 2nd, 5th & 6th, S.C., Palmetto State Sharpshooters)
  Anderson's Brigade, Brigadier General George Anderson
    (7th , 8th, 9th, 11th & 59th, Ga.)
  Law's Brigade, Brigadier General Evander Law
    (4th, 15th, 44th, 47th & 48th, Ala.)
  Gregg's Brigade, Brigadier General John Gregg
    (3rd Ark., 1st, 4th & 5th, Tex.)
  Benning's Brigade, Colonel Dudley Dubose
    (2nd, 15th, 17th & 20th, Ga.)

Hoke's Division, Major General Robert Hoke
  Corse's Brigade, Brigadier General Montgomery Corse
    (15th, 17th, 18th, 29th & 30th, Va.)
  Clingman's Brigade, Brigadier General Thomas Clingman
    (8th, 31st, 51st & 61st, N.C.)
  Johnson's Brigade, Brigadier General Bushrod Johnson
    (17th, 23rd, 25th, 44th & 63rd, Tenn.)

Hagood's Brigade, Brigadier General Johnson Hagood
  (11th, 21st, 25th & 27th, S.C., 7th S.C. Battalion)
Artillery Battalion, Lieutenant Colonel B. F. Eshleman
  (Martin's Va. Batt., Owen's La. Batt., Payne's Batt.)

Artillery Brigade, Brigadier General Edward Porter Alexander
  Huger's Battalion, Lieutenant Colonel Frank Huger
    (Fickling's Va. Batt., Moody's La. Batt., Parker's Va. Batt., J. Smith's Va. Batt.,
    Taylor's Va. Batt., Woolfolk's Va. Batt.)
  Haskell's Battalion, Major John Haskell
    (Flanner's N.C. Batt., Garden's S. Batt., Lamkin's Va. Batt., Ramsay's N.C.
    Batt.)
  Cabell's Battalion, Colonel Henry Cabell
    (Callaway's Ga. Batt., Carlton's Ga. Batt., McCarthy's Va. Batt., Manly's N.C.
    Batt.)

Notes: Anderson assumed command of the First Corps after Lieutenant General James Longstreet was wounded on May 6, and was confirmed Lieutenant General on June 1; Brigadier General Micah Jenkins was killed on May 6 and replaced as brigade commander by Bratton; Brigadier General Henry Benning was wounded May 6 and his brigade taken by Dubose; Hoke's Division was sent to Lee from the Richmond defenses by May 30 and was attached to Anderson's Corps; on May 31, Kershaw was recognized as permanent commander of the division that had belonged to Major General Lafayette McLaws; though the division brought up from the Richmond defenses by Pickett was officially attached to Anderson, its place in the Southern line along the Chickahominy was directed with Hill's Third Corps.

Second Army Corps

Lieutenant General Jubal Early

Ramseur's Division, Major General Dodson Ramseur
  Hays's Brigade, Brigadier General Zebulon York
    (1st, 2nd, 5th, 6th, 7th, 8th, 9th, 10th, 14th & 15th La.)
  Johnston's Brigade, Brigadier General Thomas Toon
    (5th, 12th, 20th & 23rd N.C.)
  Hoke's (Old) Brigade, Colonel Archibald Godwin
    (6th, 21st, 54th & 57th, N.C., 1st N.C. Battalion)

Rodes' Division, Major General Robert Rodes
  Daniel's Brigade, Brigadier General Bryan Grimes
    (32nd, 43rd, 45th & 52nd, N.C., 2nd N.C. Battalion)
  Doles's Brigade, Brigadier General George Doles
    (4th, 12th & 44th, Ga.)
  Cox's Brigade, Brigadier General William Cox
    (1st, 2nd, 3rd, 4th, 14th & 30th, N.C.)
  Battle's Brigade, Brigadier General Cullen Battle
    (3rd, 5th, 6th, 12th & 26th Ala.)

Gordon's Division, Major General John Gordon
 Gordon's Brigade, Brigadier General Clement Evans
  (3rd, 26th, 31st, 38th, 60th & 61st Ga.)
 Pegram's Brigade, Brigadier General William Lewis
  (13th, 31st, 49th, 52nd & 58th Va.)
 Terry's Brigade, Brigadier General William Terry
  (2nd, 4th, 5th, 10th, 21st, 23rd, 25th, 26th, 27th, 33rd, 37th, 42nd, 44th, 48th & 50th Va.)

Artillery Brigade, Brigadier General Armistead Long
 Hardaway's Battalion, Lieutenant Colonel R. A. Hardaway
  (Dance's Va. Batt., Graham's Va. Batt., Griffin's Va. Batt., Jones's Va. Batt., B. Smith's Va. Batt.)

 Nelson's Battalion, Lieutenant Colonel William Nelson
  (Kirkpatrick's Va. Batt., Massie's Va. Batt., Milledge's Ga. Batt.)
 Braxton's Battalion, Lieutenant Colonel Carter Braxton
  (Carpenter's Va. Batt., Cooper's Va. Batt., Hardwicke's Va. Batt.)
 Cutshaw's Battalion, Major W. E. Cutshaw
  (Carrington's Va. Batt., Garber's Va. Batt., Tanner's Va. Batt.)
 Page's Battalion, Major R. C. Page
  (W. Carter's Va. Batt., Fry's Va. Batt., Page's Va. Batt., Reese's Ala. Batt.)

Notes: Ramseur took over Early's division when that officer assumed command of Second Corps; York took over brigade command when Brigadier General Harry Hays was wounded May 9; Lewis took over Pegram's brigade from Colonel Edward Willis, killed May 30, who had previously taken the brigade from Colonel John Hoffman; Evans took Gordon's brigade when that officer succeeded to division command after Spotsylvania; the original division of Major General Edward Johnson (captured) was practically destroyed at Spotsylvania and was officially dissolved on May 14; the remaining troops were redistributed with those of Brigadier General John M. Jones and Brigadier General Leroy Stafford, both killed May 5; these were consolidated with the Virginia regiments of Brigadier General George Steuart and Brigadier General James Walker into one brigade placed under Brigadier General William Terry and into a new division led by Gordon; Steuart was captured and Walker severely injured at Spotsylvania, leaving Terry as the senior officer remaining from the old Stonewall Brigade; many of the Virginia regiments so realigned were so reduced as to be non-existent as fighting regiments; the Louisiana regiments of Stafford and Hays were consolidated into the brigade of Zebulon York; Pegram's brigade and Gordon's old brigade also were added to the new division; Johnston's brigade from Hoke's division and Hoke's old brigade from the Richmond defenses were added to Ramseur's division; Ramseur was slightly wounded May 12 but remained active; in Rodes' division, Brigadier General Bryan Grimes replaced Brigadier General Junius Daniel, killed May 12.

Third Army Corps

Lieutenant General Ambrose P. Hill

Mahone's Division, Major General William Mahone
  Perrin's Brigade, Colonel J. C. Sanders
    (8th, 9th, 10th, 11th & 14th, Ala.)
  Mahone's Brigade, Colonel D. A. Weisiger
    (6th, 12th, 16th, 41st & 61st, Va.)
  Harris's Brigade, Brigadier General Nathaniel Harris
    (12th, 16th, 19th & 48th Miss.)
  Wright's Brigade, Brigadier General Ambrose Wright
    (3rd, 22nd & 48th Ga., 2nd Ga. Battalion)
  Finegan's Brigade, Brigadier General Joseph Finegan
    (2nd, 5th, 8th, 9th, 10th & 11th Fla.)

Heth's Division, Major General Henry Heth
  Davis's Brigade, Brigadier General Joseph Davis
    (2nd, 11th & 42nd Miss., 55th, N.C.)
  Cooke's Brigade, Brigadier General John Cooke
    (15th, 27th, 46th & 48th N.C.)
  Kirkland's Brigade, Brigadier General William Kirkland
    (11th, 26th, 44th, 47th & 52nd N.C.)
  Walker's Brigade, Colonel Robert Mayo
    (40th, 47th & 55th Va., 22nd Va. Battalion)
  Archer's Brigade, Colonel William McComb
    (13th Ala., 1st Prov. Tenn., 7th & 14th Tenn.)

Wilcox's Division, Major General Cadmus Wilcox
  Lane's Brigade, Brigadier General James Lane
    (7th, 18th, 28th, 33rd & 37th N.C.)
  Scales's Brigade, Brigadier General Alfred Scales
    (13th, 16th, 22nd, 34th & 38th N.C.)
  McGowan's Brigade, Brigadier General James Conner
    (1st S.C., Prov., 12th, 13th & 14th S.C., 1st S. C. [Orr's] Rifles)
  Thomas's Brigade, Brigadier General Edward Thomas
    (14th, 35th, 45th & 49th Ga.)

Breckinridge's Division, Major General John Breckinridge
  Echols' Brigade, Brigadier General John Echols
    (22nd Va., 23rd Va. Battalion)
  Wharton's Brigade, Brigadier General Gabriel Wharton
    (26th Va. Battalion, 30th, 51st & 62nd Va.)

Pickett's Division, Major General George Pickett
  Hunton's Brigade, Brigadier General Eppa Hunton
    (8th, 19th, 32nd & 56th Va., 42nd Va. Cav. Battalion)
  Terry's Brigade, Brigadier General William R. Terry
    (1st, 3rd, 7th, 11th & 24th Va.)

Barton's Brigade, Brigadier General Birkett Fry
  (9th, 14th, 38th, 53rd & 57th Va.)
The Maryland Line, Colonel Bradley Johnson
  (2nd Md. Inf., 1st Md. Cav., 1st & 2nd Md. Batteries)

Artillery Brigade, Colonel R. Lindsay Walker
  Poague's Battalion, Lieutenant Colonel William Poague
    (Richard's Miss. Batt., Utterback's Va. Batt., Williams N.C. Batt., Wyatt's Va.
    Batt.)
  McIntosh's Battalion, Lieutenant Colonel D. G. McIntosh
    (Clutter's Va. Batt., Donald's Va. Batt., Hurt's Ala. Batt., Price's Va. Batt.)
  Pegram's Battalion, Lieutenant Colonel William Pegram
    (Brander's Va. Batt., Cayce's Va. Batt., Ellet's Va. Batt., Marye's Va. Batt.,
    Zimmerman's S.C. Batt.)
  Cutt's Battalion, Lieutenant Colonel A. S. Cutts
    (Patterson's Ga. Batt., Ross's Ga. Batt., Wingfield's Ga. Batt.)
  Richardson's Battalion, Lieutenant Colonel Charles Richardson
    (Grandy's Va. Batt., Landry's Va. Batt., Moore's Va. Batt., Penick's Va. Batt.)

Notes: Mahone went to divisional command when Anderson became head of
First Corps, and was replaced by Weisiger; Sanders led Perrin's brigade after
that officer was killed May 12; Brigadier General Edward Perry was wounded
May 6 and replaced by Finegan when that officer arrived with additional Florida
regiments on May 23; Brigadier General Henry Walker was crippled by wounds
on May 10, his brigade taken by Colonel Mayo; Brigadier General James Archer
had been captured a year before and would return to command at Petersburg,
and in his absence the brigade was led by McComb; Brigadier General Samuel
McGowan was wounded May 12, replaced by Conner; Pickett's division arrived on May 20-22 and was assigned first to First Corps, then to Hill's Third;
Hunton's Brigadier was handled as a detached unit and Barton's brigade was
brought in from Major General Robert Ransom's division to be part of Pickett's
force of just over 4,000; Brigadier General Seth Barton had been replaced by
Ransom for poor performance at Drewry's Bluff; Breckinridge came from the
Valley with two brigades and was put into the right anchor of the Third Corps
line under Lee's direct command.

Cavalry Corps

Hampton's Division, Major General Wade Hampton
  Young's Brigade, Brigadier General Pierce Young
    (17th Ga., Cobb's, Ga. Legion, Phillips Ga. Legion, 20th Ga. Battalion)
  Rosser's Brigade, Brigadier General Thomas Rosser
    (7th, 11th & 12th, Va., 35th Va. Battalion)
  Butler's Brigade, Brigadier General M. Calbraith Butler
    (4th, 5th & 6th S.C.)

Fitzhugh Lee's Division, Major General Fitzhugh Lee
  Lomax's Brigade, Brigadier General Lunsford Lomax
    (5th, 6th & 15th Va.)

Wickham's Brigade, Brigadier General Williams Wickham
(1st, 2nd, 3rd & 4th Va.)

William H. F. Lee's Division, Major General William H. F. Lee
Chambliss' Brigade, Brigadier General John Chambliss
(9th, 10th & 13th Va.)
Gordon's Brigade, Brigadier General Rufus Barringer
(1st, 2nd & 5th N.C.)

Horse Artillery, Major R. P. Chew
Breathed's Battalion, Major James Breathed
(Hart's S.C. Batt., Johnston's Va. Batt., McGregor's Va. Batt., Shoemaker's Va.
Batt., Thomson's Va. Batt.)

Notes: Following the death of Stuart on May 13, Lee was not able to appoint a successor as overall cavalry commander, therefore the three cavalry divisions were to operate under individualized command and take orders directly from Lee; Brigadier General James Gordon was killed at Yellow Tavern and his brigade taken by Barringer; Cailbraith Butler came to Hampton's division on May 28.

Sources/Acknowledgments

Some of the best writers and historians of the Civil War have dealt in some fashion with the shattering events surrounding the battle of Second Cold Harbor. The treatments of the armies' maneuvers and descriptions of the fighting from May 28 through June 12, within those sources, have ordinarily been included as only a small portion of the Rapidan to James River phase of the 1864 campaign. Some, however, have provided a clear pathway through a vague part of a much-studied conflict. I gratefully acknowledge the guidance of Bruce Catton's *A Stillness at Appomattox* and *Grant Takes Command*, as well as Clifford Dowdey's *Lee's Last Campaign*. Noah A. Trudeau's acclaimed *Bloody Roads South: The Wilderness to Cold Harbor* is one of the most daring and complete explanations of the Wilderness campaign. His charts of casualty figures for the Wilderness campaign and particularly those at Cold Harbor were very useful. Douglas S. Freeman, especially in his *Lee's Lieutenants*, provided essential material for understanding the Southern perspectives, particularly in regard to the approaches of Lee's army to the Cold Harbor arena. Shelby Foote, in volume three of his classic *The Civil War: A Narrative*, offers a section called "The Forty Days" that is without parallel in its effect.

The majority of the more than eight hundred manuscripts, books, and periodicals that I used in writing *Marching to Cold Harbor* are of eye-witness, primary-source origin. The Library of Congress, George Mason University Library, the University of Virginia, the Virginia State Library in Richmond, the Virginia Historical Society, and the Virginia Room of Fairfax County Public Libraries provided the majority of these valuable materials. The primary source collection of the Richmond Battlefield Park Headquarters was extremely valuable, adding a well-organized body of manuscript material dealing specifically with Cold Harbor. I am especially grateful for the assistance provided by Mr. David Keough and the staff at the U. S. Army Military History Institute at Carlisle Barrracks in Carlisle, Pennsylvania. The Southern Historical Collection at the University of North Carolina and the Perkins Library at Duke University in Durham, North Carolina, contributed several additional sources from their extensive holdings.

Newspapers of the period - *The Richmond Examiner, The Philadelphia Inquirer, New York Herald* and *Tribune*, and *The Washington Evening Star* - were made available by the University of Virginia Library and Georgetown University Library. For information on the almost completely forgotten Battle of Haw's Shop, I acknowledge Robert William's 1973 article for *Civil War Times Illustrated*, "Haw's Shop: A Storm of Shot and Shell." The article by Jeffrey Wert, "One Great Regret," written in 1979 for *Civil War Times Illustrated*, is an excellent, brief look at the struggle at Cold Harbor. The bound papers of the Southern Historical Society from the Virginia Historical Society collections contain two articles of value: "Grant's Change of Base and the Horrors of Cold Harbor" by William Goldsborough from 1901 (Vol. 30), and "The Cold Harbor Salient" by A. Dubois of the 7th New York Heavy Artillery, written in 1902, (Vol. 29).

In almost every source, I was able to find at least a few words or phrases concerning the fighting at Cold Harbor. The traditional guides for the Civil War historian, The *Official Records*, *The Confederate Veteran*, and *The Rebellion Record*, were especially useful. The great series, *Battles and Leaders of the Civil War*, continues to be a rich source of first-hand information. As well, tried-and-true accounts such as Horace Porter's much-used *Campaigning with Grant* and the memoirs of Philip Sheridan's and Ulysses S. Grant, as well as reminiscences of scores of common soldiers, were available and obtainable due to renewed interest in reprinting these classic works. Companies such as Morningside Press of Dayton, Ohio, Olde Soldier Books of Gaithersburg, Maryland, and Mallard Press and Fairfax Press of New York deserve much thanks from Civil War historians.

Manuscript Sources

I gratefully acknowledge the assistance of the Manuscript Division of the Library of Congress for their assistance with the following unpublished materials:

- the letters of Corporal John Arnold of the 49th Pennsylvania Volunteers
- the diary of General Cyrus Ballou Comstock, Chief Engineer and Aide-de-Camp to General Ulysses Grant at Cold Harbor
- the letters of Private David Coon of 36th Wisconsin Volunteers
- the Gist Family Collection, which includes the letters of Richard and Branford Gist of the 6th Maryland Volunteers
- the memoirs of John William Hatton of the 1st Maryland Battery, CSA
- the papers, diary, and field reports of Colonel Jedediah Hotchkiss, Cartographer, CSA
- the diary of James William Latta of the 119th Pennsylvania Volunteers
- the postwar reminiscences of Captain William Long, 44th North Carolina Volunteers
- the diary of Major Howard Malcolm Smith of the 1st New York Dragoons
- the papers of General James Harrison Wilson, U. S. Cavalry

Additionally, I would like to thank the Virginia Historical Society for their assistance with the following materials from their extensive manuscript collection:

- the autobiography of George T. Brooke of the 2nd Virginia Cavalry
- the diary of Creed T. Davis of the Richmond Howitzers
- the diary of John Warwick Daniel, Second Corps, CSA
- the memoirs of General Jubal A. Early
- the diary of Alexander C. Jones of the 44th Virginia Infantry
- the letter of Mary Sape Johnson
- the diary of Joseph H. Lambeth of the 14th North Carolina Infantry
- the manuscript and papers of Colonel Henry McClellan of Stuart's and Lee's staff
- the notes of Lieutenant Colonel David McIntosh, Commander of McIntosh's Virginia Artillery Battalion
- the letters of Gustavus Adolphus Myers
- the diary of Oscar O. Mull of the 12th Virginia Infantry
- the memoirs of Alfred Lewis Scott of the 2nd Florida Infantry
- the memoirs of John Zachary Scott of the 5th Virginia Cavalry
- the letter of W. B. Strickland of the 10th Georgia Regular Volunteers
- the diary of Reuben L. Whitehurst

Manuscript materials from the U. S. Army Military History Institute used in my research include:

- the diary of George Affitt of the 46th Virginia Infantry
- the Timothy Bateman papers
- the letter of General Joseph Finegan, CSA, June 26, 1864
- the letters of Sergeant Dayton Flint of the 15th New Jersey Infantry
- the papers of General Winfield S. Hancock
- the letters of Edward Henry of the 96th Pennsylvania Infantry
- the David Herman papers
- the diary of Charles Hobbs of the 7th New York Heavy Artillery
- the Johnson Family papers
- the Otis H. Knight papers
- the William Lind papers
- the Lewis Luckinbill papers
- the Samuel Marks papers
- the papers of General Nelson Miles
- the diary of John Noonan of the 69th New York Infantry
- the diary of Captain Isaac Plumb of the 61st New York Infantry
- the diary of Lieutenant Curtis Pollack of the 48th Pennsylvania Infantry
- the letters of Charles A. Smith of the 8th Maine Infantry
- the letters of Colonel Charles Venable of Lee's staff

From the Southern Historical Collection at the University of North Carolina in Chapel Hill, North Carolina:

- the papers of Berry G. Benson of the 1st South Carolina
- the diary of Francis A. Boyle of the 32nd North Carolina Infantry
- the papers of Bryan Grimes
- the diary of James Green of the 53rd North Carolina Infantry

I extend my thanks to the library staff of George Mason University for their assistance, and especially for the examination of their Milton Barnes manuscript collection.

My appreciation also goes to the staffs of the Richmond Battlefield National Park and the Petersburg National Battlefield Park for their kind words and advice. Material was also provided by the Department of Veterans Affairs, Richmond National Cemetery, for information on Cold Harbor National Cemetery.

The maps, five of which are included in the text, which provided detailed explanation of movements of both armies at Cold Harbor were researched and drawn by the Department of the Interior, U. S. Park Service, and made available by the Richmond Battlefield Headquarters. Manuscript material provided by Michael Andrus and the staff at the Richmond Battlefield headquarters of the National Park Service includes:

- the letters of John Robert Bagby of the 140th Pennsylvania
- the Cullen Battle papers in the collection of Rev. J. B. Hall
- the letters of James Bryant of the 13th Virginia Infantry
- the diary of John Boring of the 148th Pennsylvania Infantry

– the diary of Joseph Elliot of the 71st Pennsylvania Infantry
– the papers of Thomas J. Elliot
– the diary of John Gordon of the 2nd North Carolina Cavalry
– the letters of J. S. Graham of the 140th Pennsylvania Infantry
– the letters of Ezekial Graham of the 6th Georgia Infantry
– the diary of William Hansom
– the diary of Henry Kaiser of the 96th Pennsylvania Infantry
– the diary of James Alexander Malloy of the 3rd South Carolina Infantry Battalion
– the diary of John Robinson of the 4th Pennsylvania Cavalry
– the diary of John Tucker of the 5th Alabama Infantry

From the William Perkins Library at Duke University:

– the papers of General Richard Anderson
– the papers of Harriet B. Daniel of Arkansas (she mentions the religious habits of some Southern soldiers at Cold Harbor)
– the papers of Edwin Emory of the 17th Maine Infantry
– the memoirs of John Cheeves Haskell (the Confederate artillery officer whose published memoirs were already cited by me)
– the letters of Robert Guyton of the 139th Pennsylvania Vols.
– the letters of Henry H. Hopkins, a chaplain with the 120th New York Vols. (nothing relevant)
– the letters of Charles A. Legg of the 3rd Battalion of the Massachusetts Riflemen (discusses racism, gambling, etc., in the Army of the Potomac)
– the letters of Willie B. Stevens of the 4th Vermont Infantry (he was wounded at Cold Harbor and imprisoned)
– the diary of Joseph J. Wescoat of Charleston, South Carolina

I would also like to thank the family of Colonel Francis R. Munt (Ret.) for the use of the diary manuscripts of William Christian Munt of the 41st Virginia Infantry and of Casper B. Kent of the 1st U. S. Sharpshooters.

NOTES

Chapter One

1. William O. Stoddard, *Lincoln's Third Secretary*, Doubleday & Co., New York, NY, 1953, p. 199.

2. Grant's letter to Lincoln, May 1, 1864. See note #48, chapter one.

3. There are several excellent sources for camp life of Union soldiers at Brandy Station in the winter of 1863-64. See John Billings, *Hardtack and Coffee*, Geo. Smith and Co., Boston, Massachusetts, 1887, pp. 31-60 and 121-157 and Robert Carter, *Four Brothers in Blue*, University of Texas Press, Austin, Texas, 1978, pp. 320-370.

4. George Meade, Jr., offers some sharp details from his father in *Life and Letters of George G. Meade, Vol. 2*, Charles Scribner's Sons, New York, NY, 1913, pp. 89-90.

5. D. P. Conynham, *The Irish Brigade and Its Campaigns*, privately published, Boston, Massachusetts, 1867, pp. 425-438.

6. Frank Wilkeson, *Recollections of a Private Soldier in the Army of the Potomac*, G. P. Putnam's Sons, New York, NY, 1887, pp. 32-34.

7. *Ibid*, pp. 37-39.

8. Theodore Vaill, *History of the 2nd Connecticut Heavy Artillery*, Winsted Publishing Co., Winsted, Connecticut, 1868, p. 45.

9. D. G. Crotty, *Four Years Campaigning in the Army of the Potomac*, Dygert Brothers & Co., Grand Rapids, Michigan, 1874, pp. 117-118.

10. Bruce Catton, *A Stillness at Appomattox*, Doubleday and Co., Garden City, New York, 1953, pp. 46-48. See also, Francis A. Walker, *History of the 2nd Corps in the Army of the Potomac*, NY, 1887.

11. Philip Sheridan, *Personal Memoirs of Philip H. Sheridan*, Charles Webster and Co., New York, NY, 1888, p. 140 and John Britton, *Personal Memoirs of John Britton*, Neale Publishing Co., New York, NY, 1914, p. 247.

12. Bell Irwin Wiley, *The Life of Billy Yank: the Common Soldier of the Union*, Louisiana State University Press, Baton Rouge, Louisiana, 1971, pp. 192-223.

13. Zouave uniforms and colors were in abundance in both armies early in the war, but their use greatly decreased by spring of 1864. See Bruce Catton, *Mr. Lincoln's Army*, Doubleday and Co., Garden City, New York, 1951.

14. Hazard Stevens, *Papers of the Military Historical Society of Massachusetts, Vol. 4*, Houghton, Mifflin and Co., Boston, Massachusetts, 1895, ed. by Theodore Dwight, pp. 178-179.

15. Carter, p. 261.

16. Theodore Lyman, *Meade's Headquarters: Letters of Colonel Theodore Lyman from Wilderness to Appomattox*, Houghton, Mifflin and Co., Boston, Massachusetts, 1922, ed. by George Agassiz, p. 81.

17. Horace Porter, *Campaigning with Grant*, Mallard Press, New York, NY, 1990, reprint of 1907 edition, p. 47.

18. Charles Page, *Letters of a War Correspondent*, L. C. Page & Co., Boston, Massachusetts, 1899, p. 110.

19. George Meade, *Life and Letters of George Gordon Meade, Vol. 2*, letter of April 17, 1864, p. 166.

20. Charles Adams, Jr. in letter, April 3, 1864, from *A Cycle of Adams Letters, Vol. 2*. Houghton, Mifflin Co., Boston, Massachusetts, 1920, ed. by W. C. Ford.

21. Wilbur Fisk, from *Hard Marching Everyday: The Civil War Letters of Private Wilbur Fisk, 1861-65*, University of Kansas Press, Lawrence, Kansas, 1983, ed. by Emil and Ruth Rosenblat, p. 168.

22. John Sedgwick in letter, see *Correspondence of John Sedgwick, Major General, Vol. 2*, De Vinne Press, New York, NY, 1902, pp. 177-178.

23. There are many sources that describe U. S. Grant's behavior and personality. Three of the best that deal with early 1864 are: J. F. C. Fuller's, *The Generalship of Ulysses S. Grant*, Charles Scribner's Sons, New York, NY, 1929; Bruce Catton's *Grant Takes Command*, Little, Brown and Co., Boston, Massachusetts, 1968; and, William S. McFeely, *Grant: A Biography*, W. W. Norton & Co., New York, NY, 1981.

24. Shelby Foote, *The Civil War: A Narrative, Vol. 3: Red River to Appomattox*, Random House, New York, NY, 1974, offers a good assessment of Federal strength in early 1864 in pp. 126-145.

25. Allan Nevins, *The War for the Union, Vol. 4: Organized War to Victory*, Charles Scribner's Sons, New York, NY, 1971, p. 48.

26. Good details about 1864 guerrilla warfare in the Western theatre are found in several works, especially Jay Monaghan's *Civil War on the Western Border, 1854-1865*, Little, Brown and Co., Boston, Massachusetts, 1955.

27. Mosby's exploits in 1864 are well-documented in Virgil Carrington Jones', *Ranger Mosby*, University of North Carolina Press, Chapel Hill, North Carolina, 1944.

28. Details of the Ft. Pillow "massacre" can be found in Foote, *Vol. 3,* pp. 108-112 and Dudley Cornish's *The Sable Arm: Negro Troops in the Union Army,* Harcourt, Brace and World, New York, NY, 1956, pp. 175-178.

29. Carl Sandburg's *Abraham Lincoln: The War Years, Vol. 3,* Harcourt, Brace and World, New York, NY, 1939, pp. 96-111, offers a vivid description of Lincoln's inner circle.

30. This story is from Allan Nevins, *The New York Evening Post,* May, 1922, pp. 320-321.

31. Letter of Charles Francis Adams, April 8,1863, from the R. H. Dana Papers, Massachusetts Historical Society.

32. *New York Herald,* Jan. 7, 1864.

33. *New York Tribune,* May 13, 1864.

34. Letter from Grant to Stanton is in full-text in Benjamin Thomas and Harold Hyman, *Stanton: The Life and Times of Lincoln's Secretary of War,* Scribner's and Sons, New York, 1962 pp. 371-374.

35. *The War or the Rebellion: Official Records of the Union and Confederate Armies, Series Two, Vol. 7,* p. 607. (Hereafter cited as O.R.)

36. William Sherman quoted in *Century Magazine,* Feb., 1888.

37. Ulysses S. Grant, *Report of Lt. Gen. U. S. Grant of the Armies of the United States,* 1864-65, U.S. War Department, July 22,1865.

38. Porter, pp. 26-27

39. Ulysses Grant, *Memoirs of U. S. Grant, Vol. 2,* Bonanza/Crown Books New York, NY, 1974, reprint of 1885 edition, pp. 122-123.

40. Stoddard, pp. 197-199.

41. Lyman, p. 81.

42. *O.R., Vol. 32, Pt. 3,* pp. 245-246.

43. Bruce Lancaster and J. H. Plumb, *The American Heritage Book of the Revolution,* American Heritage Publishing Co., New York, NY, 1958, pp. 297-324.

44. Foote, pp. 100-103.

45. William Swinton, *Campaigns of the Army of the Potomac*, Charles Scribner's Sons, New York, 1882, p. 440.

46. Ulysses Grant, "Preparing for the Campaign," in *Battles and Leaders of the Civil War, Vol. 4*, BK Sales, Inc., Secaucus, New Jersey, 1985, reprint of 1888 edition, ed. by Clarence Buel and Robert Underwood.

47. *Ibid.*, p. 112

48. Elisha Hunt Rodes, May 3, 1864, *All For the Union: The Civil War Diary and Letters of Elisha Hunt Rodes*, Orion Books, New York, NY, 1985, ed. by Robert Rhodes, p. 143.

Chapter Two

1. Porter Alexander, *Fighting for the Confederacy: The Personal Recollections of General Edward Porter Alexander*, University of North Carolina Press, Chapel Hill, North Carolina, 1989, ed. by Gary Callagher, p. 345.

2. J. William Jones, *Personal Reminiscences, Anecdotes, and Letters of General Robert E. Lee.* Appleton & Co., New York, 1875, p. 196.

3. Henry Heth, *Memoirs of Henry Heth*, Greenwood Press, Westport, Connecticut, 1974, ed. by James Morrison, Jr., p. 182.

4. *O.R., Vol. 33, Pt. Two*, p. 1114.

5. *Ibid*, pp. 1114-1115.

6. McHenry Howard, *Recollections of a Maryland Soldier and Staff Officer*, Williams and Wilkins Co., Baltimore, Maryland, 1914, p. 267.

7. *O.R., Vol. 33, Pt. Two*, p.1115.

8. Douglas Freeman, *Lee's Lieutenants, Vol. 3*, Charles Scribner's Sons, New York, NY, 1944, pp. 283-292.

9. John Bell Hood led his forces to destruction at Franklin, Tennessee, in Dec., 1863 and would lead incredible charges against Sherman near Atlanta in 1864.

10. After Pickett recovered from wounds suffered at Gettysburg, he had been placed with the Dept. of North Carolina under Beauregard, where his record was not glowing. See Ezra Warner, *Generals in Grey*, Louisiana State University Press, Baton Rouge, Louisiana, 1959, p. 239-240.

11. Ewell was blamed by many for failing to seize the heights at the southern edge of the field (Little and Big Roundtops) in the first day at Gettysburg, July 1, 1863.

12. Freeman, pp. 338-341.

13. Terry Jones, *Lee's Tigers: The Louisiana Infantry in the Army of Northern Virginia*, Louisiana State University Press, Baton Rouge, Louisiana, 1987, p. 209.

14. Grant, *Memoirs, Vol. 2*, pp. 291-292.

15. Lee's health problems are discussed in D. S. Freeman's *Lee's Lieutenants, Vol. 3*, pp. 412-420 and first-hand in Walter Taylor's *Four Years with General Lee*, D. Appleton and Co., New York, NY, 1878, pp. 132-139.

16. See comments by Asbury Coward of the 5th South Carolina found in *The South Carolinians: Colonel Asbury Coward's Memoirs*, published by Vantage Press, New York, 1968, pp. 200-202.

17. Letter to Bragg, April 16, 1864. See Clifford Dowdey, *Wartime Papers of Robert E. Lee*, Litle, Brown and Co., Boston, Massachusetts, 1962, p. 738.

18. Walter Taylor, letter dated April 3, 1864, in his *General Lee: His Campaigns in Virginia, 1861-1865*, Nusbaum Book Co., Norfolk, 1906, p. 204.

19. Freeman, *Robert E. Lee, Vol. 3*, pp. 266-267.

20. *O.R., Vol. 33, Pt. Two*, p. 1144.

21. Hudson Strode, *Jefferson Davis: Tragic Hero, Vol. 4*, Harcourt, Brace, and World, New York, NY, 1964, pp. 29-36.

22. Foote, p. 126.

23. Strode, pp. 12-19.

24. Glimpses of Richmond life in the spring of 1864 can be found in Albert Kirwan's *The Confederacy: A Social and Political History*, World Publishing Co., Cleveland, Ohio, 1959, pp. 168-224 and in Raimando Luraghi's *The Rise and Fall of the Plantation South*, Franklin Watts, Inc., New York, NY, 1978, pp. 120-132.

25. *O.R, Vol. 33, Pt. Two*, pp. 1282-1283.

26. Freeman, *Robert E. Lee, Vol. 3*, p. 266.

27. Robert E. Lee, Jr., *Recollections and Letters of Robert E. Lee*, Doubleday, Page & Co., New York, NY, 1904, p. 123.

28. *Confederate Veteran, Vol. 28*, p. 68.

29. *O.R., Vol. 36, Pt Two*, p. 226.

30. Charles Venable is quoted by both Walter Taylor and Moxley Sorrel in those officers' memoirs. His own account is in *Battles and Leaders, Vol. 4*, pp. 240-246.

31. James Wadsworth in Lyman, p. 118.

32. Stanton Allen, *Down in Dixie: Life in a Cavalry Regiment in the War Days*, D. Lothrop Co., Boston, Massachusetts, 1888, p.206.

33. Foote, pp. 118-122.

34. Augustus Dickert, *Kershaw's Brigade*, Morningside Bookshop, Dayton, Ohio, 1976, reprint of 1899 edition, p. 340.

Chapter Three

1. Alexander, p. 385.

2. Wilkeson, p. 49.

3. Porter, p. 73.

4. *Histories of Several Regiments and Battalions from North Carolina in The Civil War, Vol. 5*, E. M. Uzell, Publishers, Raleigh, North Carolina, 1901, ed. by Walter Clarke, p. 97.

5. Meade wrote years later that this was the only major point of disagreement with Grant. See *Newsletter of Ulysses S. Grant Association, No. 3*, April, 1966.

6. Andrew A. Humphreys, *The Virginia Campaign of 1864-65*, Scribner's and Sons, New York, NY, 1883, p. 23.

7. Grant, p. 183.

8. Porter, p. 43.

9. Warren Goss, *Recollections of a Private Soldier: A Story of the Army of the Potomac*, Thomas Crowell and Co., New York, NY, 1890, pp. 49-51.

10. There were few units still wearing the Zouave costumes in battle by this time. There were no more than six regiments in the Federal forces and no full units at all in Lee's army. The New York and Pennsylvania Zouaves suffered dreadful casualties and there were few regiments in service by Cold Harbor. Two exceptions were the 114th Pennsylvania, which served as a headquarters guard until Petersburg and saw no direct combat, and the 164th New York which was slaughtered at Cold Harbor.

11. *O.R., Vol. 34, Pt. Two*, pp. 218-219.

12. Samuel Buck, *With the Old Confederates: Actual Experiences of a Captain of the Line*, Houck and Co., Baltimore, Maryland, 1925, p. 115.

13. Goss, pp. 268-276.

14. G. Moxley Sorrel, *Recollections of a Confederate Staff Officer*, McCowat-Mercer Press, Jackson, Tennessee, 1958, p. 221.

15. Lyman, p. 94.

16. James Longstreet, *From Manassas to Appomattox: Memoirs of the Civil War in America*, J. B. Lippincott and Co., Philadelphia, Pennsylvania, 1896, pp. 560-561.

17. Douglas Freeman gives an excellent explanation of this "road-bed" that figured so much in the war in Virginia in *Lee's Lieutenants, Vol. 3*, pp. 360-362.

18. Sorrel, p. 235.

19. Porter, p. 65.

20. Benjamin F. Jones, *Under the Stars and Bars: A History of the Surrey Light Artillery*, Morningside Bookshop, Dayton, Ohio, 1975, reprint of 1890 edition, pp. 246-248.

21. Fisk, pp. 278-279.

22. Porter, pp. 73-74.

23. Lyman, p. 106.

24. J. Cutler Andrews, *The North Reports the War*, University of Pittsburgh Press, Pittsburgh, Pennsylvania, 1955, pp. 524-525.

25. Romeyn Ayres in *Military History Society of Massachusetts Papers, Vol. 6*, p. 389.

Chapter Four

1. Nevins, p. 23.

2. George Washburn, *Military History and Record of the 108th New York Volunteers*, Press of E. R. Andrews, Rochester, New York, 1894, p. 174.

3. Gregory Jaynes, *The Killing Ground: The Wilderness to Cold Harbor*, Time/Life Books, New York, NY, 1986, p. 39.

4. James Wilson, *Under the Old Flag*, Greenwood Press, Westport, Connecticut, 1971, reprint of 1912 edition, p. 346.

5. Lyman, p. 101.

6. Wilkeson, pp. 91-93.

7. Charles Dana, *Recollections of the Civil War*, Collier Books, New York, 1963, reprint of 1902 edition, p. 179.

8. Charles Banes, *History of the Philadelphia Brigade*, J. B. Lippincott and Co., Philadelphia, Pennsylvania, 1876, p. 235.

9. Porter, p. 176.

10. *O.R., Vol. 36, Pt. One*, p. 2.

11. *New York Tribune*, May 13, 1864.

12. Bruce Catton, *Grant Takes Command*, pp. 215-216.

13. There are many references to the fact that two years before, the Federal military under George McClellan had attempted an amphibious conquest of Richmond from landings on the James and York Rivers. His maneuvering had taken his armies through the region east and north of Richmond during the Seven Days' Battles.

14. Lyman, pp. 99-100.

15. Gen. Thomas Hyde, *Following the Greek Cross*, Houghton, Mifflin and Co., Boston, Massachusetts, 1894, pp. 191-192.

16. Ulysses S. Grant in *Battles and Leaders, Vol. 4*, p. 436.

17. Porter, p. 98.

18. Heth, pp. 178-179.

19. Other occurrences in the Wilderness were described by Longstreet. John Gordon gives a vivid account of Lee's presence at the "Bloody Angle" in his *Reminiscences of the Civil War*, Charles Scribner's Sons, New York, NY, 1903, pp. 276-277.

20. *O.R., Vol. 36, Pt. One*, pp. 704-706.

21. John Noonan, letter, 5/16/64, U.S. Army Military History Institute, Carlisle, Pennsylvania (USAMHI) archives.

22. *O.R., Vol. 36, Pt. One*, p. 4.

23. Meade, pp. 197-198.

24. *Battles and Leaders, Vol. 4*, p. 182.

25. *O.R., Vol. 36, Pt. One*, p. 706.

26. Terry Jones, pp. 210-211.

27. Fisk, pp. 218-221.

28. Rhodes, pp. 152-153

29. Benjamin W. Jones, p. 176.

30. Dana, pp. 178-179.

Chapter Five

1. *O.R., Vol. 36, Pt. One*, p. 83.

2. William Shreve, *Massachusetts Historical Society Papers, Vol. 4*, p. 317.

3. Lyman, p. 172.

4. Taylor, p. 132.

5. John Haley, *The Rebel Yell and the Yankee Hurrah: A Civil War Diary of a Maine Volunteer*, Down East Books, Camden, Maine, 1985, ed. by Ruth Silliker, p. 152.

6. Sheridan, p. 279.

7. Catton, *Grant Takes Command*, p. 245.

8. Porter, p. 135.

9. Haley, p. 153.

10. Crotty, p. 132.

11. Stephen Weld, *War Diary and Letters of Stephen Minot Weld, 1861-1865*, Massachusetts Historical Society, Boston, Massachusetts, 1979, p. 297. An excellent account of this episode appears in Warren Wilkinson's *Mother, May You Never See the Sights I've Seen: The Fifty-Seventh Massachusetts Veterans Volunteers in the Last Year of the Civil War*, Harper & Row, New York, NY, 1990, pp. 137-143.

12. Walter Taylor, *General Lee: His Campaigns in Virginia, 1861-1865, with Personal Reminiscences*, Nusbaum Book Co., Norfolk, Virginia, 1906, p. 249.

13. For a clear explanation of North Anna fighting from the Southern perspective, see James I. Robertsons, *A. P. Hill: The Story of a Confederate Warrior*, University of South Carolina Press, Columbia, South Carolina, 1988, pp. 274-277.

14. Haley, p. 155.

15. *Battles and Leaders, Vol. 4*, p. 135.

16. Crotty, p. 132.

17. Wilkeson, pp. 91-93.

18. Alfred Scott, memoir, 5/29/64, VHS.

19. Frassinato, p. 158-159.

20. Grant, p. 176.

21. Charles Venable in *The Army of Northern Virginia: A Memorial Volume*, J. W. Randolph and English, Richmond, Virginia, 1880, ed. by Rev. J. William Jones, p. 168.

22. Several sources including personal aides Taylor and Venable, as well as Jubal Early and his son Robert, Jr., testify to the fragile condition of Lee's health in late May, 1864.

23. Lee, Jr., p. 90.

24. Gen. John Gibbon, *Recollections of the Civil War*, Putnam's and Sons, New York, NY, 1926, p. 226.

25. Bruce Catton, *A Stillness at Appomattox*, Doubleday and Co., Garden City, New York, 1953, p. 142.

26. Wilson, pp. 240-243.

27. Clifford Dowdey, *Lee's Last Campaign*, Broadfoot Pub. Co., Wilmington, North Carolina, 1960, pp. 34-41.

28. Edward Pollard, *A Southern History of the War*, Mallard Press, New York, NY, 1977, pp. 277-279

29. These scenes and Lincoln's words to Brooks are found in Andrews, pp. 539-544.

30. Wilkeson, p. 97.

Chapter Six

1. Robert Stiles, *Four Years Under Marse Robert*, Neale Publishing Co., New York, NY, 1910, p. 284.

2. Austin Stearns, *Three Years with Company K of the 13th Massachusetts Infantry: The Diary of Sergeant Austin Stearns*, 1976, ed. by Arthur Kent, p. 274

3. Gibbon, p. 228.

4. *O.R., Vol. 36, Pt. One*, p. 828.

5. Rhodes, p. 155.

6. Evander Law, "From the Wilderness to Cold Harbor," *Battles and Leaders of the Civil War, Vol. 4*, p. 137.

7. Grant, p. 258.

8. Rawlins was Grant's chief-of-staff who exerted a great influence over the commanding general. His staff reports make up much of this portion of the *Rebellion Record*, a compendium of Union documents of war-time activities. A 1980 reprint edition of the Arno Press compilation, done in 1868 and edited by Frank Moore, is invaluable for study of the Wilderness Campaign.

9. *Ibid,* Vol. 10, p. 555.

10. Jubal Early, *Autobiographical Sketch and Narrative of the War Between the States*, J. B. Lippincott Co., Philadelphia, Pennsylvania, 1912, p. 361.

11. Freeman, *Lee's Lieutenants, Vol. 3* , p. 499.

12. *O.R., Vol. 36, Pt. One*, pp. 821-822, p. 1031. See also, Robert Williams "Haw's Shop: A Storm of Shot and Shell," *Civil War Times Illustrated*, Jan., 1971.

13. George Brooke, memoir, 5/28/64, VHS.

14. See Harry Hansen, *The Civil War: A History*, Penguin Group, New York, NY, 1961, pp. 591-595 and Ralph W. Donnelly, *The Confederate States Marine Corps*, White Mane Pub. Co., Shippensburg, PA., 1989, pp. 57-63, for two of the best descriptions of the Battle of Drewry's Bluff.

15. Horace Porter, *Campaigning with Grant*, p. 162.

16. *O.R., Vol. 51, Pt. Two*, pp. 952-953.

17. John Pullen, *The 20th Maine: A Volunteer Regiment in the Civil War*, J. B. Lippincott, Philadelphia, Pennsylvania, 1957, pp. 205-206.

18. George Eggleston, "Notes on Cold Harbor", in *Battles and Leaders, Vol. 4*, pp. 231-232.

19. John Hatton, memoir, 6/1/64, Library of Congress Manuscript Collection (LBM), Washington, D.C.

20. Stearns, p. 276.

21. John Haley in *The Rebel Yell and the Yankee Hurrah*, ed. by Ruth Silliker, p. 165.

22. *O.R., Vol. 36, Pt. One*, p. 998.

23. Porter Alexander, *Fighting for the Confederacy: The Personal Recollections of Gen. Edward Porter Alexander*, ed. by Gary Gallagher, p. 397.

24. Freeman, p. 508. See also *O.R., Vol. 36, Pt. Three*, p. 828.

25. *O.R., Vol. 52, Pt. Two*, p. 975.

26. Early, p. 362.

27. R. E. McBride, *In the Ranks: From the Wilderness to Appomattox Court House*, Walden and Stowes, Cincinnati, Ohio, 1881, pp. 70-71

28. Grant, p. 262.

29. *O.R., Vol. 36, Pt. Three*, p. 850.

30. *O.R., Vol. 36, Pt. Three*, p. 857.

31. *Ibid*, p. 858.

32. Sheridan, *Memoirs*, p. 406.

Chapter Seven

1. U. S. Grant, *Memoirs, Vol. 2*, pp. 258-259.

2. Augustus Dickert, *Kershaw's Brigade*, p. 369.

3. Virginius Dabney, *Virginia: A History*, Algonquin Books of Chapel Hill, Chapel Hill, North Carolina, 1986, p. 444.

4. George Meade, *Life and Letters of George G. Meade*, p. 198.

5. Page, p. 96.

6. Theodore Lyman in his *Letters of Col. Theodore Lyman*, p. 136 and Horace Porter in *Campaigning with Grant*, p. 156, discuss this Cold Harbor debate.

7. William Frassinato is the premier historical expert on Civil War photography. For his study of original photographs from Cold Harbor, see *Grant and Lee: The Virginia Campaigns, 1864-65*, pp. 160-167.

8. William Farrar Smith published the official orders in "The Eighteenth Corps at Cold Harbor" in *Battles and Leaders, Vol. 4*, pp. 222-226. Brigadier General Adelbert Ames was left in charge of force left at New Castle.

9. *Ibid*, p. 225.

10. William Farrar Smith is the best source for study of that incredible confusion. See his *From Chattanooga to Petersburg under Grant and Butler*. His soldiers – Asa Bartlett, Ernest Waitt, and others support most of his account.

11. W. P Derby, *Bearing Arms in the Twenty-Seventh Massachusetts*, Wright and Potter, Boston, Massachusetts, 1883, p. 309.

12. Porter, p. 161.

13. *O.R., Vol. 36, Pt. Three*, p. 858.

14. Alexander M. Stewart, *Camp, March, and Battlefield or Three and a Half Years with the Army of the Potomac*, p. 302.

15. *Rebellion Record, Vol. 10*, p. 555.

16. Alexander, p. 399.

17. Dickert, p. 368.

18. *Ibid*, p. 370.

19. Dickert adds this account to his own, p. 371.

20. Stiles, p. 289.

21. See Thomas Clingman's account in *Histories of Several Regiments and Battalions from North Carolina in the Civil War, 1861-65*, pp. 198-206.

22. Alexander, p. 400.

23. Robert Krick, *Parker's Virginia Battery*, Virginia Book Company, Berryville, Virginia, 1975, p. 255.

24. *O.R., Vol. 36, Pt. Two*, p. 851.

25. *O.R., Vol. 36, Pt. One*, p. 86.

26. *Rebellion Record, Vol. 10*, p. 556.

27. Vaill, p. 58.

28. Edwin Haynes, *History of the Tenth Regiment, Vermont Volunteers*, Tenth Vermont Regimental Association, Lewiston, Maine, 1870, p. 79.

29. Wilkeson, p. 103.

30. *Battles and Leaders, Vol. 4*, pp. 222-223.

31. Lyman, p. 138.

32. *Battles and Leaders, Vol. 4*, p. 226.

33. Glenn Tucker, *Hancock the Superb*, Bobbs-Merrill Co., Indianapolis, Indiana, 1960, p. 219.

34. Vaill, p. 61.

35. *Ibid,* pp. 61-62.

36. Vaill, p. 66.

37. Clingman, p. 204.

38. Vaill, p. 66

39. Martin McMahon, *Battles and Leaders, Vol. 4*, p. 219.

40. Clingman, pp. 206-207.

41. George Stevens, *Three Years in the Sixth Corps: A Concise Narrative*, S. R. Gray Co., Albany, New York, 1866, pp. 347-348.

Chapter Eight

1. George Eggleston, *The History of the Confederate War, Its Causes and Conduct, Vol. 2*, William Henneman Co., London, 1910, p. 254.

2. John Pullen, *The 20th Maine: A Volunteer Regiment in the Civil War*, p. 206.

3. Robert Krick, *Parker's Virginia Battery*, p. 133.

4. *O.R., Vol. 36, Pt. One*, p. 864.

5. Andrew Humphreys, *The Virginia Campaign of 1864-1865*, p. 181.

6. *O.R., Vol. 36, Pt. One*, p. 344.

7. *Ibid*, p. 87.

8. Porter, p. 167.

9. Theodore Lyman, *Letters of Theodore Lyman*, p. 136.

10. *Ibid*, p. 138.

11. George Meade, *Life and Letters*, p. 200.

12. J. F. Caldwell, *A History of a South Carolina Brigade: McGowan's Brigade,* King and Baird Co., Philadelphia, Pennsylvania, 1866, p. 157.

13. Of all his corps commanders at this point, Lee had the most confidence in Jubal Early. Alexander, Venable, Taylor, and Early's reports in the *Official Records* refer to Early's tacit permission to attack wherever he chose.

14. Henry G. McClellan, memoir, 6/3/64, VHS.

15. The Confederate trenches at Cold Harbor were some of the most intricate seen in the entire war. Bruce Catton's descriptions in *A Stillness at Appomattox*, pp. 152-156, remain invaluable.

16. Jennings Wise, *The Long Arm of Lee*, Oxford University Press, New York, NY, 1959, p. 817.

17. Warren Wilkinson, *The Fifty-Seventh Massachusetts Veteran Volunteers in the Last Year of the Civil War*, pp. 150-151.

18. *History of the 116 Pennsylvania: The Corn Exchange Regiment*, Pennsylvania Infantry Association/J. L. Smith Co., Philadelphia, Pennsylvania, 1905, pp. 478-479.

19. William S. Long, letter, 1902, LCM.

20. William F. Smith in *Battles and Leaders, Vol. 4*, p. 224.

21. *O.R., Vol. 36, Pt. One*, pp. 478-479.

22. Jedediah Hotchkiss Papers, diary, Mar.-May, 1864, LCM. The Hotchkiss Papers also contain field reports with drawings of the defenses.

23. Wise, p. 819.

24. *Ibid*, pp. 820-821.

25. Evander Law in *Battles and Leaders, Vol. 4*, p. 139.

26. Johnny Scott, *The 23rd Virginia Infantry Battalion Regimental History*, H. E. Howard Virginia Regimental History Series, Lynchburg, Virginia, p. 31.

27. U.S. Grant, *Personal Memoirs, Vol. 2*, p. 269.

28. Frank Wilkeson, *Recollections of a Private Soldier*, p. 104.

29. John Anderson, *History of the 57th Massachusetts Volunteers*, E. B. Stilling Co., Boston, Massachusetts, 1896, p. 115.

30. Porter, pp. 174-175.

31. William Smith in *Battles and Leaders, Vol. 4*, p. 225.

32. Charles Banes, *The History of the Philadelphia Brigade*, p. 269.

Chapter Nine

1. Martin McMahon in his article, "Cold Harbor" in *Battles and Leaders, Vol. 4*, p. 213.

2. John Haley in *The Rebel Yell and the Yankee Hurrah*, ed. by Ruth Silliker, p. 166.

3. *O.R., Vol. 36, Pt. Two*, p. 671.

4. Terry Lowry, *26th Battalion Virginia Infantry Reg. History*, Howard Virginia Regimental History Series, Lynchburg, Virginia, 1991, p. 43.

5. *O.R., Vol. 36, Pt. Two*, p. 367.

6. Freeman, *Robert E. Lee, Vol. 3*, p. 524.

7. For complete text, see Clifford Dowdey, *Wartime Letters of Robert E. Lee, Vol. 2*, p. 701.

8. *Soldier of the South: General Pickett's Letters to His Wife*, Houghton, Mifflin and Co., Boston, Massachusetts, 1928, ed. by Arthur Inman, Letter of June 3, 1864, pp. 91-92.

9. First-hand accounts of Lyman, Porter, and Dana, among others, discuss the fact that V and IX Corps did very little moving or fighting from June 1 through June 12.

10. J. D. Smith, *History of the 19th Maine Volunteer Infantry*, Great Western Print Co., Minneapolis, Minnesota, 1909, p. 186.

11. Glenn Tucker, *Hancock the Superb*, p. 233.

12. John Gibbon, *Recollections of the Civil War*, p. 232.

13. *O.R. Vol. 36, Pt. Two*, p. 435.

14. Foote, p. 291.

15. Noonan, letter, 6/14/64, USAMHI.

16. Frank Wilkeson, *Recollections of a Private Soldier*, pp. 104-106.

17. J. D. Smith, p. 187.

18. *Ibid*, p. 188.

19. Lowry, p. 45.

20. Ernest Waitt, *History of the 19th Regiment Massachusetts Volunteers*, The Salem Press Co., Salem, Massachusetts, 1906, pp. 318-319.

21. Banes, p. 271.

22. Waitt, p. 319.

23. Wilkeson, p. 107.

24. Lowry, p. 46.

25. A. Du Bois in Vol. 29, *Southern Historical Society Papers*, 1902, pp. 276-279.

26. Lowry, p. 47.

27. William Goldsborough, *The Maryland Line in the Virginia States Army*, Butternut Press, Gaithersburg, Maryland, 1978, reprint of 1869 edition, pp. 127-128.

28. Hatton, memoir, 6/16/64, LCM.

29. Wilkeson, pp. 109-110.

30. Tucker, p. 231.

31. Theodore Lyman, *Meade's Headquarters, 1863-65: Letters of Colonel Theodore Lyman from the Wilderness to Appomattox*, pp. 143-144.

32. Edwin Houghton, *The Campaigns of the Seventeenth Maine*, Short and Loring Co., Portland, Maine, 1866, p. 217.

33. Thomas Hyde, *Following the Greek Cross*, Houghton, Mifflin and Co., Boston, Massachusetts, 1894, p. 211.

34. Stiles, p. 289.

35. Dickert, pp. 370-371.

36. Lyman, p. 146.

37. *O.R., Vol. 36, Pt. Two*, pp. 707-708.

38. McMahon, *Battles and Leaders, Vol. 4*, p. 215.

39. William F. Smith, "The Eighteenth Corps at Cold Harbor," in *Battles and Leaders, Vol. 4*, p. 227.

40. Thomas Mears Eddy, *Connecticut During the Rebellion: Military and Civil History of Connecticut During the War of 1861-1865*, privately published, Hartford, Connecticut, 1868, p. 597.

41. Asa Bartlett, *History of the Twelfth Regiment, New Hampshire Volunteers in the War of Rebellion*, I. C. Evans, Printer, Concord, New Hampshire, 1897, pp. 204-206.

42. *Ibid*, p. 207.

43. Bartlett, pp. 207-208.

44. William Oates, *The War Between the Union and Confederacy and Its Lost Opportunities*, Neale Publishing Co., New York, NY, 1905, p. 369.

45. William Dame, *From the Rapidan to Richmond*, Owens Publishing Co., Richmond, Virginia, 1987, reprint of 1920 edition, pp. 203-204.

46. Samuel Putnam, *The Story of Company A, Twenty-Fifth Regiment, Massachusetts Volunteers in the War of Rebellion*, Putnam, Davis, & Co., Worcester, Massachusetts, 1886, pp. 286-287.

47. William Derby, *Bearing Arms in the Twenty-Seventh Massachusetts Regiment*, pp. 302-303.

48. Oates, pp. 370-371.

49. Rossiter Johnson, *Campfire and Battlefield: A History of the Civil War*, Fairfax Press, New York, NY, 1978, p. 365.

50. Johnson Hagood, *Memoirs of the War of Secession*, The State Co. Columbia, South Carolina, 1910, p. 231.

51. Evander Law, "The Wilderness to Cold Harbor" in *Battles and Leaders, Vol. 4*, p. 141.

52. John S. Graham, letter, 6/4/64, Richmond Battlefield Park Collection (RBP), Richmond, Virginia.

Chapter Ten

1. William Oates, *The War Between the Union and Confederacy and Its Lost Opportunities*, p. 367.

2. William Derby, *Bearing Arms in the Twenty-Seventh Regiment*, p. 317.

3. Thomas Hyde, *Following the Greek Cross*, p. 214.

4. Charles Venable, *Memorial Volume*, p. 62.

5. Evander Law, "Wilderness to Cold Harbor," *Battles and Leaders, Vol. 4*, p. 142.

6. Jefferson Davis, *Rise and Fall of the Confederate Government, Vol. 2*, Charles Scribner's Sons, New York, NY, 1881, p. 524.

7. This familiar quote is from John Cooke's *Wearing the Gray*, privately published, New York, NY, 1867, p. 406.

8. *Battles and Leaders, Vol. 4*, pp. 224-225. See also *O.R., Vol. 36, Pt. Two*, pp. 1000-1001.

9. Noah Trudeau, *Bloody Roads South: The Wilderness to Cold Harbor*, Fawcett Colombine, New York, NY, 1989, p. 292.

10. William F. Smith, *Battles and Leaders, Vol. 4*, p. 225.

11. Porter, p. 177.

12. Cyrus Comstock, diary, 6/6/64, LCM.

13. This story is told by several Alabama veterans. See William Oates' section on the 4th Alabama, pp. 775-781 as well as T. Botsford, *A Sketch of the 47th Alabama Regular Volunteers*, pp. 388-391.

14. Ambrose Burnside in *O.R., Vol. 36, Pt. Two*, p. 914.

15. Glenn Tucker, *Hancock the Superb*, p. 226.

16. Martin McMahon in his "Cold Harbor" in *Battles and Leaders, Vol. 4*, p. 218.

17. Porter, p. 177.

18. See Porter Alexander and Robert Stiles of the Confederate artillery command deny mutiny. Most Federal accounts, particularly McMahon, claim mutiny.

19. Frank Wilkeson, pp. 109-110.

20. Cullen Battle, memoir, 1878, Hall Collection, Virginia State Library, copy from RBP collection.

21. Dickert, p. 375.

22. *Battles and Leaders, Vol. 4*, p. 138.

23. David McIntosh, memoir, 1911, VHS.

24. Porter Alexander, *The Personal Recollections of General Porter Edward Alexander*, p. 405.

25. Asa Bartlett, *History of the Twelfth Regiment, New Hampshire Volunteers*, p. 210.

26. William F. Smith, *Battles and Leaders, Vol. 4*, p. 226.

27. George Stevens, *Three Years in the VI Corps*, p. 354.

28. McMahon, *Battles and Leaders, Vol. 4*, p. 219.

29. Oates, p. 367.

30. *Ibid*, p. 367.

31. Derby, pp. 321-322.

32. George Meade, *Life and Letters of George G. Meade*, p. 200.

33. McMahon, *Battles and Leaders, Vol. 4*, p. 220.

34. Theodore Lyman, *Meade's Headquarters: Letters of Colonel Theodore Lyman from the Wilderness to Appomattox*, p. 147.

35. *Ibid*, p. 149.

36. Oates, p. 368.

37. Robert Stiles, *Four Years Under Marse Robert*, p. 290.

38. Eddy, p. 597.

39. Lee's Message is given in full in Clifford Dowdey's *Wartime Papers of Robert E. Lee*, p. 752.

40. Hudson Strode, *Jefferson Davis: Tragic Hero*, *Vol. 4*, Harcourt, Brace, and World, New York, NY, 1964, p. 51.

41. John B. Jones, *A Rebel War Clerk's Diary at the Confederate State's Capital*, *Vol. 2*, J. B. Lippincott, Philadelphia, Pennsylvania, 1866, p. 224.

42. John Reagan, *Memoirs*, W. Flavius McCaleb/Neale Publishing Co., New York, NY, 1866, pp. 191-192.

43. Strode, pp. 52-53.

44. Dowdey, Wartime Papers of Robert E. Lee, p. 753.

45. Banes, p. 273.

46. Bartlett, p. 212.

47. Lyman, pp. 149-155.

48. Grant, p. 273.

49. Dowdey, p. 753.

50. Jones, p. 226.

51. Grant, p. 275.

52. *Ibid*, p. 276.

53. Hyde, pp. 212-213.

54. Haynes, p. 82.

55. Hagood, p. 238.

56. Derby, pp. 322-323.

57. Lewis Bissell, *The Civil War Letters of Lewis Bissell*, ed. by Mark Olcott and D. Lear, Field School Education Foundation Press, Washington, D.C., 1981, p. 248. Letter to his father, June 4, 1864.

Chapter Eleven

1. Samuel Putnam, *The Story of Company A, Twenty-Fifth Massachusetts Volunteers in the War of Rebellion*, p. 291.

2. Gideon Welles, *Diary of Gideon Welles, Vol. 2*, Houghton, Mifflin and Co., Boston, Massachusetts, 1911, p. 45.

3. Charles Venable, *The Army of the Potomac: A Memorial Volume*, ed. by Rev. J. William Jones, p. 62.

4. George Meade, *Life and Letters of George G. Meade*, p. 200.

5. James Bryant, letter, 6/4/64, RBP.

6. James Clark, *The Iron-Hearted Regiment: Accounts of the 115th New York Volunteers*, privately published, Albany, New York, 1865, p. 131.

7. Bissell, p. 249.

8. Gustavus A. Myers, letter, 6/6/64, VHS.

9. William Derby, *Bearing Arms in the Twenty-Seventh Massachusetts*, p. 324.

10. John Anderson, *History of the 57th Regiment of Massachusetts Volunteers*, p. 117.

11. Alexander, pp. 411-412.

12. William Swinton, *Campaigns of the Army of the Potomac*, pp. 481-487.

13. Peter Mitchie, *Life and Letters of Emory Upton*, Appleton & Co., New York, NY, 1885, p. 108.

14. James Wilson, *Under the Old Flag*, p. 398.

15. *Ibid*, p. 400.

16. Andrew Humphreys, *The Virginia Campaign of 1864 and 1865*, pp. 198-200.

17. See Noah Trudeau, *Bloody Roads South*, p. 341, and Glen Tucker, *Hancock the Superb*, pp. 220-221, for charts and figures.

18. Putnam, p. 292.

19. Stephen Weld, *War Diary and Letters of Stephen Weld, 1861-1865*, p. 302.

20. Derby, p. 324.

21. Porter, p. 179.

22. Trudeau, p. 341.

23. Richard Drum, "The Army of the Potomac at Appomattox" in *Battles and Leaders, Vol. 4*, p. 182.

24. Humphreys, pp. 194-195.

25. *O.R., Vol. 36, Pt. Three*, p. 598.

26. Smith expressed those feelings to several comrades after the war and gave vent to them in his *From Chattanooga to Petersburg Under Grant and Butler*, Houghton, Mifflin and Co., Boston, Massachusetts, 1893. Caution on this source is recommended, as in all accounts by Smith, who was cashiered out of service at Petersburg not long after the Cold Harbor action.

27. The best source on that often-repeated story is Cutler Andrews, *The North Reports the War*, pp. 548-549.

28. Sylvanus Cadwallader, *Three Years with General Grant*, Alfred Knopf and Co., New York, NY, 1955, p. 209.

29. *Ibid*, pp. 209-210.

30. Andrews, pp. 549-550. Another description is given in Louis Starr's *Bohemian Brigade: Civil War Newsmen in Action*, Knopf, NY, 1954.

31. Hansen, p. 537.

32. *Corn Exchange Regiment*, pp. 466-467.

33. *Ibid*, p. 468.

34. *Lee's Lieutenants, Vol. 3*, pp. 510-513.

35. Porter, p. 189.

36. *Rebellion Record, Vol. 10*, p. 561.

37. *Corn Exchange Regiment*, pp. 469-470.

38. *O.R. Vol. 36, Pt. One*, p. 1035.

39. Stiles, pp. 308-309.

40. Alexander, pp. 421-422.

41. Grant, pp. 276-277.

42. Thomas Hyde, *Following the Greek Cross*, pp. 214-215.

Selected Bibliography

Of the thousands of published and unpublished accounts and references to Second Cold Harbor, these listed materials were of special use. They served particularly well in setting the stage and providing the voices for the soldiers and officers who were the main participants at Cold Harbor.

Agassiz, George W. ed. *Meade's Headquarters 1863-65: Letters of Colonel Theodore Lyman from Wilderness to Appomattox*. Houghton, Mifflin, Co., Boston, Massachusetts, 1922.

Allen, Stanton P. *Down in Dixie: Life in a Cavalry Regiment in the War Days*. D. Lothrop Co., Boston, Massachusetts, 1888.

Ambrose, Stephen E. *Upton and the Army*. Louisiana State University Press, Baton Rouge, Louisiana, 1964.

Anderson, Capt. John. *History of the 57th Regiment of Massachusetts Volunteers*. E. B. Stilling Co., Boston, Massachusetts, 1896.

Anderson, Dwight and Nancy Scott. *The Generals: U. S. Grant and Robert E. Lee*. Alfred Knopf, New York, NY, 1988.

Andrews, J. Cutler. *The North Reports the Civil War*. University of Pittsburgh Press, Pittsburgh, Pennsylvania, 1955.

Banes, Charles H. *History of the Philadelphia Brigade*. J. B. Lippincott & Co., Philadelphia, Pennsylvania, 1876.

Bartlett, Asa W. *History of the Twelfth Regiment, New Hampshire Volunteers in the War of the Rebellion*. I. C. Evans, Printer, Concord, New Hampshire, 1897.

Berkely, Henry R. *Four Years in the Confederate Cavalry: The Diary of Private Henry Berkely*. University of North Carolina Press, Chapel Hill, North Carolina, 1901.

Bicknell, George W. *History of the 5th Maine Regiment* MacDonald's Maine Mementoes, Eustis Maine, 1988.

Billings, John. *Hardtack and Coffee*. Geo. Smith and Co., Boston, Massachusetts, 1887.

Blake, Henry Nichols. *Three Years in the Army of the Potomac*. Lee and Shepard Co., Boston, Massachusetts, 1865.

Botsford, T. F. *A Sketch of the 47th Alabama Regular Volunteers, CSA*. Privately published, Montgomery, Alabama, 1909.

Brainard, Mary G. Green. *Campaigns of the 146th Regiment New York State Volunteers*. G. Putnam's Sons, New York, NY, 1915.

Brinton, John. *Personal Memoirs of John Brinton*. Neale Publishing Co., New York, NY, 1914.

Brown, Philip F. *Reminiscences of the War of 1861-1865*. Privately published, 1912.

Buck, Captain Samuel. *With the Old Confederates: Actual Experiences of a Captain of the Line*. Houck and Co., Baltimore, Maryland, 1925.

Buel, Clarence Clough and Robert Underwood, eds. *Battles and Leaders of the Civil War, Vol. 4*. B.K. Sales, Inc., Secaucus, New Jersey, 1985 reprint of the 1888 Edition.

Cadwallader, Sylvanus. *Three Years with General Grant*. Alfred Knopf, New York, NY, 1955.

Caldwell, J. F. *A History of a South Carolina Brigade: McGowan's Brigade*. King and Baird, Co., Philadelphia, Pennsylvania, 1866.

Carter, Robert Goldthwaite. *Four Brothers in Blue*. University of Texas Press Austin, Texas, 1978.

Catton Bruce. *A Stillness at Appomattox*. Doubleday and Co., Garden City, New York, 1953.

.... *Grant Takes Command*. Little, Brown and Co., Boston, Massachusetts, 1968.

Clark, James. *The Iron-Hearted Brigade: Being an Account of the Battles, Marches, and Gallant Deeds Performed by the 115th New York Volunteers.* Privately published, Albany, New York, 1865.

Clarke, Walter, ed. *Histories of Several Regiments and Battalions from North Carolina in the Civil War, 1861-65.* E. M. Uzell, Publishers, Raleigh, North Carolina, 1901.

Cleaves, Freeman. *Meade of Gettysburg.* Morningside Bookshop, Dayton, Ohio, 1980.

Conynham, Capt. D. P. *The Irish Brigade and Its Campaigns,* Houghton, Mifflin and Co., Boston, Massachusetts, 1867.

Coppee, Henry. *Grant and His Campaigns.* C. B. Richardson Co., New York, NY, 1906.

Coward, Col. Asbury. *The South Carolinians: Memoirs of Colonel Asbury Coward.* Vantage Press, New York, 1968.

Crotty, D. G. *Four Years Campaigning with the Army of the Potomac.* Dygert Brothers & Co., Grand Rapids, Michigan, 1874.

Curtis, O. B. *History of the 24th Michigan of the Iron Brigade.* Winn and Hammond Co., Detroit, Michigan, 1891.

Dame, William Meade, D. D. *From the Rapidan to Richmond.* Owens Pub. Co., Richmond, Virginia, 1987 reprint of 1920 edition.

Dana, Charles A. *Recollections of the Civil War.* Collier Books, New York, NY, 1963 reprint of 1902 edition.

Daniel, John Moncure. *The Richmond Examiner During the Civil War.* Privately Published, New York, NY, 1868.

Davis, Jefferson. *The Rise and Fall of the Confederate Government, Vol. 2.* Charles Scribner's Sons, New York, NY, 1881.

DeLeon, Thomas Cooper. *Four Years in Rebel Capitals: An Inside View of Life in the Confederacy.* University of Alabama Press, Tuscaloosa, Alabama, 1890.

Denny, Waldo. *Wearing the Blue in the 25th Massachusetts Volunteer Infantry*. Putnam & Davis, Worcester, Massachusetts, 1879.

Derby, William P. *Bearing Arms in the Twenty-Seventh Massachusetts Regiment*. Wright & Potter Co., Boston, Massachusetts, 1883.

De Trobriand, P. Regis. *Four Years with the Army of the Potomac*. Tichnor and Co., Boston, Massachusetts, 1889.

Dickert, D. Augustus. *History of Kershaw's Brigade*. Morningside Bookshop, Dayton, Ohio, 1976 reprint of 1899 edition.

Dowdey, Clifford. *Lee's Last Campaign*. Broadfoot Publishing Co., Wilmington, North Carolina, 1988.

.... and Louis Manarin, eds. *The Wartime Papers of Robert E. Lee*. Little, Brown Co., New York, NY, 1962.

Drake, James Madison. *History of the Ninth New Jersey Veteran Volunteers*. Journal Printing House, Elizabeth, New Jersey, 1889.

Dwight, Theodore F., ed. *Papers of the Military History Society of Massachusetts, Vols. 4 and 5: Campaigns in Virginia, 1861-1865*. Houghton, Mifflin and Co., Boston, Massachusetts, 1895.

Early, Jubal A. *Autobiographical Sketch and Narrative of the War Between the States*. Lippencott Co., Philadelphia, Pennsylvania, 1912.

Eddy, Thomas Mears. *Connecticut During the Rebellion: Military and Civil History of Connecticut During the War of 1861-1865*. Privately Published, Hartford, Connecticut, 1868.

Eggleston, George Cary. *A Rebel's Recollections*. Hurd and Houghton, New York, NY, 1875.

.... *History of the Confederate War: Its Causes and Conduct, Vol. 2*. William Hennemann Co., London, 1910.

Emmerton, James A. *The Record of the 23rd Regiment Massachusetts Volunteers*. W. Ware & Co., Boston, Massachusetts, 1886.

Evans, Clement Anselm, ed. *Confederate Military History, Vol. 4: North Carolina*. Blue and Grey Press, Secaucus, New York, 1976 reprint of 1889 edition.

Fleming, Sgt. Major V. M. *Campaigns of the Army of Northern Virginia*. W. C. Hill Co., Richmond, Virginia, 1921.

Foote, Shelby. *The Civil War: A Narrative: Vol. 3, Red River to Appomattox*. Random House, New York, NY, 1974.

Frassinato, William A. *Grant and Lee: The Virginia Campaigns, 1864-1865*. Scribner's and Sons, New York, NY, 1983.

Freeman, Douglas Southall. *Lee's Lieutenants, Vol. 3*. Charles Scribner's Sons, New York, NY, 1944.

.... *R. E. Lee: A Biography, Vols. 2 & 3*. Charles Scribner's Sons, New York, NY, 1936.

Fuller, Edwin H. *Battles of the 77th New York State Foot Volunteers*. Privately published, New York, NY, 1901.

Fuller, Col. J. F. C. *The Generalship of Ulysses S. Grant*. Da Capo Books, New York, NY, 1989 reprint of 1929 edition.

Gallagher, Gary, ed. *Fighting for the Confederacy: The Personal Recollections of General Edward Porter Alexander*. University of North Carolina Press, Chapel Hill, North Carolina, 1989.

Gavin, William G., ed. *Infantryman Pettit: The Civil War Letters of Corporal Frederick Pettit*. Avon Books, New York, NY, 1990.

Gibbon, John. *Recollections of the Civil War*. Putnam's and Sons, New York, NY, 1926.

Goldsborough, William. *The Maryland Line in the Confederate States Army*. Butternut Press, Gaithersburg, Maryland, 1978 reprint of 1869 edition.

Gordon, Gen. John B. *Reminiscences of the Civil War*. Charles Scribner's Sons, New York, NY, 1903.

Goss, Warren Lee. *Recollections of a Private: A Story of the Army of the Potomac*. Thomas Crowell and Co., New York, NY, 1890.

Grant, Ulysses S. *Personal Memoirs of U. S. Grant, Vol. 2*. Charles Webster and Co., New York, NY, 1886.

.... *Report of Lt. Gen. Ulysses S. Grant of the Army of the United States: July 22,1865*. U.S. War Dept./U.S. Government Printing Office, Washington, D.C.

Greeley, Horace. *The American Conflict: A History of the Great Rebellion in the United States of America, 1860-1865, Vol. 4*. O. D. Case & Co., Chicago, Illinois, 1866.

Hagood, Johnson. *Memoirs of the War of Secession*. The State Co., Columbia, South Carolina, 1910.

Haines, Alanson A. *History of the Fifteenth Regiment, New Jersey Volunteers*. Jenkins & Thomas, Printers, New York, NY, 1883.

Hansen, Harry. *The Civil War: A History*. Penguin Group, New York NY, 1961.

Hardin, M. D. *History of the 12th Regiment Pennsylvania Reserve Volunteer Corps,* Privately published, Philadelphia, Pennsylvania, 1890.

Haskell, John Cheeves. *The Haskell Memoirs*. Putnam, Inc., New York, NY, 1960.

Haynes, Edwin M. *The History of the Tenth Regiment, Vermont Volunteers*. Published by the Tenth Vermont Regimental Assoc., Lewiston, Maine, 1870.

Haynes, Martin A. *History of the 2nd Regiment New Hampshire Volunteers*. C. F. Livingston Co., Manchester, New Hampshire, 1865.

Houghton, Edwin. *The Campaigns of the Seventeenth Maine*. Short and Loring Co., Portland, Maine, 1866.

Howard, McHenry. *Recollections of a Maryland Soldier and Staff Officer*. Williams and Wilkins Co., Baltimore, Maryland, 1914.

Huffman, James. *Ups and Downs of a Confederate Soldier of the 10th Virginia Infantry.* W. Rudgies and Sons, New York, NY, 1940.

Humphreys, Gen. Andrew A. *The Virginia Campaign of 1864 and 1865.* Scribner's and Sons, New York, NY, 1883.

Hyde, Thomas Worcester. *Following the Greek Cross.* Houghton, Mifflin and Co., Boston, Massachusetts, 1894.

Inman, Arthur C., ed. *Soldier of the South: General Pickett's War Letters to His Wife.* Houghton-Mifflin Co., Boston, Massachusetts, 1928.

Jackson, Donald Dale. *Twenty Million Yankees: The Northern Home Front.* Volume no. 14, in Time/Life series "The Civil War" from Time/Life Books, New York, NY, 1986.

Jaynes, Gregory. *The Killing Ground: The Wilderness to Cold Harbor.* Volume no. 19, in Time/Life series "The Civil War" from Time/Life Books, New York, NY, 1986.

Jennings, Cropper Wise. *The Long Arm of Lee: A History of the Army of Northern Virginia.* J. P. Bell Co., Lynchburg, Virginia, 1915.

Johnson, Rossiter. *Campfire and Battlefield: A History of the Civil War.* Fairfax Press, New York, NY, 1978.

Jones, Benjamin Washington. *Under the Stars and Bars: A History of the Surrey Light Artillery.* Morningside Bookshop, Dayton, Ohio, 1975.

Jones, Evan Rowland. *Four Years in the Army of the Potomac.* Tyne Publishing Co., London, 1881.

Jones, John B. *A Rebel War Clerk's Diary at the Confederate States Capital, Vol. 2.* J. B. Lippincott, Philadelphia, Pennsylvania, 1866.

Jones, J. William. *Personal Reminiscences, Anecdotes, and Letters of General Robert E. Lee.* D. Appleton & Co., New York, NY, 1875.

Jones, Rev. J. William. *The Army of Northern Virginia: A Memorial Volume.* J. W. Randolph and English, Richmond, Virginia, 1880.

Jones, Paul. *The Irish Brigade.* Robert Luce, Co., New York, NY, 1969.

Jones, Terry L. *Lee's Tigers: The Louisiana Infantry in the Army of Northern Virginia*. Louisiana State University Press, Baton Rouge, LA, 1987.

Kent, Arthur. *Three Years with Company K of the 13th Massachusetts Infantry: The Diary of Sergeant Austin Stearns*. Associated University Presses, Cranbury, New Jersey, 1976.

Kidd, J. H. *Personal Recollections of a Cavalryman of the 6th Michigan Cavalry*. Sentinel Press, Ionia, Michigan, 1908.

Kirwan, Albert D., ed. *The Confederacy: A Social and Political History*. World Pub. Co., Cleveland, Ohio, 1959.

Krick, Robert. *Parker's Virginia Battery*. Virginia Book Co., Berryville, Virginia, 1975.

Lee, Capt. Robert E. *Recollections and Letters of General Robert E. Lee*. Doubleday, Page & Co., New York, NY, 1904.

Linderman, Gerald. *Embattled Courage: The Experience of Combat in the Civil War*. MacMillan, Inc., New York, NY, 1987.

Longstreet, Gen. James. *From Manassas to Appomattox: Memoirs of the Civil War in America*. J. B. Lippincott and Co., Philadelphia, Pennsylvania, 1896.

Lowry, Don. *No Turning Back: The Beginning of the End of the Civil War*. Hippocrene Books, New York, NY, 1992.

Lowry, Terry. *26th Battalion Virginia Infantry, Regimental History*. Virginia Regimental History Series, H. Howard, Inc., Lynchburg, Virginia, 1991.

Luvaas, Jay, ed. *Col. G. F. R. Henderson: The Civil War - A Soldier's View*. University of Chicago Press, Chicago, Illinois, 1958.

Luraghi, Raimondo. *The Rise and Fall of the Plantation South*. Franklin Watts, Inc., New York, NY, 1978.

McBride, R. E. *In the Ranks: From the Wilderness to Appomattox Courthouse*. Walden and Stowes, Cincinnati, Ohio, 1881.

McKim, Randolph. *Leaves From the Diary of a Young Confederate.* Zenger Publishing Co., New York, NY, 1910.

Matter, William. *If It Takes All Summer: The Battle Of Spotsylvania.* University of North Carolina Press, Chapel Hill, North Carolina, 1988.

Meade, Capt. George. *The Life and Letters of Gen. George G. Meade, Vol. 2.* Charles Scribner's Sons, New York, NY, 1913.

Menge, W. S. and J. A. Shirmak, eds. *The Civil War Notebook of Daniel Chisolm: A Chronicle of Daily Life in the Union Army, 1864-65.* Ballantine Press, New York, NY, 1989.

Miers, Earl Schenk. *The Last Campaign.* Lippincott and Co., Philadelphia, Pennsylvania, 1972.

Miles, Gen. Nelson. *Memoirs of the Civil and Military Life of Nelson Miles.* Harper & Brothers Co., New York, NY, 1911.

Miller, Delevan. *Drum Taps in Dixie: Memories of a Drummer Boy, 1861-1865.* Hungerford-Holbrook Co., Watertown, New York, 1905.

Mitchell, Reid. *Civil War Soldiers: Their Expectations and Their Experiences.* Simon and Schuster, Inc., New York, NY, 1988.

Mitchie, Peter. *Life and Letters of Emory Upton.* Appleton & Co., New York, NY, 1885.

Moore, Frank, ed. *The Rebellion Record: A Diary of American Events, Vols, 10 and 11.* Arno Press, New York, NY, 1868.

Morrison, Jr., James L., ed. *The Memoirs of Henry Heth.* Greenwood Press, Westport, Connecticut, 1974.

Nevins, Allan. *The War for the Union: Vol. 4, The Organized War to Victory, 1864-65.* Charles Scribner's Sons, New York, NY, 1971.

.............................ed. *A Diary of Battle: The Personal Journals of Colonel Charles S. Wainwright, 1861-1865.* Harcourt, Brace & World, New York, NY, 1962.

New Jersey Civil War Centennial Commission. *The Civil War Letters of General Robert McAllister*. Rutgers University Press, New Brunswick, New Jersey, 1965.

Nichols, G. W. *A Soldier's Story of His Regiment (61st Georgia): and Incidently of the Lawton-Gordon-Evans Brigade, Army of Northern Virginia*. Continental Book Co., Kennesaw, Georgia, 1961.

Niven, John. *Connecticut for the Union*. Yale University Press, New Haven, Connecticut, 1965.

Oates, Col. William C. *The War Between the Union and Confederacy and Its Lost Opportunities*. The Neale Pub. Co., New York, NY, 1905.

Olcott, Mark and D. Lear, eds. *The Civil War Letters of Lewis Bissell,* Field School Education Foundation Press, Washington, D.C., 1981.

Page, Charles. *Letters of a War Correspondent*. L. C. Page & Co., Boston, Massachusetts, 1899.

Parker, John and Robert Carter. *History of the 22nd Massachusetts Infantry*. Boston, Massachusetts, 1887.

Pennsylvania Infantry Association. *History of the 118th Pennsylvania Volunteers Corn Exchange Regiment from Their First Engagement at Antietam to Appomattox*. J. L. Smith Co., Philadelphia, Pennsylvania, 1905.

Pollard, Edward A. *The Early Life, Campaigns, and Public Services of Robert E. Lee*. E. B. Treat & Co., New York, NY, 1871.

.... *A Southern History of the War*. Fairfax Press, New York, NY, 1977 reprint of 1866 edition.

Porter, Gen. Horace. *Campaigning with Grant*. Mallard Press, New York, NY, 1990 reprint of 1907 edition.

Prowell, George Reeser. *History of the 87th Regiment Pennsylvania Volunteers*. Regimental Association Press, York, Pennsylvania, 1901.

Pullen, John. *The 20th Maine: A Volunteer Regiment in the Civil War*. J. B. Lippencott, Inc., New York, NY, 1957.

Putnam, Samuel Henry. *The Story of Company A, Twenty-Fifth Regiment, Massachusetts Volunteers in the War of Rebellion.* Putnam, Davis & Co., Worcester, Massachusetts, 1886.

Reagan, John H. *Memoirs.* W. Flavius McCaleb/Neale Pub. Co., New York NY, 1866.

Rhodes, Robert Hunt, ed. *All For the Union: The Civil War Diary and Letters of Elisha Hunt Rhodes.* Orion Books, New York, NY, 1985.

Robertson, James, Jr. *Soldiers Blue and Gray.* University of South Carolina Press, Columbia, South Carolina, 1988.

.... *General A. P. Hill.* University of South Carolina Press, Columbia, South Carolina, 1987.

Rosenblat, Emil and Ruth, eds. *Hard Marching Every Day: The Civil War Letters of Private Wilbur Fisk, 1861-65.* University of Kansas Press, Lawrence, Kansas, 1983.

Roth, Margaret Brobst. *The Civil War Letters of a Wisconsin Volunteer.* University of Wisconsin Press, Madison, Wisconsin, 1960.

Sandburg, Carl. *Abraham Lincoln: The War Years, Vol. 3.* Harcourt, Brace, and World, New York, NY, 1939.

Schiller, Herbert M. *A Captain's War: The Letters and Diaries of William H. S. Burgwyn, 1861-1865.* White Mane Publishing Co., Inc., Shippensburg, Pennsylvania, 1993.

Scott, Johnny Lee. *23rd Battalion Virginia Infantry, Regimental History.* H. E. Howard Virginia Regimental History Series, Lynchburg, Virginia, 1977.

Sheridan, Philip H. *Personal Memoirs of Philip Sheridan, Vol. 2.* Charles Webster and Co., New York, NY, 1888.

Silliker, Ruth, ed. *The Rebel Yell and the Yankee Hurrah: A Civil War Diary of a Maine Volunteer.* Down East Books, Camden, Maine, 1985.

Smith, John Day. *The History of the Nineteenth Regiment of the Maine Volunteer Infantry.* Great Western Print Co., Minneapolis, Minnesota, 1909.

Smith, Gen. William Farrar. *From Chattanooga to Petersburg under Grant and Butler.* Houghton-Mifflin Co., Boston. Massachusetts, 1893.

Sorrel, A. Moxley. *Recollections of a Confederate Staff Officer.* McCowat-Mercer Press, Jackson, Tennessee, 1958.

Sprague, Homer B. *History of the 13th Infantry Regiment of Connecticut Volunteers During the Great Rebellion.* Case, Lockwood Co., Hartford, Connecticut, 1867.

Stepp, John and William Hill. *A Mirror of War: The Evening Star During the Civil War.* Prentice-Hall, Inc., Englewood Heights, New Jersey, 1961.

Steere, Edward. *The Wilderness Campaign.* The Stackpole Co., Harrisburg, Pennsylvania, 1960.

Stevens, George Thomas. *Three Years in the VI Corps: A Concise Narrative.* S. R. Gray Co., Albany, New York, 1866.

Stewart, Alexander Morrison. *Camp, March, and Battlefield or Three and a Half Years with the Army of the Potomac.* J. B. Rogers, Printer, Philadelphia, Pennsylvania, 1865.

Stiles, Robert. *Four Years Under Marse Robert.* The Neale Publishing Co., New York, NY, 1910.

Stoddard, William O. *Lincoln's Third Secretary.* Doubleday Co., New York, NY, 1955.

Strode, Hudson. *Jefferson Davis: Tragic Hero, Vol. 4.* Harcourt, Brace and World, New York, NY, 1964.

Swinfen, D. B. *Ruggles' Regiment: The 122nd New York Volunteers in the American Civil War.* University Press of New England, Hanover, New Hampshire, 1982.

Swinton, William. *Campaigns of the Army of the Potomac.* Charles Scribner's Sons, New York, NY, 1882.

Taylor, Walter H. *Four Years with General Lee.* D. Appleton and Co., New York, NY, 1878.

.... *General Lee: His Campaigns in Virginia, 1861-1865, with Personal Reminiscences*. Nusbaum Book Co., Norfolk, Virginia, 1906.

Thomas, Emory. *The Confederate Nation, 1861-1865*. Harper & Row, New York, NY, 1979.

Trudeau, Noah. *Bloody Roads South: The Wilderness to Cold Harbor*. Fawcett Columbine, New York, NY, 1989.

Tucker, Glenn. *Hancock the Superb*. Bobbs-Merrill Co., Indianapolis, Indiana, 1960.

Vaill, Theodore F. *History of the Second Connecticut Volunteer Heavy Artillery*. Winsted Printing Co., Winsted, Connecticut, 1868.

Vandiver, Frank, ed. *The Civil War Diary of Josiah Gorgas*. University of Alabama Press, Tuscaloosa, Alabama, 1947.

Waitt, Ernest Linden. *History of the Nineteenth Regiment of Massachusetts Infantry*. The Salem Press Co., Salem, Massachusetts, 1906.

The War of the Rebellion: A Compilation of the Official Records of the Union and Confederate Armies, Vols. 32, 36 and 51, Part 2, Series 1; Vol. 36, Part 3, Series 1.; Vol. 7, Series II, Part 1; Vol. 3. Series IV, Pt. 1. United States Government Printing Office, Washington, D.C., 1880-1901.

Ward, Joseph R. C. *History of the One Hundred and Sixth Regiment, Pennsylvania Volunteers, 2nd Brigade, 2nd Division, 2nd Corps, 1861-1865*. F. McManus, Jr., Philadelphia, Pennsylvania, 1906.

Walker, Francis Amasa. *The History of the 2nd Corps in the Army of the Potomac*. Charles Scribner's Sons, New York, NY, 1887.

Warner, Ezra J. *Generals in Blue: Lives of the Union Commanders*. Louisiana State University Press, Baton Rouge, Louisiana, 1964.

.... *Generals in Gray: Lives of the Confederate Commanders*. Louisiana State University Press, Baton Rouge, Louisiana, 1959.

Washburn, George. *Military History and Record of the 108th New York Volunteers*. Press of E. R. Andrews, Rochester, New York, 1894.

Welles, Gideon. *Diary of Gideon Welles*. Houghton-Mifflin Co., New York, NY, 1911.

Weld, Stephen. *War Diary and Letters of Stephen Minot Weld, 1861-65*. Massachusetts Historical Society, Boston, Massachusetts, 1979.

Wheeler, Richard. *On Fields of Fury: From the Wilderness to the Crater*. Harper Collins, Inc., New York, NY, 1991.

.... *Voices of the Civil War*. Penguin Books, New York, 1990.

Wiley, Bell Irwin. *The Life of Billy Yank: The Common Soldier of the Union*. Louisiana State University Press, Baton Rouge, Louisiana, 1952.

.... *The Life of Johnny Reb: The Common Soldier of the Confederacy*. Louisiana State University Press, Baton Rouge, Louisiana, 1943.

Wilkeson, Frank. *Recollections of a Private Soldier in the Army of the Potomac*. G. P. Putnam's Sons, New York, NY, 1887.

Wilkinson, Warren. *Mother, May You Never See the Sights I've Seen: The Fifty-Seventh Massachusetts Veterans Volunteers in the Last Year of the Civil War*. Harper & Row, New York, NY, 1990.

Williams, Kenneth P. *Lincoln Finds a General: A Military Study of the Civil War, Vol. 4*. MacMillan Co., New York, NY, 1956.

Williams, T. Harry. *Lincoln and His Generals*. Alfred Knopf, Inc., New York, NY, 1952.

Wing, Henry Ebeneezer. *When Lincoln Kissed Me: A Story of the Wilderness Campaign*. Privately published, New York, NY, 1913.

Wilson, Gen. James Harrison. *Under the Old Flag*. Greenwood Press, Westport, Connecticut, 1971.

Index

Adams, Capt. Charles, Jr., 6
Adams, Charles Francis, 9
Alabama troops: 4th Infantry, 127, 146, 152, 166; 15th Infantry, 127, 146, 152
Alexander, Brig. Gen. Edwin Porter, 15, 24, 78, 98, 125, 126-127, 187, 203
Alsop's Farm, Spotsylvania, 42
Anderson, Brig. Gen. George, 127, 134, 150
Anderson, Capt. John, 130, 187
Anderson, Lt. Gen. Richard, 17; assumes command of First Corps, 41-42; at the Wilderness, 34; at Spotsylvania, 41-42; at Cold Harbor 80, 81, 86, 94-96, 98-99, 105, 165, 203
Andersonville, Georgia prison camp, 8
Appomattox River, 78
Army and Navy Journal, 43
Army of Northern Virginia, 15 16-18; Wilderness losses, 37; losses at Spotsylvania, 49, 68; total losses, 200
Army of the James, 74-75, 199
Army of the Potomac, 1-4, 18, 38, 49, 75; losses at Wilderness, 37; at Spotsylvania, 49; at North Anna, 63; at Cold Harbor, 108-109, 125-126, 131, 204
Ashland, Virginia, 69
Atlee Station, Virginia, 69, 94
Averell, Brig. Gen. William, 199
Ayres, Brig. Gen. Romeyn, 28, 37, 60

Banes, Pvt. Charles, 131, 140, 177
Barlow, Brig. Gen. Francis, at Spotsylvania, 46-47; at Cold Harbor, 133, 138, 136-139, 141, 169, 174
Bartlett, Sgt. Asa, 151-152, 169
Barton, Col. William, 149
Batchelor, Charles, 18
Battle, Brig. Gen. Cullen, 168, 200
Beauregard, Gen. Pierre G. T., 8, 116; at Drewry's Bluff, 73-75; at Atlee Station, 78; at Petersburg, 199-200, 203
Beaver Dam Station, Virginia, 55
Bennett, James G., 9

Bermuda Hundred, Virginia, 21, 74, 75
Bethesda Church, Virginia, battle, 80-82, 95, 108
Birney, Maj. Gen. David, 33, 99, 135
Bissell, Pvt. Lewis, 183, 186
Blake, Capt. Fred, 105
Block House Bridge, 42, 44, 55
Block House Road, 42
Bloody Angle (Spotsylvania), 47-49, 50, 59
Boatswain's Swamp, 119, 135
Bolton's Bridge, 176
Bowles, Col. P. D., 166
Bowling Green, Virginia, 56
Bragg, Gen. Braxton, 73, 83, 203
Brandy Station, Virginia, 5, 20, 188
Breckinridge, Maj. Gen. John, 49, 57, 94; at Cold Harbor, 119, 120, 127-128, 134, 141, 169, 174, 177; sent to Valley, 199-200
Brices Cross Roads, Mississippi, battle, 199
Brock Road, 25, 33, 40-41
Brook, Pvt. George T., 73
Brooke, Col. John, 136, 141, 142
Brooks, Noah, 65
Brooks, Brig. Gen. William, 149, 154, 157
Bryant, Pvt. James, 185
Buck, Capt. Samuel, 30
Burnside, Maj. Gen. Ambrose, 33, 47; at North Anna, 57, 99; at Cold Harbor, 120, 122, 125
Butler, Gen. Benjamin, 8, 25, 166, 187; at Drewry's Bluff, 49, 74-75
Butler, Brig. Gen. Calbraith, 71
Byrnes, Col. Richard, 136, 144-145

Cabell, Col. Henry (artillery battery), 126
Cadwallader, Sylvanus, 196
Carroll, Col. Samuel, 34
Carter, Pvt. Robert, 5
Catharpin Road, 32
Catton, Bruce, 62
Chancellorsville, Virginia 25, 37, 39, 40